An Introduction to Phenomenological Psychology

An Introduction
To
PHENOMENOLOGICAL
PSYCHOLOGY

By

DREYER KRUGER

with a contribution by
CHRISTOPHER R. STONES

DUQUESNE UNIVERSITY PRESS
PITTSBURGH

First Published in the United States of America in 1981
by DUQUESNE UNIVERSITY PRESS
600 Forbes Avenue, Pittsburgh, Pa. 15219

Copyright © 1979 by Juta & Co. Limited
P.O. Box 123, Kenwyn 7790, South Africa

Library of Congress Cataloging in Publication Data

Kruger, Dreyer.
    An introduction to phenomenological psychology.

    Bibliography: p.
    Includes index.
    1. Phenomenological psychology. I. Stones,
Christopher R., joint author. II. Title.
BF204.5.K78   150.19'2   80-29203
ISBN 0-8207-0150-5 (pbk.)

76051

Let us ever hold fast to what it means to be a human being.

—Søren Kierkegaard

Ins ersehnte Himmelreich einer wahren Psychologie werden wir nicht kommen, es sei denn, dasz wir werden wie die Kinder.

—Edmund Husserl

Ons is 'n blinde en middernagtelike vrees
wat al die ligte dae van ons lewe
die helder weë van die aarde gaan en weet
dat stilte en verskrikking weerskant lê. . . .

—N. P. van Wyk Louw

Acknowledgements

The idea for writing this book has been germinating over the years. Since 1974, Introductory courses in phenomenological psychology have been offered at Rhodes University and phenomenology has gradually seeped into other graduate and pregraduate material offered as well. From the first, the lack of a text suitable for undergraduate teaching was a handicap. Few of the introductory texts available offered a full explication of the main categories of being human. Those that did were either not available in English or were written more from the psychiatric than from the psychological point of view. It is in the hope of filling this gap that the present offering is being made.

A deep indebtedness to the pioneers in this field is gladly acknowledged and here the names of Medard Boss of Zürich, Jan Hendrik van den Berg of Leiden and Amedeo Giorgi of Duquesne University in Pittsburgh should be specially mentioned.

I am indebted to Chris Stones who contributed chapter IV, to Jacqueline Dreyer who typed the manuscript and to Tony Frank who compiled the bibliography and assisted with proof-reading.

Contents

CHAPTER I

Images of Contemporary Man and the Challenge to Modern Psychology

1. REFLECTIONS ON WHERE MODERN MAN IS AT AND THE PROBLEM OF UNDERSTANDING

We live in a time in which man has become problematic to himself as never before. Psychology, ambivalent about being a science of man, can take refuge in an attitude that its task is to comprehend and systematically describe behaviour, in other words, to be empirical and objective without further ado and hence, in this way, may define itself as being not necessarily concerned with man's fate although not thereby precluding its results from being used to improve human conditions. Psychology can, and often does, define itself in such a way that it can, as a science, be indifferent to the human condition. On the other hand, psychology may well ask itself whether it can be a *meaningful* science of man if it is indifferent to the question of what it means to be a person in our time and if it refuses to research and grapple with the human realities of the twentieth century.

To speak of modern man as being alienated, anomic, living in a Godless, meaningless universe, of being in despair and so on, is not new. Certainly, these terms were already used in the nineteenth century by people such as Søren Kierkegaard and Friederiech Nietzsche, as well as others. Nietzsche dramatically proclaimed the death of God and the coming transvaluation of values. Today, the discussion of the death of God hardly raises a ripple in sophisticated intellectual circles, and a statement that life is absurd only arouses strong emotions in the 'squarest' members of society. Man's dislodgement from a meaningful relation to the world was accurately prognosticated in the nineteenth century, but in the twentieth century the malaise has grown deeper. The conception of progress which includes a belief in the perfectibility of man in the nineteenth century has become a purely materialistic, vapid and empty term in the moral, human and cultural catastrophe of the twentieth century.

Hegel's secure system of thought which seemed to be able to encompass all of human reality was passionately attacked by Kierkegaard, Nietzsche and Marx, each from a different point of view. Organized Christianity which seemed to be a secure custodian of Western man's spirituality was bitterly attacked by Kierkegaard for its hypocrisy. This he expressed in the biting irony that whilst it was most unjust that America was not named after

1

Columbus it was even more unjust that Christianity *was* named after Christ.

The twentieth century has seen the emergence of new criticisms and pessimisms concerning the human condition. In 1930 Freud published *Das Unbehagen in der Kultur* (literally the *dis*-ease in culture) somewhat misleadingly translated as *Civilization and its Discontents*. The chief thrust of this book is that civilization is achieved at too high a price which is being paid for by a feeling of guilt whenever the human being tries to actualize the pleasure principle. However, Freud felt that we are unable to liberate ourselves from this because the repression of our aggressive and erotic strivings is the price we have to pay to have a civilization at all.

In the nineteenth century already, Karl Marx had pointed out in his early writings (mostly de-emphasized and abnegated in the official Communist states) that the abolition of property could lead to the abolition of human self-alienation, and therefore the real reappropriation of human essence by and for man. For Marx the stress on man's social aspect served to enhance his individuality. He thought that alienation vitiated all human faculties so that the supersession of this alienation would be a total liberation. He pointed out that humanity's sensibility had been so blunted that people could imagine objects to be there only when they actually possessed them, all physical and intellectual senses having been replaced by the single alienation of having. It would seem then that Marx has touched here on a truth in so far as man restricts himself in his relationship with the world (McClellan, pp. 35–6). However, it is clear that Marx, in concentrating on property relations, is defining alienation too narrowly.

Since the last world war, Herbert Marcuse, continuing Freud's and Marx's thinking in works such as *Eros and Civilization* and *One dimensional Man*, has argued that the dis-ease which Freud saw in culture mainly stems from surplus repression emanating from the productive principle. Furthermore, it seems that man has become one-dimensional, able to relate to nature in socially organized fashion only in terms of manipulation. He also speaks of this one-dimensionality being so strong that it cannot be overcome because all deviant or creative and non-conformist ways of living and relating to the world are smoothly reassimilated into the dominant life style by the repressive tolerance of contemporary capitalist society (Marcuse 1970, 1972).

Unlike Marx and Marcuse, Martin Heidegger does not see the roots of our contemporary malady in capitalism and the present social structure, but goes much further back. He characterizes the human condition in terms of a forgetfulness of being which he traces back to Socrates and the post-Socratic philosophers. Man is prevented from seeing the world as something which is there for him. The world is stripped of meaning because a long tradition of rationalist positivist thinking has degraded the thing into mere object. Heidegger sees it as the task of philosophy to rescue the consciousness of being out of our forgetfulness and to explicate it again for our time. The basic feature of the pre-Socratic Greek conception of being can be summarized in that thought and knowledge are saturated with the emphatic care concerning the light which emanates from the totality of the things-that-are, to heed this and to oppose mere appearance. Man therefore does not stand over against the things-that-are as mere uninvolved observer. Rather he is always the one who feels himself drawn into being as that which is continually in a process of creation. Words such as thinking, knowing and understanding did not have a purely rational meaning for pre-Socratic thinkers, but included an involvement, appreciation and differentiation. Such an understanding of being includes much more than mere logic and empirical thinking. It means that the cognition of the things-that-are was pervaded by an 'ought-to' and there could be no talk of value-free thinking. The split between logical thinking and ethics did not exist here, but this starts in the thought of Plato where the idea is for Plato the archetype of the essential thing which is an incomplete image of the *ideal* (derived from idea). Every idea orientates itself on a certain example and the highest norm is then the idea of the good (Kanthack 1959; Steiner 1978).

A value-free science, which, in our time at any rate, is a servant of technology, easily leads to the increasing organization and bureaucratization of life, control of production, distribution and eventually to control of human consciousness through the mass media. Theodor Roszak made this point cogently: 'Whatever the role of Reason may still be in defending the open society, it should by now be abundantly clear how easily the rationality of contemporary science passes over into a mere instrumental expertise within the technocratic hierarchy' (Roszak 1972, p. 241). Whether it is appropriate for natural scientists in circumstances such as these to continue to practise their quest as a value-free enterprise is an agonizing question. However, the question is whether psychology should be involved in augmenting these trends or whether it should be so constituted that it can, potentially, provide at least part of the answer to these problems. In other words, can psychology merely define itself as an observational endeavour not concerned with the direction of predominant cultural trends or should psychology involve itself in the sense of getting to know what areas of life require study most urgently and then 'giving itself away'? John Shotter, in fact, pleads that psychology should be a science which turns itself into a dialogue with the human being as to the question 'where should you and I go?' Unless the psychologist has a pretty clear idea of the human image that he would like to see realized, he will find that society and more specifically technocracy will dictate to him his frame of reference for research and, in this way, he may be contraproductive in bringing about the sort of change which thoughtful people can see is needed. If we define ourselves as being involved in questions like these, then surely psychology should become a science not only of man, but a science *for* man. Sigmund Koch speaks of 'the mass dehumanization process which characterizes our time – the simplification of sensibility, homogenization of taste, attenuation of the capacity for experience [that] continues apace. Of all fields of community in scholarship, it should be psychology which combats this trend. Instead, we have played no small role in augmenting and supporting it. It should be a matter of embarrassment that the few who are effectively working against the deterioration of culture are the physicists, the biologists, philosophers, historians, humanists, even administrators, participating in the re-definition of knowledge . . . but not *ourselves*. Is it not time that we raise the courage to relent?' (Koch 1968, p. 38).

John Shotter (p. 17) points out that man's 'bewilderment at his own nature has been growing for some quite long time now. But recently, with the creation of modern psychology, it has reached the final stage of its growth, and the condition has now become acute. For we live in a scientific society, and yet our scientific scheme of things has no place in it for our selves; in scientific terms they have no reality at all.' Shotter further indicates (p. 19) that 'unless we can formulate for ourselves an account of the world, which has in it a proper place for ourselves, it is of course, difficult to give any rational answers to questions such as these'. The questions John Shotter refers to are questions like 'what are the things in my world?' and 'what can I do to change things and change my condition, why am I like I am?' etc.

There can be no doubt that the early experimental psychologists anticipated that, by using the natural scientific method which recorded such resounding triumphs in the nineteenth and twentieth centuries, they too would be able to achieve great progress so that psychology could take up its rightful place next to the established biological and physical sciences, in fact, itself become a biological science using the natural scientific method. Thus, in 1890 one of the pioneers Theodor Ziehen (1924, p. 1) writes that the new psychology has banished metaphysics entirely. He says that it deserves the term physiological psychology in a double sense. Firstly, because it uses the methods of physiology rather than those of philosophy and, secondly, because it always looks at the physical parallels of what is experienced in consciousness. Moreover, he anticipates that through this new method the old contradiction between the material and the psychic can be overcome.

Two decades later, Watson (Woodworth 1931, p. 45) stated in his book *Behaviour: An Introduction to Comparative Psychology* that 'psychology as the behaviourist views it, would be a purely objective branch of natural science using experimental methods. Its theoretical goal is the prediction and control of behaviour.' Watson stated that psychology should discard reference to consciousness and forget about trying to make mental states the object of observation. This can be done, Watson continues, 'in terms of stimulus and response, in terms of habit formation, habit integration and the like . . .'. The aim would be to learn general and particular methods by which behaviour may be controlled. Watson also promised that if this plan was followed the educator, the physician, the jurist and the businessman could utilize the data in a practical way as soon as it could be experimentally obtained. In fact, Watson also claimed that this new psychology would make philosophy unnecessary, turning it into the history of science; furthermore an experimental ethics would be developed instead of an ethics based on theology, and behaviourism would develop scientifically-based ways of child-rearing and education and thus prevent neuroses which arose in childhood and had to be treated at great cost in adulthood. Watson in *Behaviourism* claims to put forward not only a new methodology, or a mere body of psychological theory, but a system which would revolutionize ethics, religion, psychoanalysis – in fact, make a natural science of what used to be known as the mental and moral sciences. Significant for the high hopes that were held out for the man who had won the public ear as a representative of science, was that a New York newspaper, *The Tribune*, wrote at the time 'perhaps this is the most important book ever written; one stands for an instance blinded with a great hope' (Woodworth 1931, p. 97).

Skinner, in his book *Beyond Freedom and Dignity* (1973) calls for a new design for our culture in order to avert the catastrophes emanating from man's antisocial behaviour. In order to achieve this, Skinner finds it necessary to demolish the idealistic view of autonomous man and transfer his functions one by one to the environment. To Skinner, man is a person in the sense that he is a body which displays a complex repertoire of behaviour. He believes that what he is doing in this book is an essential conceptual step to clear the deck for a fully scientific study of behaviour and hence for the reconstruction of man's life mainly by means of positive reinforcement. At this stage, we may note the faith of both Watson and Skinner in the efficacy of science (defined as natural science) to overcome man's problems. They seem to believe in the perfectibility of man which had been the essential component of the concept of progress in the nineteenth century. Neither of these scientists seems to have assimilated the significance of the cultural catastrophe of the First and Second World Wars, the tyrannization of consciousness, the dehumanization of man going on in the large-scale technologizing and bureaucratization of everyday life; but propose to meet the needs of contemporary man by reducing him to a mere object or organism to whom a set of behavioural technologies will be applied.

Although not all psychologists were as optimistic as Wundt, Ziehen and Watson, it does seem that most pioneers anticipated that if psychology became a scientific project it would succeed in becoming a science leading us to a greater understanding of man. The question may well be asked whether the project of natural scientific psychology can really succeed. If it has not succeeded in more than a hundred years since establishing itself, then can it succeed at all? Is it perhaps not more appropriate to ask whether, in fact, Wundt took the wrong turning? Should we not revise the entire project of scientific psychology, renounce Wundt, Watson and their followers and start anew using a different basis? This book is essentially an attempt to delineate an alternative basis for the project of a scientific psychology.

In addressing ourselves to this question, we must question to what extent psychology has really succeeded in confronting its basic subject-matter. In this connection G. M. Allport (1968, p. 4) has stated that 'In present day psychology, specialization is in the saddle, theorizing on the grand scale is frowned out of court and there are plenty of miniscule theories but scarcely any that are comprehensively human in their reference. Because of the stress on research methods, students operationalize the problem till it fits some measurement model and having thus operationalized the problem out of existence, they then go and test a highly artificial set of hypotheses.' When we look at the journals, the position remains equally depressive. One may read right through the journals for a number of years and find hardly any two things which can clearly connect up with one another. We find petty little experiments made to ascertain things such as the sensitivity to light of a certain type of fish, but how this connects up with some of the major problems of psychology remains obscure.

Contemporary psychology may be characterized as a series of almost discrete disciplines, some having only tenuous ties with other ramifications of the science. Theories have ranges of convenience and different foci; different sets of prescriptions seem to apply, depending on the field being investigated and the researcher's orientation. As regards Ziehen's promise to banish all metaphysics from psychology, Abraham Maslow (1961, p. 54) has suggested that we should refurbish our basis by turning back to philosophy, especially philosophical anthropology. Although Maslow is not uncritical of existentialist philosophy, he states that logical positivism has been a failure, that the basic philosophical presuppositions will have to be considered anew and that psychologists should stop relying on 'unconscious, unexamined philosophies that they picked up as children'.

Thorpe (1975), an eminent clinical psychologist, is so dissatisfied with what he called anti-mentalistic, 'nothing but' and dehumanizing trends in American psychology departments, that he calls for a unilateral declaration of independence for applied psychology by demanding separate departments.

Very few psychologists seem to be really hopeful that scientific psychology will sooner or later have something definitive and decisive to say about man and the human condition. Psychology seems to have put its faith in what we may call an accumulative fragmentalism. It is almost as if we feel that if we continue undertaking research programmes of various types without a central paradigm or a grand theory, we will somehow accumulate enough material for a consistent image of man to emerge at the end thereof. Some psychologists prefer not to think of that at all and see themselves either as practitioners who cannot be bothered too much about theory or as research scientists who cannot be bothered too much about understanding man as man. It could even be that some scientific psychologists think that their problem is not to understand man at all, but to understand something about a science of man. As against this, the phenomenologist would aver that psychology must define itself as a science in such a sense that it can contribute substantially and in a coherent and logical fashion to our understanding of the phenomenon man. It is therefore inevitable that a phenomenological psychologist will define psychology in a manner different from that of a Gestaltist, a behaviourist or a psychoanalyst.

2. DOMINANT IMAGES OF MAN IN PSYCHOLOGY AND PSYCHOLOGICAL RESEARCH

Allport had said that almost every psychological theory carries with it some presupposition regarding the body–mind relation, the function of consciousness, the issue of freedom, the nature of the self – to name a few of our riddles of the sphinx. He further goes on to say (1968, p. 19) that we can never have a fully systematic eclecticism until we can resolve two central antimonies in psychology, namely that of dualism and that of purpose. I shall restrict myself here to the problem of dualism. That a phenomenological approach can also help us to tackle the other problems consistently should become clear as we go along.

René Descartes (1595–1650) whose influence on Western thought and culture has been so profound, has bequeathed to psychology two images of man because of his radical dualism, namely the duality between mind and body and man and world. In his discourse on method he used a methodological doubt. He starts by doubting everything possible, e.g. he could doubt the reality of the world, the reality of his own body, etc. He noted that our senses sometimes delude us, therefore it is possible, in principle, that they can *always* delude us. Similarly we have dreams, he said, in which we have images of our bodies and the world which, we have to acknowledge, do not correspond to reality. However, in the end he could not doubt the fact that he was doubting; furthermore, he could hardly be doubting if he did not exist, i.e. the fact of himself as a subject could thus be secured as a truth. Hence we should start with the fact that we can doubt, i.e. think. From this comes his famous dictum '*cogito ergo sum*'; I think therefore I am.

However, what do we think about? Descartes, having put the human body and the world in brackets, i.e. having suspended judgement in his radical methodological doubt concerning the reality of these, could hardly have stated that it is the world that we think about. He could only reply: '*Sum cogitans cogitationes meas* – I think my own thinking, I am conscious of the contents of my consciousness, I know my own cognitive images, and that is what I am' (Luijpen 1969, p. 53). This means that God, the body and the things are not lost to thinking but have only been tainted by the qualifications 'thinking about'. Thus, even if my body and the chair I am sitting on are unreal, it is indisputable that I have the body-idea and the chair-idea.

Descartes then asked himself what conferred the quality of indubitability to the foregoing statements and concluded that nothing convinced him of the truth of his statements except that he had this clear and distinct idea that in order to think, one must *be*. Clearness and distinctness are therefore the criteria for truth.

As far as materiality is concerned only one quality met the criterion of being clear and distinct and that was extension. This then goes for everything in the world that is not the *res cogitans*, man's body and the world, in fact, everything tangible by what-ever sense or means, becomes part of the *res extensa*, therefore quantitative. However, it is only the natural sciences which operate with materiality as quantity. In Cartesian thinking then whatever natural sciences cannot speak about may have some meaning for everyday life, but none at all for the 'marvellous science' which concerns itself with what is real and what is true.

According to Theodor Roszak, Descartes related that in November 1619 an angel descended and revealed to him the possibility of a *marvellous* new *science*, based upon mathematics. Roszak makes the wry comment 'And here perhaps we have the fateful assumption which has made science what it is, and our culture the captive audience of the scientist's single vision that the angel of truth can speak but once and then only as a mathematician' (Roszak 1972, pp. 294–5).

In Cartesian terms then, man, his body and his world, has a twofold reality, namely that of *res cogitans* and *res extensa*. Let us first look at the *res extensa*. It should also be clear now that in so far as science always works on declared or undeclared philosophical presuppositions, it has certainly flourished on the nourishment thus afforded it by Descartes. All scientific terms can in the last analysis be reduced to spatiality, e.g. weight, speed, colour, etc. Looking at the cultural impact of Cartesian philosophy then we note that Western man has been notable and unique through his unparalleled conquest of space. The vast edifice of science and technology is built entirely upon measurement procedures. But such a world is at a most basic level of thought a dehumanized one. Descartes took man entirely out of the world and science in Cartesian terms is only possible in so far as man keeps himself out of his observations. No one can gainsay the unparalleled success of the scientific endeavour that has been erected on this basis.

But now what about psychology? Psychology inherited first the *res cogitans* part of Descartes vision. Mind or soul, Descartes said, was an insubstantiality, or rather an immaterial substance. He then had to explain to himself how it was that if I think, or if I decide that I could lift my hand, this could actually be done because the decision to lift the hand is a psychic operation whereas lifting the hand itself is a physical operation. Descartes supposed that the two entities could interact and he designated the pineal gland which is situated in the middle of the brain as the locus of this interaction. It never became clear exactly how this interaction could take place and, accordingly, we find that this division of man into a physical and material part and the radical differentiation of the mind, or self, or soul, from the world has placed psychology in an unbearable dilemma. Contemporary schools of psychology are all too clearly attempts to get away from this basic dilemma.

3. FREUD'S PERSONALITY THEORY

Freud's personality theory started essentially as an attempt to erect a structure of personality within the confines of Descartes' *res cogito*. It is an intrapsychic theory, an inner view of man.

The discovery and development of psychoanalysis is usually traced back to the years 1880–2 when Joseph Breuer was treating a neurotic patient, known in the literature as Anna O. The main symptom in Anna's case was a paralysis of the right arm and of the right leg. She also later developed paralyses of the left leg, anaesthesia of several parts of the body, a functional visual disorder and a disorder of consciousness which was akin to a state of hypnosis. In this last state, Breuer could converse with Anna. After these cathartic sessions (called 'chimney-sweeping' by Anna), the patient felt better. In the summer of 1882, she developed a new symptom which was cured in an interesting and dramatic manner. This was cytophobia, which is a fear of liquid. Every attempt on Anna's part to drink something led to nausea. She got rid of the symptom in one of her sessions in which she was in a state of spontaneous hypnosis. Talking about her new symptom, Anna suddenly remembered that she had seen how a dog had been drinking from a vessel out of which a woman had just slaked her thirst. While Anna was telling this, she expressed the most extreme nausea. However, immediately afterwards she asked for a glass of water, drank the water and the symptom was gone.

Now let us have a look at what this case meant for Freud and Breuer, who were collaborators for quite a time. First of all, it meant that there was a certain affect or emotion which was associated with a certain experience. In the case of Anna's last symptom, it was the experience of seeing what to her (as to most nineteenth-century people of the upper classes) must have been a disgusting event. The glass was contaminated for her and the emotions that went with it were repressed together with the experience. They were forgotten but, and this is the important thing, although the emotions as well as the experience were forgotten, they continued to exert a dynamic influence from somewhere. 'Where' was this somewhere? This, Freud thought, showed that there must be some sphere of the psychic life in which experiences etc. which were no longer conscious could go on affecting the life of the patient. Hence, there must be an unconscious sphere of the psyche and, moreover, there must be a mechanism by which conscious experiences or memories could become part of the unconscious. Repression is the prototypical defence mechanism; later on a wide variety of other mechanisms were elaborated. From the way in which Anna recovered, came the idea of the dynamic influence of past events on the present consciousness of the patient and the idea that cure was to be effected by recovering the contents of the unconscious. Initially Freud tried to help the patient recover unconscious contents by means of hypnosis; however, he soon substituted the method of free association. Psychoanalysis, Freud later said, could be likened to the process of draining the Zuider Zee in Holland.

The following are the main principles of the psychoanalytic approach to personality:

(1) The principle of psychic determinism

According to Freud, it was possible for outer random events to influence one's life. For instance, crossing the street at the same time as a lorry fails to stop at the robot may bring about an accident. On the other hand, stated Freud, there was no *inner* randomness. Impulses coming from within the person were *determined* by prior conditions. These were often unconscious as he could demonstrate through the analyses of dreams, slips of the tongue and errors in writing and action.

(2) The principle of unconscious determination

Freud's depth psychology rests upon the assumption that the inner life of the individual is built up in layers. The deeper layer is unconscious and is controlled by its own laws of time, space and logic. The unconscious is timeless; whether a thing happened 50 years or half a day ago, is immaterial for the unconscious. It is also indifferent to any idea of spatiality. In other words, whether the person spoken to or referred to is far or near, for the unconscious it makes no difference. Thirdly, the unconscious is totally illogical: opposites like love and hate, admiration and contempt, can exist side by side.

There is intense relationship between the conscious and the unconscious and the unconscious can sometimes make us do things which are completely contrary to our conscious intentions. The unconscious consists of contents which were never conscious, but this content is added to by repression of those experiences and thoughts which are not acceptable to the individual's image of himself.

(3) The historical or genetic principle

Although Freud changed his theory on many occasions, he never relinquished the idea that the present symptom or manifestation of personality can be explained by reference to early happenings in life. When he found that his early traumatic theory of the origin of neurosis was no longer tenable, he substituted a genetic theory and thus retained the principle that present events can be explained by what happened in the past. Freud never gave any great significance to the present tense, nor was his metapsychology able to accommodate the future *as* future.

(4) The individualistic principle

Although Freud did not deny the role of parents and other significant adults, he never sought the causes of neurosis or present mental states in the actions of people other than the patient. In Freud's theory, the difficult parent could not be held responsible for the difficulties experienced by his child. The Oedipus complex in fact serves to illustrate the family triangle, but Freud saw this complex in terms of the internalized *representations* of father and mother, not in terms of the *acts* of father and mother.

(5) The principle of determination by passion rather than by reason

It is clear that Freud's entire psychology involved the primacy of emotion rather than reason and certainly his psychology helped to overthrow the view of rational man which had been current in certain schools of philosophy and political economy.

(6) Determination by drive or instinct

Freud saw the human being as being fundamentally a driven creature – a creature who has a limited amount of energy at his disposal and seeks to discharge such energy. Although Freud did not deny the validity of drives such as those of hunger and thirst, he felt that these needs could be easily satisfied in most societies so that the dynamic element would usually be sex. Sex had, for Freud, a wide erotic meaning and he saw the human being in the first place as being pleasure driven or hedonistic. As time went on, it became difficult for him to explain phenomena such as nightmares, depressions and the war neuroses of the First World War (so-called shell-shock cases) in these terms. In his book *Beyond the Pleasure Principle* published in the early 1920s he observed the need for repetition as basic to the pleasure principle. Thus, a child may play at throwing away a thing and retrieving it and do this over and over. Freud actually observed this in a child whose mother worked and he interprets this as a need to hold on to the love object, the departing mother. In other words, the child was using his play as a magic equivalent to having control of his mother. This means that the pleasure drive is essentially a holding on to and an attempt to re-establish an earlier state of affairs. *The drive bends back*. This means that man paradoxically wants to restore the state when he was not yet born. All organic life show a tendency towards breaking down into more simple forms. This means that the aim of life is death. The Id therefore embodies not only the eros or life-drive, but the death or aggressive drive as well.

(7) The reductionistic principle

We may note that Freud's theory starts out as an attempt to explain the meaning of symptoms. It then becomes a comprehensive theory of psychic life. The psyche is seen here as some sort of immaterial container in which the drama of life is being played out. To this extent, then, Freud remained well within the confines of the Cartesian 'inner man'. However, the positivistic philosophy of Freud's time was a strong one as it still is. Apart from the general scientific climate of the time, Freud was also personally influenced by one of his mentors, Ernst Brücke, who was a member of the Helmholtz school of medicine, in which reduction to material properties was not just an explanatory principle but an article of faith. Reductionism means that higher principles are reduced to those lower on the scale. In the last instance, all human reality is to be found in physiological, chemical and physical processes. For instance, Freud believed that there was no reality in what we call moral principles, values or religion. This could be reduced in the last instance to the basic physiological needs of a person. For instance, great emphasis on cleanliness could be reduced to reaction formation against anal strivings, or a great emphasis on religion could be reduced to a defence against aggressive impulses directed on the father. In the last instance, everything reduces to libido, which is fundamentally a form of physical energy which drives the body-mind machine called man.

It is Freud's immortal merit that he saw that symptoms had meaning. In other words, Freud was the first both to see and build into a systematic system the fact that man's problems in living were not simply a feature of his imagination, were not simply due to malingering, but constituted a reality of his life. The method of psychoanalysis makes it possible for one person called analyst to share in the human reality of another person called patient. The tragedy, however, of Freud's development, from the phenomenological point of view, is the fact that these insights were then forced into the procrustean bed of the empiricistic-positivistic science of his time so that eventually everything 'psychic' had to be forced into a frame of reference in which the basic life and death drives could be resolved into physiology. Medard Boss has tried to show that in the psychoanalytic practice there is already an unmediated and concrete understanding of the fellow human being. For instance, if we speak of repression, then we are talking about the fact that the human being has the capacity to either accept the life potentialities offered in free responsibility to himself or to deny them (Boss 1957, p. 47).

Also in the development of the concept of transference, as the cornerstone of psychoanalytic therapy, Freud showed that he understood the fact that the possibility of being with-one-another, of sharing, of being open with one another points towards our primary openness to each other (Boss 1957, p. 48). In fact, Freud said that transference and counter-transference went together. In other words, the personal relationship between patient and psychoanalyst would be a mutual thing. Secondly, Freud already saw clearly that the analyst had to have great respect for the peculiar character of the analysis and that it was therefore necessary for the analyst to be careful that he did not directly influence the patient and, moreover, in no way violated the individuality of the patient.

We have been so used to thinking in psychoanalytic terms that it is as well at this stage to look at a couple of them and see what validity and use they may have as explanatory concepts. A young man who was said to be in the initial acute stages of schizophrenia once came to me and impressed me as being in a very agitated and highly anxious state. He sat down and told me that he had some absolutely inexplicable and uncanny experiences, that he never felt like this before and was very puzzled by what was going on in his inability to understand himself. I asked him how he felt right now and, looking around the office, he stated that when he looked at a certain chair it was uncanny because he felt that the chair was controlling him. I then asked him to go and sit on the chair, to handle the chair, feel his weight on it. He did this and I asked him then how he felt; he said he felt better. He no longer felt that the chair was controlling him. However, he added, my table was now controlling him. I then asked him to sit at my table, handle the papers on the table, open and close the drawers, etc.; after doing this, he no longer had the feeling that the chair or the table was controlling him. Psychoanalytically, this could be explained in terms of projection. There is no way in which the chair could be said to be controlling my client and certainly I could not experience the table or the chair as controlling me. The answer must then be that the client was projecting his own feelings on to the table or the chair. But how would such a projection take place? How is it possible that something like a feeling of being controlled can somehow be inside an encapsulated subject living within the boundaries of his own skin, can then leave him to attach itself to a thing like a chair or a table, in other words, become united to these things to such an extent that the patient sees this change as reality. I shall come back to this example later in my discussion of the spatializing aspect of existence in which it will be possible to understand this client's being in the world. For the moment, we shall have to conclude that projection as an explanatory principle cannot stand the scrutiny of experience, because no one has ever experienced detaching a feeling from himself and making it adhere to something else. Similarly, when the client complains of psychosomatic symptoms for which no organic basis can be found, it is said that he converts. A similar argument can be used to criticize this concept, because no one has ever explained how it is possible for a purely subjective feeling existing in the 'mind' of a subject to attach itself to his body seen as an object. Similarly, the concept of transference is also explained in that an affect or emotion which used to be experienced in relation to one person is now transferred to another person. This means that contact problems are transferred from one person to another, in which case the first one was the one with whom the patient really had the trouble, whilst the second one is the person with whom he is not having trouble. Now the experiential test of these conceptions are disqualified by the psychoanalytic insistence that the projection, conversion and transference happens unconsciously. In other words, a series of concepts which are inexperienceable and unprovable are justified by another concept which is just as unprovable.

The Measurement Option

The marvellous science of which Descartes had a vision was a science which ultimately resolves itself into mathematics so that all statements can eventually be moulded into quantitative form. For psychology to be able to comply with this requirement man has to be conceived as being measurable. It is also true that we have a certain natural scientific dogmatism which lays claim to the nature of reality itself as reflected in the statement by Max Planck that the real is that which is measurable. A similar absolutism is seen in the statement by Thorndike that all that exists, exists to a certain degree and anything that exists to a certain degree can be measured. The measurability of the human personality is also the perspective of Raymond Cattell who indicated that '. . . the scientists of psychology are peering into a hyper-space. In this multi-dimensional world into which we have, at any rate, taken a passing glance, the great discoveries of psychological mathematics remain to be made' (Cattell 1970, p. 366). The 'passing glance' to which he refers is his own extensive analysis of variance of questionnaires, ratings, objectives tests, etc., which he built into a comprehensive personality theory – a really impressive structure. But on what grounds does Cattell decide that one can understand man better if one is able to measure him? Presumably he does this because it is the only possible way he sees of being scientific. To what extent, we may ask, however, does Cattell's indubitably brilliant use of his methods and mathematical analyses comply with the more basic scientific requirement to be true to that which is being observed? Supposing one is in a lecture room and wants to make a study of the attitude of students who are facing the table. One may argue that some of them will like the table, others will dislike it and a third group will be indifferent. The researcher can now assign to each different attitude a numerical value of, let us say, one, two or three. He can similarly ask the students how they feel about the dean of the faculty and they can again be given a choice: like, indifferent, or dislike and he can, logically again assign the value of 1, 2 and 3 to these differentials. We are using two very superficial examples which sound rather arbitrary, but with various refinements this is really the basis on which we have erected the enterprise of measurement in psychology. But now we come to the important question: in this piece of research where research may have found that the average attitude of the class towards the dean equals 2,1 and towards the table 2,2 can it still be said that 1 = 1, 2 = 2 and 3 = 3 as one would have been able to say if one had measured the physical length of the dean and of the table with a calibrated ruler? If the reply to this question is no, then the project of a measurement psychology or psychometrics in the sense that experience and behaviour are quantifiable cannot be successful. If the reply is yes, then one has equalized the dean with the table. To put this more precisely, one has then equalized human experience of the table with human experience of the dean. This last postulation, however, so clearly contradicts the experienced reality that it need not be discussed further.

Arguing from this rather slender basis, one can make the more general statement that, with a view to understanding the human being, natural scientifically oriented measurement psychology is not a suitable endeavour. We cannot understand man as man rather than as object by means of the measurement approach. It is only after we have an understanding of what it really means to be a student in the classroom in relation to a piece of furniture or in relation to another person such as the dean, that we may be able to devise a measurement procedure in order to study certain aspects of this complex relationship. In this sense, then, phenomenological research is propaedeutic to other forms of research. We believe, however, that after looking through the matter phenomenologically, it may, in many cases, be unnecessary to do a measurement study as well. That is because, in order to understand our fellow man, we shall have to look mainly at the quality of his experience, in other words, how he feels about it or what he experiences, or what it is in the world which really speaks to him, e.g. what is the meaning of the phenomenon (table or dean) for him. However, these qualities and nuances of meaning cannot be quantified. They can only be quantified in the rather arbitrary way shown above.

Do we thereby limit ourselves to ideographic research? Everybody has his own style of life; the experience of the table and of the dean of person A is his *own* and can never be the same as that of person B. Can we also do nomothetic research using a phenomenological approach? The answer is yes: for details please refer to the chapter on Research. In the present section I want to consider the possibilities of nomothetic research in natural scientific psychology.

Nomothetic research in psychology aims to arrive at general statements concerning the nature of experience and behaviour, i.e. regularities which are valid for at least all members of at least a certain defined group of people. Now it is a fact that in the hundred years of psychology as a separate experimental science, no such law has yet been found. We are inclined to ascribe this state of affairs to the youthfulness of psychology as a science, but we forget that we chose the date 1879 as the beginning of scientific psychology because the first laboratory for psychology was established then. However, psychology, as an experimental natural science, developed its basic foundations long before Wundt in the work of Herbart, Weber, Fechner and others. The historical fact of which we usually remain silent is that the date 1879 is approximately only 75 years later than the date on which other sciences such as chemistry got their own laboratories. We now have to put this question in a more direct and painful manner. If the project of a natural scientific psychology has not succeeded after more than a hundred years of experimental research, is it perhaps because psychology on this basis cannot succeed? The reason why we cannot find scientific laws in the accepted sense is, firstly, that the experiment on a natural scientific basis requires, in principle, the possibility of identical repetition of the original experiment. One could, for instance, design an experiment in which one induces fear in a group of people by startling them in various ways, e.g. by a gunshot, a snake which appears unexpectedly, etc. One can then make certain objective observations, e.g. one can photograph facial expressions, measure changes in heartbeat and blood vessel expansion, etc. In this manner one can posit a general scientific hypothesis concerning the effect of such stimulation on the human being. It is in principle, however, impossible for me to raise this hypothesis to a law, because I cannot conceivably repeat the experiment exactly. It is not a question here of an obstacle which eventually can be overcome. On the contrary, the repetition of the experiment in such a manner that it complies with the requirements of natural scientific verification is, in principle, impossible for reasons which are obviously part and parcel of human existence, namely: (a) One cannot use the same group of people in order to repeat the experiment because if they come into the same situation they will already have changed. The human being, unlike a stone, is changed by the experiment. (b) A second group cannot be used because it is simply impossible to find a second group of people who are exactly equal to the first group. (*c*) What we find in the laboratory is not easily generalized into life in general. If we weigh a stone in the laboratory, we have no reason whatsoever to surmise that such a stone will have a different weight outside the laboratory. The human being in the laboratory, however, is not an isolated self which can be deposited in a specific place like a stone or a piece of flesh; man usually lives a certain set of relationships and in the laboratory he lives another set of relationships. The laboratory as situation, his relationship vis-à-vis the experimenter and even the space of the laboratory which, with its apparatuses and general atmosphere, cannot be experienced as the usual form of lived space; all those circumstances define the human being in the laboratory as being different from the way he is constituted in everyday life.

It is a fact that any psychological experiment involves a relationship between the subject and the experimenter and this has made it impossible to achieve the ideal of objectivity in psychology. Objectivity means that the subjects must only be affected by the variables controlled by the experimenter and not by him as a person to whom the subject relates. It has, however, become clear that this is impossible. Lyons (1970, p. 21) has suggested that there is a hidden dialogue in experimental research:

'E does not tell S everything there is to tell and so S responds with two communications. On the overt level he "answers" E by appearing to following the experimental instructions; and on the covert level he makes his own guess as to what E is really after and then acts with that assumption. Conversely since S does not tell E everything that he has to tell, E responds to him with two communications. On the overt level he recites the instructions and carries out his duties as experimenter; and on the covert level, suspecting that there is something S is not telling, he makes his own guess as to how much S really knows, and although he may not vary his behaviour during the experimental session, he quite probably allows this guess to enter into his final interchange with S and his interpretation of the data.'

Psychophysiology

There is a very strong train of thought in psychology that, to understand what is going on with the human being, we have to make a study of his glands as well as his autonomic and central nervous systems. From this point of view it is argued that consciousness is really just an epiphenomenon of the brain or, differently formulated, that there is only brain action and that the study of consciousness as such is scientifically of no particular value because, in order to be scientific, we must restrict ourselves to that to which the consciousness can be reduced. This point of view, sometimes called central state materialism or the mind–brain identity thesis, has a fairly long history. About 150 years ago a French physician, La Mettrie, wrote a book called *L'Homme machine* and in the present century, the brain was first seen as a very complicated switchboard, later, however, as a computer, and nowadays we are told that we should master the metaphor of the brain code as used by molecular biologists. In other words, we are being asked to get to know the language of the brain. But, asks D. N. Robinson, who are the *'we'* who are being asked to undertake this learning process? Is the brain being asked to learn its own language? In other words, the language which I am using in order to write this sentence, if it is a reduced or translated version of brain language and if the consciousness and the brain are identical, then that must mean that this sentence is being written by my brain. But who can read a codified language without the knowledge of the original language on which the code was based? In other words, we are saying that the real language is not the language we speak, but the code. However, the code is based upon the language which we speak. This, in turn, means that if we are saying that we have to get to know the language of the brain, we are then saying something which is totally paradoxical such as that the language which I have to teach myself is the language which I have been taught and am using now. The reality of the situation is that if we go through the brain, we find no meanings, no words, no conscious contents, in short, we find nothing of that which makes human existence meaningful. All we shall be able to find will be movements of electrical impulses and chemical reactions of brain matter. We shall find no neuron which is in possession of a noun and we shall also be unable to find a combination of cells or synapses which display a motive. Neither shall we be able to find a piece of cortex which is in possession of a memory (Robinson 1976, p. 397). What we may find is that certain conscious processess will be impossible without certain brain processes, but it is totally wrong to infer that the necessity for the brain means that the brain, as such, is consciousness. I do not sit in my head just as I am not sitting in my left or my right foot. It seems as if this type of research is being given a privileged position because of psychology's endeavour to comply with the norms of high scientific standing. Natural scientific procedures require *res extensae* (spatial things) and in the case of the 'mind' the brain is the only candidate. It is undoubtedly true that a neurological investigation can throw much light on certain conditions or preconditions for human existence, but the nervous system as such does not embrace human existence. It seems to me that the materialistic view of consciousness has not been proved by experimental findings and, in fact, is not provable by such findings. Even if I should succeed in bringing out emotions by means of electrical stimulation of the reticular formation of the brain, such as found by the Swedish researcher Holger Hyden, I shall always still have to ask the person whether it is rage or joy which he is now experiencing. In other words, even in this type of research, I do not remain independent of communication. It is not possible for me to activate a certain set of nerves and then to be able to say that what the person is experiencing is this or that. I have to ask him at least once what it really means to him, that is, how he is experiencing it. It is, of course, possible to leave out the meaning of the person's experience and to concern ourselves exclusively with the physiology of brain processes, but then we are no longer psychologists but physiologists, i.e. not even physiological psychologists.

Behaviourism

Compared to psychoanalysis and central state materialism, both behaviourism and phenomenology are attempts to move away from an intrapsychic theory of man. I say here that central state materialism representes an intrapsychic view of man although it moves away from the psyche altogether, but does so only by assigning the functions of the psyche to a physical entity, the brain. Behaviourism does not try to localize behaviour in the central nervous system, but tries to locate it between the individual and the environment. Radical behaviourism goes further by saying that the individual is entirely under the control of the environment of which an important component (Skinner 1964) is the verbal community. The radical behaviourist such as Skinner declares himself uninterested in events that go on inside the skin and explicitly rejects the intrapsychic or representational theory of consciousness. Thus, Skinner says, 'If a real world is, indeed, scrambled in transmission, but later reconstructed in the brain, we must then start all over again and explain how the organism sees the reconstruction' (Skinner 1964, p. 87). It is, in fact much easier to hold that the world we see is simply the world out there and here phenomenology would be in agreement with radical behaviourism. A difference of opinion will, however, arise when the nature of the world out there is explicated. Skinner says the world out there is what is studied by the physical sciences. This means that the profile of the world delineated by the physical sciences is absolutized as *the* reality. However, the phenomenologist would tend to deny that the world out there is a system of bare facts. He would point to the limitation of science which can operate only within its own view of the world in terms of which the object is defined implicity and explicitly as that which can be described by using the parameters of space as pure extensionality and time as linear progression. As we shall see later, the phenomenologist will deny that this is the only valid delineation of time and spatiality. Because Skinner and other behaviourists see the world out there as a system of bare facts, the relationship between the organism and the environment is described in terms of stimuli and responses. However, a careful reading of behaviourist literature will reveal that a consistent explanation of what a stimulus and a response is, and how these two are to be clearly distinguished under all circumstances, is lacking. A circular definition seems mostly to be used, in terms of which a stimulus is something which elicits a response whereas a response is something elicited by a stimulus.

Furthermore, behaviourism does not try to develop a method which is adequate to its subject-matter, namely man. Behaviourism simply says that there is already in existence a pre-existent body of methodology, namely that of the natural sciences, which should be applied to the human object as well. Thus, although behaviourism takes man out of his skull and sees him as being in relation to the world, it tries to describe the phenomena of being a person in terms of a purely objective observation of the behavioural expression of such phenomena. For instance, the phenomenon of anger is not studied directly, but, instead, an attempt is made to define anger operationally in terms of angry behaviour such as balling the fist, getting involved in fighting, shouting, etc. A behavioural description will thus specify the observable contingencies of what is usually understood by being angry, but it will not give us a description of what the term anger means experientially and in action.

From the foregoing, we can see that various strategies used to overcome the Cartesian dilemma have been characteristic of four major approaches in psychology. We have also noted that none of these seems to have an adequate answer as to how to study the human being in order for experience and behaviour to emerge in meaningful terms and to be systematically described and subsumed in a comprehensive unified body of knowledge called psychology. It will therefore be the task of the next chapter to indicate how phenomenology tackles the problem and to weigh its adequacy in terms of whether it remains true to its subject-matter.

CHAPTER II

Man, his World and the Task of Psychology

In order to understand the phenomenological approach to psychology, it is necessary to understand something about its history. Contemporary existential phenomenology (Luijpen 1969, pp. 31–5) is derived from two main sources. The first is Søren Kierkegaard, a Danish theologian and thinker who may be regarded as the founder of existentialism but who could hardly be called a phenomenologist. Outside of Kierkegaard's field, theology, one could refer to the work of F. Nietszche as existentialist and also to the novels of Dostoeivsky which were preoccupied with man, in all his ecstatic and tortured ramifications, with his painful choices and relationships. On the other hand, the father of phenomenology is Edmund Husserl, who could hardly be called an existentialist. Husserl and Kierkegaard have something in common though, in that they both rejected the reductionistic tendencies of natural science and both denied that man could be understood by regarding him as a system of atoms.

Kierkegaard made penetrating studies of self and anxiety and spoke from intense direct personal experience. Rollo May cogently remarked that whilst Freud had a vast knowledge *about* anxiety, Kierkegaard *knew* anxiety. Kierkegaard regards man as existence, as subject involved with God. Man, not being a self-sufficient, spiritual atom, is a subject which is authentically himself in his relation to the God of Revelation. Existence in the philosophy of Kierkegaard is absolutely original and unrepeatable, radically personal and unique. By his emphasis on the uniqueness of existence, it is impossible for this branch of the movement to speak of generalized knowledge which is the claim of every science. In this emphasis on the unique and particularity of each existence, one has to accept as a consequence that everything that is thought about such an existence can in principle not be applicable to any reality other than the reality of the existence of the thinker himself and therefore have no broader validity. In this sense, then, the thinking of Kierkegaard is both consciously and voluntarily anti-scientific and does not and cannot reach further than a monologue. However, the fact that the existentialist in the Kierkegaardian sense does not want to be scientific could also be seen as the reaction against a certain definite attitude over what scientific is meant to be. Kierkegaard was reacting mainly to Hegel in whom scientism was such that the original and unique in human subjectivity was simply argued out of the picture.

Husserl, however, was not anti-scientific in the same sense that

Kierkegaard was, but there were certain correspondences. Husserl was not satisfied with the state of the philosophy of his time. He did not think, as some scientists and even philosophers did and do, that philosophy was an unnecessary luxury and should make way for the empirical methods of natural science. He denied that natural science was the only form of science that could exist. In this, the work of Dilthey was also salient. Dilthey, before Husserl's publication of *Logical Investigations* (1900), had indicated that the sciences concerned with man should regard themselves as Geisteswissenschaften, should define their task as that of understanding and that these should be differentiated from the natural sciences which had as their task the job of explaining (Van den Berg 1973, p. 42). Husserl similarily denied that natural science was the only form of science that could exist and he wanted to make philosophy also into a strict science. Philosophy therefore could not allow natural science to prescribe its methods. Phenomenology then, although not a natural science, also strives for inter-subjectivity and general laws. Husserl investigated consciousness as intentionality, a term derived from Franz Brentano who was one of Wundt's numerous critics. Brentano had criticized Wundt's approach of trying to analyse consciousness into its elements. This, according to Brentano, was a futile endeavour because consciousness does not exist in and for itself. Consciousness he said, always intends an object – I do not just love, I love someone, I do not just see, I see something. In order to attain his aim, Husserl took over Brentano's concept of intentionality and expanded it. He investigated consciousness as intentionality, i.e. consciousness as being directed on to that which is not consciousness itself. In this conception Husserl showed a close relationship to Kierkegaard's view of man as existence, in that both turned their faces against an atomistic conception of man and consciousness.

Now it is easy to see why Husserl's approach is called phenomenology. If consciousness intends an object, then the focus should be on the object itself. Husserl said that one should allow a phenomenon to speak for itself. In other words, if we are investigating our perception of the tree, we should try to look at this tree without any preconceptions and we should then explicate our primary experience of the *tree*. One of Husserl's better-known slogans is 'back to the things themselves' (*'Zurück zu den Sachen'*).

To be quite clear on this point: if we say consciousness intends an object, then we are not trying to suggest that consciousness is some homuncule, some organ or substantiality which operates a function. It would be more accurate to say that consciousness is not a substance, immaterial or otherwise, that intends, but that being conscious means an intentional act through which man lets the world appear to him. It is an irrefutable fact that we are conscious of the things and people around us and of ourselves. All that we know and basically need to know at the outset is that it is in the nature of man to be able to reveal the world to himself. Consciousness must therefore not be seen as any sort of entity closed in upon itself but as an act of revealing.

It is also easy to see that when one speaks of man's continuous intentional acts one can hardly study man as an entity isolated from the world. If consciousness is not absolute, then it is hard to see how man can be seen as existing within himself. If consciousness is the act of revealing the world and if this act is always directed towards an object, then the encapsulated view of man must fall away. This has very important implications for psychology. Martin Heidegger is the philosopher who tries to explicate this basic question. In this philosopher, then, the two streams of existentialism and phenomenology are joined together. Influenced by Husserl's epistomology, existentialism shed its anti-scientific bias while phenomenology was enriched by existential themes. Heidegger tried to develop a philosophy of man; a philosophy which starts with the ancient question of being. Instead of focusing on the 'I' of Descartes in the phrase 'I think therefore I am', he focused on the 'am' or *being* question. In terms of Heidegger's thinking one would rather say 'I am, therefore I think'. Our consciousness of being, i.e. of being in the world, precedes all our thinking about the world. Man is both the question and the questioner and therefore he must be the starting point of all questions concerning being. Man is the being who is in the world consciously and thus illuminates being. Using Husserl's conception of intentionality, Heidegger overcomes the subject/object dichotomy and thus gives us a philosophy of man which avoids the pitfalls of both idealism (which absolutizes mind) and materialism (which absolutizes man's spatial–measurable existence).

The picture is slightly complicated because Heidegger refuses to identify himself as an existentialist or a phenomenologist, in spite of the fact that it was he who first elaborated the various dimensions of standing out to the world or existence. Heidegger prefers to call himself a thinker of being. He sharply distinguishes his hermeneutic phenomenology from Husserl's phenomenology of consciousness.

Heidegger's explication of being in his major work *Sein und Zeit* which first appeared in 1927 does not directly concern us here. However, the major dimensions of his ontology have been adapted for psychology as a philosophical anthropology, especially by Medard Boss, following on earlier attempts in this direction by Ludwig Binswanger and others. In the next section we shall be expounding Heidegger's view of man's being in the world. Heidegger makes a clear-cut distinction between Sein (being) and the Seiende (the totality of things that are – it must be understood that the things-that-are includes everything of which man can speak, e.g. stones, animals, people, thoughts, emotions, music, etc.). In using these translations, I am following Thomas Langan (1959) in order to avoid the confusion engendered by other translations using 'being' for both of Heidegger's terms.

BEING-IN-THE-WORLD

It belongs to the essence of man that the totality of things-that-are is always showing itself to him in some or other of its manifold forms or particularities, e.g. plants, animals, rivers, mountains, buildings, fellow human beings, his own body, thoughts, emotions, etc. Man must, in some or other way, be so constituted or extended that all these can 'appear in the light' or become apparent to him. This includes not only seeing (optically) but also hearing or using the other senses. The things-that-are may also offer themselves to us as a dream or something fantasied, imagined or thought about. Man is therefore a being which is always open for all the other things-that-are. He is a locale or instance where the totality of that which announces itself can be taken up and held fast (Kanthack 1959, pp. 1–8).

We are unable to think of man in such a way that nothing, but nothing, shows itself to him not even in the way of a vague feeling of something. We do not know what man would be like if it would not have been possible for him to be like this. As a place to which something can offer itself, he is never so isolated and abandoned that he may be described as an emptiness that is waiting to be filled up.

I am deliberately using the phrase 'that which shows itself' to overcome the built-in dualistic tendencies in language. Due to our dualistic language, one tends to say 'I see a tree or flowers or the doggy', rather than to say that the tree and all other things-that-are can show themselves to me.

It is not necessary that things show themselves with the same amount of clarity all the time. If I walk along a landscape, I shall notice this or that feature of the scene in turn, but those which I have noted and which are now out of focus do not thereby vanish entirely. It goes into a backgroundedness but it is still there for me in the sense that it can be made present again. From this we may see that the wholeness of the things that are can, in principle, be made present to us.

We have to emphasize man as the openness of being who 'catches' that which shows itself in its potential allness. Man can only be a torso if we try to pull him out of his cohesion with the things-that-are. He remains bracketed with these until his death. However, when he dies, the cohesion is broken. With that something falls away which was unique. The things that appeared in his life can never show themselves again in the very same manner to anyone else. In this manner, then, the things-that-are are involved in an unrepeatable cohesion with a specific individual. This is the same as saying that each human life is a unique and for ever unrepeatable series of experiences.

In order to clarify being, Heidegger goes back to one of the most original of all questions, namely, what is the way of being of the things-that-are. The answer to this must be presence in both senses of the word (temporarily as well as spatially). Presence, however, has duration and therefore being and being human must be understood from the perspective of time.

If being as such is a presence it has to be characterized from the very beginning by a certain clarity. Something like presence or being-present can happen only in the clarity of being. Man then is that presence which steps forward in a clearly delineated manner as the necessary lighting of being. This means that if we look at man apart from prejudiced characterizations in terms such as consciousness, soul, body as a material entity, or person, etc., and if we approach man in such a way that he shows himself only through himself, his true core comes forward as the open domain of being. It is true then to say that the most characteristic and fundamental aspect of man is the fact that in this light he has an originary understanding of being as such. This understanding of being characterizes and carries his whole existence. Since man is the 'locale' where that which shows itself can show itself and be comprehended, man can also be called the 'there' of being. Hence the term Dasein (Boss 1957, pp. 58–61). Heidegger himself says that 'that Seiende which is myself and that has, *inter alia*, the being possibility of questioning, we subsume under the term Dasein' (Heidegger 1972, p. 7).

Man can be compared with physical light. Man cannot exist without the things just as we can recognize light only as such if it strikes something which we can recognize. No individual asked to be born and none can control the place, time and circumstances of his birth. He therefore stands as thrownness in the openness of being and it is this openness which we may call world. We can also say therefore that Dasein needs the things in order to become visible in the openness of being. In this approach we understand Dasein as openstandingness towards the world. It is impossible to speak of a world without man and everything that comes into being can only be apprehended by and make itself manifest to man.

In such a formulation the subject/object dichotomy is overcome. The fact that man is a locale where the things-that-are announce themselves can thus be seen to mean that to be man is fundamentally and essentially to *ex*-ist and hence to be in the world. It should already be clear to use expressions such as I think, I do, I feel, I imagine, I dream, etc., all imply being-in-the-world, always presuppose something which is more than an encapsulated process or entity called being conscious.

IMPLICATIONS FOR PSYCHOLOGY

I have never met a psychologist or anyone else who experiences himself or herself as pure mechanism, thing or mere organism. If I do not experience myself as such, then I do not think one can build a meaningful psychology by starting with a premise of man as thing or organism. Although I deny neither the substantiality of my body, nor the fact that it has much in common with that of an animal, nor the materiality of the things around me, I am in dialogue with my world and fellow man in the way that a thing or even an animal is not.

At the same time psychology should not accept the view of man emanating from idealistic philosophy where man is seen as isolated subjectivity who can only perceive the world by taking it into himself (so to speak), who sees relating to the world in terms of a statement that reality has appearances in the mind or the brain, etc. I am not a self sitting in my brain, on the contrary, I exist; I am always already out there interacting with others and the world.

Let me further clarify the statement that I am not in the world in the way that an animal or an object is. For instance, we can see that an ashtray relates to nothing outside itself. The ashtray is completely contained within its own boundary. I, however, am not contained within my own skin. If I look at a tree outside, then in a sense, I really am with the tree. On the other hand, if you look at me looking at the tree and ask me why I am looking at the tree and not doing my work, I may feel self-conscious, in which case I shall then come back to where my body is. To try to contain me within my skin or even within a so-called territorial imperative or demarcated, measurable, personal space, still does not do justice to me as Dasein. As regards the animal, it is clear that it, too, is not contained within its skin. The work of biologists and ecologists have clearly pointed to the fact that an animal relates to that segment of the world which is meaningful to him. Wolfgang Köhler's experiments with chimpanzees show that even these animals do not experience things as functionally neutral which can therefore fulfil *different* functions, but as Landmann (1974, p. 195) expresses it 'they experience each thing in terms of only one function . . . and therefore arrive only with difficulty at the insight that one can also attach other functions to it'. The 'aha experiences' of these animals in being able to use a stick or a blanket for more than one purpose were very *rare*.

However, it is impossible for man to explicate how the animal stands out towards the world and what meanings are generated in this intercourse. It is difficult to see how research on animal behaviour can usefully be transposed to the understanding of human experience and action. Phenomenology must therefore be in this sense also a *human* psychology.

In view of my originary understanding of being, it should also be realized that I am from the very first conscious of other beings who are in the world in the same way as I am. We can say then that the world we live in is Mitwelt, a world which we share with others. I know and trust my experience. That we can know and understand the experience of others is a premise basic to the operation of our whole social world. We can communicate with each other. To say that we cannot understand a person is usually the same as saying that we cannot communicate with him.

All psychology rests upon communication. The task of the psychologist is to understand people by making explicit what people can communicate to him concerning their experience and behaviour. In order to make meaningful explications, he will continually draw on his own experience which will have been built up out of his own dialogue with the world and fellow man. Through the intercourse between body and world, body and significant others, the child builds up a pre-reflective world, pregnant with meaning. What is meant through terms such as mother, at-homeness, father, hard, soft, etc., is already part of our preverbal encounter with the world. It is therefore also the task of psychology to make these pre-reflective meanings communicated through the living body reflectively clear. It should be clear by now that such a psychology will have to develop new research methods, and this is dealt with in a subsequent chapter.

The world is not a system of bare facts. It would be more accurate to say that for the phenomenologist the world is a system, a cosmic totality, of *meanings*. The basic supposition of behaviourism, namely that we perceive stimuli, must fall away. We perceive meanings, e.g. trees, people chatting, rather than light or sound waves impinging on the senses. 'Stimulus' is a physicalistic abstraction highlighting one profile of a Gestalt imbedded in meaning. Facts acknowledged as such in our society are based upon consensual validation. If one grew up in an entirely different sort of society, one would probably not see a bench or table in the lecture room, but possibly a sacrificial table or even a piece of wood. Even the most sophisticated instruments to measure the table or the movements of its atoms are certainly not independent of consensual validation. The millimetre is not found in nature; the metre is a spatial concept agreed upon by scientists. This also goes for being human as such: we are always dependent on others in order to confirm us in our specific humanity and individuality. The point I am trying to make is that the structure of being human can develop only in dialogue with others, and only in dialogue with others, and a special type of dialogue at that, can it be articulated. It is not possible for me to make explicit in word, image or sound any feeling, thought or any other psychic structure other than in dialogue with someone else. I cannot be myself other than to be myself in relation to another. Even when I feel so rejected and isolated that I write a monologue and shut it up in a drawer, the other still remains present in principle in the sense of a future or incidental reader or in the negative sense of being meant for a cold rejecting individual or humanity who does not realize the loneliness of my life and my lack of acceptance by others.

Although it is true that my existence is not *only* a dialogue *with* others, I actualize myself on a *reflective* level only in relation to others. I can achieve the sort of reflection needed in order to explicate my experience only, on condition that I can assume the possibility of this being understood by another fellow human being whether present or absent. From this it follows that I plug myself into the horizon of comprehension of the individual to whom I am revealing my experience. This means, then, that research which has as its goal an understanding (in the sense of Verstehen) cannot be done where the research psychologist cannot create optimal conditions for the subject to explicate his experience of a phenomenon.

It is important to understand that first person statements are in a sense indisputable. For instance, I may complain of toothache. It could be that the dentist finds that there is no organic basis for this complaint. However, the dentist cannot dispute the fact that I am suffering pain from a source located by me as the tooth. No one but myself can reveal the state of my existence. However, I shall reveal myself only to a trusted fellow man. Moreover, even if I trust A as well as B, I shall not reveal myself to A in exactly the same way as I reveal myself to B.

The task of the psychologist is to create the conditions to make it possible for all the subjects to reveal that which is their openness towards the world which is the same as being conscious. The research psychologist must therefore create an atmosphere in which the subject is *free* to explicate. This corresponds with Martin Heidegger's conception that the essence of truth is freedom. The essence of truth is the freedom to reveal that which is in principle already open. This point will be further elaborated upon later on when we come to the conception of man as a being who is able to keep certain aspects of his experience in the dark and who can in fact hide himself behind a mask, but whose life structure remains in principle open. From the foregoing, we can therefore also make the statement that research based on communication is necessarily participant observation.

In the foregoing, we have already mentioned a few categories in terms of which we can attempt to base our understanding of man. We have spoken of man's bodiliness, man's being in the world with other fellow human beings and his communication within Mitwelt, the world and the things which show itself to him and that we have to understand being in terms of presence as temporality and in terms of spatiality. Man, of course, has a life history, and this constitutes another dimension of his existence. Moreover, man is mortal and his knowledge of mortality is given to him at a very early stage in his life. Furthermore, man experiences this himself as a being who is free, who can make choices. Freedom, it will be contended, is a basic dimension of existence.

HUMAN BODILINESS

Since the Renaissance, man's view of his body has come to be more and more completely dominated by the natural scientific point of view according to which the body is a machine (although a wonderful machine) completely controlled by biochemical processes and the pattern of life stamped upon the genes. Although the intra-organism point of view is disputed by the behaviourists, these theorists would nevertheless agree that man is a person in the sense that he is a *body* with a wide repertoire of behaviours (Skinner 1973) the laws of which can be traced in accordance with a mechanistic point of view. This point of view has completely dominated medicine and inasmuch as clinical psychology is a derivative of psychiatry, which is supposed to be a medical discipline, this view of the body has found entrance into some psychotherapeutic circles as well. In his theoretical writings Freud did not escape it. This point of view would regard what is called man's self, mind or soul, etc., as being merely epiphenomena of brain action or indeed simply superfluous verbiage in view of our limited understanding of the brain. The most consistent point of view along these lines would hold that once brain action is fully understood, psychology itself will become superfluous.

However, there are strong oppositions to this point of view. First of all, there is the argument that one can control bodiliness consciously. A striking instance of this is to be found in the often quoted example of the Yogi master or Swami (Pines, p. 81–3) who can control the temperature of his body, e.g. he can make one half of his hand a few degrees warmer than the other half. In a salient EEG experiment, it was found that this Yogi master, H.H. Swami Rama, was able to produce a high volume of alpha and theta waves and in fact produced the characteristic delta waves of deep sleep while remaining fully conscious. This sets quite a poser. If the answer to man's self is sought in brain-action, then one would have to explain how the Swami was able to control his consciousness in such a way. Would he then control one level of brain-action by another level of brain-action and how would this last level of brain-action be controlled in turn? It is easy to see that this leads us into an infinite regress, leading, in fact, nowhere. But why go into that? Why not stay at the beginning? Let us put it this way: the Swami has a brain. The brain has not got the Swami. The Swami is not sitting in his head just as he is not sitting in his hand or in his toes. Another criticism of the mechanistic as well as the interactionistic view of man comes from having a long, hard look at the so-called psychosomatic disorders. Here it is accepted, but with increasing conceptual and philosophical confusion, that mind and body somehow influence each other. It is said that factors such as rage, conflict, anxiety, etc., can cause psychosomatic disorders such as peptic ulcer, asthma, etc. However, it has never been made quite clear how a so-called immaterial substance such as an emotional 'state of mind' can translate its conflicts into bodily dimensions. Nor has it been made clear how the impersonal state of the body expressed in biochemical formulae can bring about discomfiture in the mind. Appeals to mind and body as different aspects of some vague holistic entity does not solve the problem at all. A much more explicated version of what bodiliness means is needed.

Medicine, as has been said, has been dominated by this view and medical progress has justly congratulated itself on its profound achievements. However, in this impressive record of medical progress, there are one or two dark points. First of all, there are inexplicable cures and failures which no amount of medical research seems able to comprehend or predict. Furthermore, medical science has signally failed in any attempts to strengthen man's resistance against disease. This seems strange in view of the fact that medicine claims its expertise from a wide knowledge of the body as object and, if so, it should surely have been possible by now to strengthen the body against ravages brought about by environmental agents such as germs, climatic upsets, etc.

Man is a body and ordinarily does not unduly worry himself about the fact. Man becomes aware of the fact that he has a body only when the body becomes an object for him; this happens only under certain circumstances, e.g. when he is being medically examined or when he knows that he is sick. The body in which he lived so unawarely, so matter-of-factly, suddenly becomes a barrier to the fulfilment of his needs. Man then becomes conscious of the fact that he has a body as an object, rather than of his pre-reflective mood of being a body.

I stand out toward the world in being a body. I take my body for granted and I am always bypassing my body towards the task that I have in the world. The body, in fact, shapes itself according to its task in the world. There is the clear aggressive stride of the determined, dominant person versus the uncertain shuffle of the downtrodden and the oppressed. There is the loud voice of the man who is used to dominating everyone and everything around him versus the soft pleading voice of those who are submissive or who prefer more subtle ways of manipulation. The nature of one's bodiliness shows itself in the glance, the handshake, the gait, the gesture, the upright or slouching bearing, etc.

A client in psychotherapy (Eppel 1978) dreamt of a rag-doll which was being thrown around by her parents and others, and she realized that she herself was in fact the rag-doll: she was allowing significant others to live her life for her and she didn't have the courage to say what she really wanted. After therapy, this young woman said that she used being sick or psychosomatic illnesses to protect herself from people so that they couldn't make any demands upon her. Her body became a way in which she could refuse to execute the task in the world that her parents gave her. She recovered her bodily self as a satisfying and healthy aspect of her being once she was able to throw off her psychosomatics which she described as a crutch which enabled her to be a rag-doll. In other words, once she had the courage to stand on her own, she was no longer a 'rag-doll' body neither did she 'need' psychosomatics. She said that prior to her recovery she hated her body as a thing that represented her and she didn't want to be inside her body, because it represented her failed marriage (in her own words): her 'whole sickness sort of psychosomatic thing'.

During the period of her neurosis, her body just became her shell – sexually as well – she actually became totally frigid. She couldn't stand any entrance into her body like having an injection or even using tampons. Once she overcame her problems, she was able to have a new body, a body which did not need psychosomatics, which was not frigid but receptive to the advances and embraces of a member of the opposite sex, a body which did not feel heavier after each session of psychotherapy, but which in fact became lighter for her as she shed more and more of what she called her 'dirty linen'.

The body shapes itself in accordance with its task in the world. As long as the aforementioned client saw her task in the world as one in which she had to face unbearable demands, as demands imposed upon her by outside authority, her body remained to her strange, something that she didn't want to be in, something that had to be sick, had to be used as a barrier against others. In fact, she felt any intrusion into her personal space as a physical intrusion. When she was at school she, along with the other children, experienced the admonitions of the teachers that every time that they were naughty they were hammering new nails into the suffering body of Christ: a criticism which she could respond to with her own bodiliness. When people made intrusive remarks about her, she felt it in her body.

However, when she recovered, she still had this big personal space, but she no longer experienced the arguments and intrusions of others as physical intrusions into her body. On the contrary, she consciously defended her personal space and, if people intruded, she could switch them off suitably.

It is one of Freud's undoubted merits that he saw the great importance for our ease or dis-ease in living in the way we were in the world through our bodiliness. Unfortunately, Freud, in terms of the positivistic science of his time, tried to anchor this in 'hard' empirical facts such as the body-orifices, namely mouth, anus and the sexual organs. In his pan-sexual meta-psychology, Freud fully realized that the mouth was not simply an organ for taking in food, that the anus had more than mere eliminating functions and that the genital, urethral area was of much greater psychological importance than merely passing urine and sexuality in the sense of sexual intercourse. He certainly widened our understanding of these by introducing the conception of erogenous zones. Moreover, Freud indicated that the Victorian denial of the reality of sexuality, especially sexuality in women, was greatly to blame for much of the dis-ease which found expression in the various neuroses which Freud and his followers treated by means of psychoanalytic methods. However, what Freud tried to reduce to the mechanism of repression of sexuality should be seen in a more comprehensive fashion as contemporary Western man's alienation from his body. Moreover, Western man, by stressing sexual liberation, has simply fallen into another trap in that genital sexuality is now made to stand for the liberation of the entire body.

It is wrong to limit the erogenous zones to the obvious candidates of mouth, anus and sexual organs. The whole body, in fact, is an instrument receptive to all sorts of pleasures. One has only to watch little pups playing or cuddle a little child to realize that the entire body is a singing vibrant dimension of living and not a mere organic machine. However, through a long process rooted in

Judaic-Christian religion and later augmented and reinforced by scientific and technological progress, especially since the industrial revolution, man has become progressively more alienated from his body. In particular, Western man rejects the lower pole of his body and has been taught through his socialization processes to deny certain aspects of his body. Cleanliness being placed next to godliness, body odours are considered to be offensive. The child is toilet trained as early as possible and even though the child tends to play with its own faeces, it is made ashamed of this very early on as contrary to cultural norms. The child's attempts to retain the pleasurableness of his own body are thus soon wiped out by cultural sanctions.

In *The Divided Self*, Laing quotes the case of Peter in whom we can see a dramatic instance of man's alienation from what might be called the lower poles of the bodily self. 'Peter was a large man of 25, and he looked a picture of health. He came to see me complaining that there was a constant unpleasant smell coming from him. He could smell it clearly, but he was not sure whether it was the sort of smell that others could smell. He thought that it came particularly from the lower part of his body and genital region. In the fresh air, it was like the smell of burning, but usually it was the smell of something sour, rancid, old, decayed, he likened it to the sooty, gritty, musty smell of a railway waiting room; or the smell that comes from broken down "closets" of the slum tenements of the district in which he grew up. He could not get away from this smell although he had taken to having several baths a day' (Laing, p. 120). Laing further mentioned that for his two self-absorbed parents, Peter was an intrusion. Peter's mother was vanity personified in that she treasured the clothes her husband bought her and had great anxieties about the possibilities of being disfigured through childbirth. When Peter's mother caught him playing with his penis, she said that it wouldn't grow if he did that. Her husband belittled Peter by calling him useless Eustace and saying that he was just a big lump of dough.

Peter's problem is an extreme instance of the cultural devaluation of the body coupled with a sociological schema which requires us to have a body for others.

In this dimension of being a body for others, one deodorizes oneself and one's dog, becomes anxious if one dresses in clothes not approved of by the peer group, feels anxious and devaluated if one's body build deviates from the ideal norm, one is terrified of being too fat or too thin, not pretty enough or if one is a male, if one does not fit in the cultural ideal of masculinity which is the norm in Western countries.

John Berger in his little book *Ways of Seeing*, has delineated the details of how the female body has become a body for others during and following the Renaissance.

Bodiliness and the Upright Posture

Man's upright posture is constitutive of his humanness at a most basic level. Although man shares most of his organs and inner bodily processes with animals, it would be a mistake to understand man from the reductionistic point of view, i.e. from his animalness. Rather, we should see that the human *structure*, also in the aspect of bodiliness, is first of all a *human* structure and is to be understood from this point of view. In other words, to understand the human being, we should understand the human structure not from the point of view of the physical elements to which it can be reduced, but rather by trying to understand the function of parts of the human body based on an understanding of the whole.

The upright posture in man is not something automatic like breathing. Even when all the physical conditions, e.g. maturation of tissues, the development of postural reflexes, etc., are fulfilled, the infant still has to accomplish the upright posture and certainly it is regarded by the significant others in his life as an important first achievement. To quote Erwin Straus, from whose seminal essay (p. 141) I have derived most of the ideas in this section, 'upright posture characterizes the human species. Nevertheless, each individual has to struggle in order to make it really his own. Man has to become what he is. . . . While the heart continues to beat from its fetal beginnings to death without our active intervention and while breathing neither demands nor tolerates our voluntary interference beyond narrow limits, upright posture remains a task throughout our lives.'

Awakeness is characteristic of the upright posture. Awakeness is necessary for counteracting gravity. To maintain the upright posture is to live in perpetual opposition to the force of gravity.

Upright posture removes us from the ground and places us at a distance from the world. The proximal senses of smell and taste become much less definitive for orientation than seeing or hearing. Straus says: 'upright posture removes us from the ground, keeps us away from things, and holds us aloof from our fellow man. All of these three distances can be experienced either as gain or as loss.'

It is characteristic of the human infant that he starts using the pronoun 'I' for himself once he has firmly acquired the upright posture. In the early years the child is much more likely to refer to himself by his given name. In using the pronoun 'I', I oppose myself to fellow man and also distinctly differentiate myself from the world. Awakeness and the upright posture seem to be different faces of the same coin. It is impossible to maintain the upright posture when asleep (discounting for the moment the rather rare cases of somnambulism). In contrast to the activity implied in the upright posture, we experience lying down in sleeping, in sex and in drug use as voluptuous. Straus says: 'there is the voluptuous gratification of succumbing. Sex remains a form of lying down or, as language says, of lying or sleeping with. Addicts, in their experience, behaviour, and intention, reveal the double aspect of sinking back in its contrast to being upright.'

As a result of the upright posture, we are verticals who, in a sense, never meet. Our typical posture to others is the face-to-face situation; again emphasizing the distant sense of seeing.

The upright posture correlates with the development of the human hand and arm. In describing or defining the five senses, we speak of separate senses of touch, pain, feeling, seeing, etc., but we do not describe the human hand as a sense organ. In fact, in a certain way of speaking, the human hand is a sense organ, but only in movement. Thus, to assess the texture of a material, we cannot simply put our hand on the material, we have to move our hand in order to sense its texture. The hand becomes, as Straus puts it, an organ of 'active gnostic touching – the epicritic, discriminative instrument *par excellence*' (p. 150).

To return to the point that the parts should be understood from the whole: upright posture is constitutive of being human in a definitive sense, also in that we note that man, unlike the an-thropoids, has a head which is actually mounted on the spinal column whereas in the case of the latter the head *hangs* from the spinal column. Moreover, having achieved the upright posture, the human hands and arms are freed and man can become a tool-using being. The existence of tool-using has often been ascribed to the opposition between thumb and the other fingers, but this is only part of the story. The fact that the hands are not needed for walking is a more basic given in our existence. Moreover, the human face is changed by the upright posture or, more accurately put, we can have a human face only if we have an upright posture. Thus, since the mouth is no longer an organ for fighting, the massive jaw muscles can be dispensed with and the mouth becomes a much more limited and sensitive organ. Moreover, because the jaw is now less important in the self-preservation of the individual, the human skull can develop differently, thus enlarging the brain-case.

Because of upright posture, smell has lost its orientative func-tion and seeing and hearing have assumed domination. The interests of animals are limited to the proximate whereas the interests of the human being are spread over a much wider area. Straus says (p. 162) 'the relation of sight and bite distinguishes the human face of those of lower animals. Animal jaws, snout, trunk, and beak—all of them organs acting in the direct contact of grasping and gripping—are placed in the "viceline of the eyes". With upright posture, with the development of the arm, the mouth is no longer needed for catching and carrying or for attacking and defending.' It can therefore sink down from the viceline of the eyes which can now concentrate with an open look on distant things and rest fully upon them, viewing them with the detached interest of wondering. This turning or changing of the human face into a seeing face is well expressed in the German word 'Gesicht', the Afrikaans 'gesig' and the English 'visage'. Having transformed the prominent primate jaws into mouths, one of the conditions for the development of language are fulfilled. The other concerns the ear: in the upright posture, the ear is no longer attuned to sounds and their origin as such and the external ear loses its mobility. This capacity, says Straus, 'to separate the acoustical Gestalt from the acoustical material makes it possible to produce purposely and to reproduce intentionally sounds articulated according to a pre-conceived scheme' (p. 163).

In other words, having achieved the upright posture, man is able to develop language because he is able to get away from the necessity of being attuned to the significance of sound and he can then achieve articulated sound. At the same time when speech connects speaker and listener, it also keeps them at a distance.

It will thus be seen that the upright posture is definitive for human bodiliness and to understand anatomy and physiology from the phenomenological-existential point of view, we must argue from the holistic understanding of the specific human structure to understanding the function of the parts of the body.

We may now return to the statement that the body shapes itself in accordance with its task in the world. Thus, the soldier must stand rigidly erect on parade and have a completely symmetrical attitude. Van den Berg comments that this must be so otherwise the soldier could be given half an order! The soldier marches in step with his comrades to the accompaniment of the drum-beat. The task of the soldiery is to act as a unified corps in executing aggressive acts. Moreover, repetitive marching and drilling are necessary because in battle the soldier is required to act on an order without thinking.

In prayer, too, we see how the body shapes itself in accordance with its relation to the cosmic totality which it sees as God or the Divine. Thus, a Christian, being a child of God, makes himself small by kneeling when speaking to God, i.e. in prayer. The Moslem goes to the fatalistic extreme of submission by prostrating himself on the ground. The classic Greek prayed in the upright position, with his arms lifted and open and thus widened his body space in an enthusiastic gesture. Straus points out the derivation of this word from en-theos-iastic which means to 'to receive the God' or 'to be possessed by Him' (Straus, p. 154).

In traditional Xhosa religion the ancestor is prayed to in the upright position. This is because the ancestor is close to God but is not, as in Christianity, even where we pray through Christ, seen as being at one with God, but rather as a being who can be pleased or placated; with whom one can negotiate.

Straus points out that neither the completely supine position nor the erect posture promotes communication. One cannot really reach people when standing up. That is why a cocktail party is such a frustrating experience because one is in a state of superficial communication and one easily slips into a stereotype or role. The true posture for communication, for Western man anyway, is the sitting-down position. One sits down in a chair in order to discuss, to enjoy a cup of coffee together, etc. On the other hand, if one lies down, one relaxes too much and may easily fall asleep or enter a reverie whereas in the upright position, communication becomes harder and harder to maintain.

SPATIALITY, THE WORLD AND THE THINGS

First of all, let it be reiterated that the conception of space as pure measurable extension is an assumption generated by Cartesian philosophy and accepted by physical science which has been convenient and productive for these sciences. This, however, is not how we really experience space except in so far as our consciousness has largely been conditioned by this particular conception of space so that it is sometimes difficult for us to *think* of it in any other way. A blueprint made by an architect or other designer is entirely based on this. Here again, as in the case of bodiliness, it is imperative that we should realize that we cannot build a meaningful human science unless we are prepared to start with our own primary experience. Thus, in relation to bodiliness, we may say that 'my heart bleeds for you', or 'I can jump with joy', or 'his glance went through me'; these metaphors should be taken seriously as describing the realities of being human.

There is an intimate interlocking between man's bodiliness and his spatiality. We speak of the personal space or bodily space. In psychological research on the traditional pattern, a large number of studies have been made in order to try to measure this bodily space. However, none of these methods has, so far, led to significant results in that a comprehensive theoretical framework for bodily space could be adumbrated. For Straus, there is an intimate connection between bodiliness and spatiality in that he speaks of the bodily 'three mile zone'. This bodily three-mile zone, for him, goes with the upright stature. Having our arms free, we are able to gesture. To be ourselves, which means the same as

being thoroughly at home in our own bodies, we must have a
certain space in which we can move, act, express and gesture. The
arms being released from their functions for locomotion (as in the
animal) then describe a lateral space which is directly experienced
as being bound up with me acting, with me as orienting myself
rather than as neutral space out there. Children who move into a
new classroom have a feeling of where they want to sit and do not
assign themselves randomly. Once a child has decided on a
certain desk he is not indifferent when someone claims the same
place. However, it would be wrong of us to limit human spatiality
to the lateral space of the arms and hands. Rather we should see
human spatiality for the individual as being synonymous with his
personal horizon at a particular time. Thus, if I am sitting in a
lecturing room concentrating on what the lecturer is saying, then
in a sense I am closer to the lecturer than to the person sitting
beside me. On the other hand, if we glance across a crowded room
in a cocktail party, and we see a friend or a loved one coming in at
the door, then one depasses or 'leaps over' the intervening
measurable space and one is with such a person at that time.

The client of whom we have been speaking previously said that
'that was significantly part of my experience of therapy. I slowly
learnt to make my personal space more logical, that in fact, it is
not my body, you know. I am allowed my personal space. Now I
am this thing that is overflowing out of my body, it's *me*. You see
that's what I mean when I say that this personal space thing I
have is not really a physical thing. You see when you make
spiritual contact with me, like you make demands on me, I can
withdraw from overflowing out of my body into that corner
again.'

We note that Sara states that her body is not a physical thing
and that she speaks of her body and personal space as concretely
experienced in terms which are incompatable with physical science language.

We are always the centre of our world. Up, down, above,
below, left, right, these are dimensions in which we live inevitably.
Whilst it is true that left and right remain dependent upon the
body, up and down are spatial. Whether we stand up or lie down,
up remains above and down remains below. When we are really
interested in a book we live in that book, we no longer have a
distance from the book as the written word apart from us, we live
the story. When we say that we sit at the feet of someone, or we
are hanging on his lips, it means that we are there with him,
looking up at him even though we may be sitting in a measurable
sense at a higher level in a lecture theatre.

Robert M. Pirsig (1977, pp. 289–90) describes the importance of merging with the object if one is to do a successful

maintenance or repair job on a motorcycle or any other machine. He says that we all have moments when we are doing something that we really want to do. These moments, he says, do not often seem to occur to us in our work. He goes on to say that the mechanic he is talking about does not make this separation and 'one says of him that he is interested in what he is doing, that he is involved in his work. What produces this involvement is, at the cutting edge of consciousness, an absence of any sense of separateness of subject and object' (p. 298). Pirsig further points out that there are certain idiomatic expressions such as being 'with it', being 'a natural', 'taking hold' and others which point to the absence of a subject – object duality. He further states that if one is dominated by feeling separate from what one is doing, then one cannot be said to care about what one is doing. This caring, he says, really is a feeling of identification with what one is doing. Perceiving, acting, loving, responding, are all forms of being-with things or persons which have momentary or lasting significance for one.

As we shall see later, part of our being in relationship with another human being is the extent to which we can share the nearness and farness of things known or unknown, trusted or not trusted with such a person. Part of the difficulty that the therapist has in handling silences on the occasion when his client does not speak, is his ability to remain with the client none the less, to keep on sharing his world although he is not communicating. It is only too easy for the therapist to drift away from the client when verbal communication is thus broken off.

As a further illustration of how we live our lives in terms of the physiognomy of world and spatiality let us consider the following dream of a client in therapy: 'I am standing on a slope somewhere with buildings around me. These buildings look like university residences or hotels or boarding-houses, a sort of a concrete jungle with doors and corridors, etc. I see some people or possibly one person coming up the hill. Then I find that they are chasing me and I run in and out through the buildings and corridors and in the end it just fades away. I do not know whether I really escaped them.' This gives us an insight into the landscape of the world in which this client lives. We see that the buildings are impersonal yet they are places where one is supposed to live. His life therefore, at the moment, is in a sense a concrete jungle. He sees people approaching; however, in this impersonal landscape of his life, people are threatening in a vague way. He is not able to confront these people and determine his relationship with them. He does not feel at home. He is insecure in his world which is a somewhat denuded one.

A home is much more than a building with four outer and a

number of inner walls. For the vast majority of people, home means a building of some sort. However, for a building to be considered a home, it must offer habitable space. Cathedrals are magnificent buildings but one would hardly feel at home in them for purposes of everyday living. This is the same as saying that a structure would hardly be a habitable space except in so far as one is truly able to experience it as a place for one's day-to-day life. Similarly, one would not be able to carry out laboratory experiments in a cathedral unless one has already destroyed the cathedral as cathedral. It is not possible for one to pray in a laboratory in the same sense as one is able to pray in a church.

Every form of spirituality requires a different form of spatiality. The traditional Nguni culture in South Africa entailed a certain form of spirituality. This form of spirituality includes contact with the ancestors who are seen as residing in the river or in the forest, but who are also seen as being present on certain occasions such as when a ritual feast is being held in honour of the birth of a new member or in order to remember one who has died. In such a case, the spirituality cannot thrive in the enclosed space of a church, because this spirituality is at one with the vitality of nature. For the Nguni, life and vitality mean the same thing and his cosmology requires the vital principle. The true life is the life in which power is at the disposal of the human being and the cosmos is seen in terms of lower and higher orders of power. Health and good living mean to him having more power, that is, having more life. Therefore, his spirituality will be bound up with the forces of nature as he sees them, i.e. plant, animal, human being and ancestors will form an unbroken chain of being. For their spirituality Nguni people do not need a special building. Traditionally ritual slaughtering and accompanying ceremonies took place in the cattle-kraal to which certain taboos (e.g. on woman) apply but the ancestors are present also at other parts of the feast or ceremony. We may surmise then that the spatial arrangements in the kraal and during the other ceremonies correspond to what Westerners used to experience as the sacred, sanctified space of the cathedral.

However, in the West, as J. H. van den Berg has so eloquently shown, the various epochs of spirituality are correlated with the forms of church architecture. Architecture, according to Van den Berg, is the art of boundary. The church, in presenting a clear-cut boundary between a sacral inside and a profane outside, created a devotional, spiritual space but, according to Van den Berg, this boundary fell away round about 1740 when the baroque church style came to an end and no new styles were generated. Since then, we have built churches in pseudo-gothic, pseudo-classic styles and have been unable to establish a new form of spirituality; we have accordingly been unable to develop a new architecture to encompass our spirituality. When Frank Lloyd Wright in 1906 built Unity Hall in Chicago in the factory style, this was an honest admission that the Western church can no longer offer any form of spirituality (Van den Berg 1968). Alternatively, one may say that, although Western man indubitably is a spiritual being, a person with spiritual needs, Frank Lloyd Wright's factory style shows without pretence that, as an institution, the Church of the West no longer offers a space for such spirituality to unfold.

The depth of the contemporary spiritual dilemma shows up in the experience of Simone Weil for whom the 'absence of God' became, by the dialectic of negation, precisely a sign of God so that God shows His presence only in the form of his absence (Weil, 1974).

Even though denied spiritual expression, Western man struggles with his spiritual needs, trying to give it some sort of shape. Great ones, such as Charles Peguy and Simone Weil, were able to express and live their spirituality creatively outside the church. However, the following dream from a fellow psychologist in his late twenties was told to me and my reaction to this dream led to the dreamer's own interpretation that it was an expression of his spirituality. (He was not in therapy.) The dream now follows:

'I am standing next to a man in a white coat. He is older than I am. Together we stare intently at a fish floating just below the surface of the water in a fish-tank. We are looking through the end piece of the tank (which is at eye-level); the tank somehow extends "right out of the dream". The fish is motionless, perhaps dead.

As I stare at the fish, I wish with my total being that it is alive but yet it seems dead. I say to the man in the white coat something about "I'm sure it is alive", but I really don't believe my words. He shakes his head. This happens a few times. Then with a surge of joy I think I see it moves. Elated I turned to him but he shakes his head. Again we stare at the fish. It gives a wriggle. Joy surges through me. Then very gently and slowly the fish swims off towards the end of the tank which is "beyond the dream". The dream ends.'

The immediate reaction of the author when told this dream (no associations were asked for) was that the dreamer at the beginning of the dream somehow needs the authority of the man in the white coat embodying scientific status. It is possible that the dreamer has been conditioned to a reality in which truth is supposed only to emerge within a scientific setting (a laboratory). However, the most striking aspect of the dream was the open-ended nature of the tank, as if this shows the dreamer's existence in the spatial sense to somehow extend into the infinite. What is more, he is anxious to see the fish move, in other words, he is anxious to see movement within this infinite open life space. The fact that the fish eventually swims off towards the end of the tank, which is somehow beyond the dream, shows that this aspect of his life is definitely still within his reach and could, in fact, be opening up right now.

The dreamer then told me that this dream elucidates his core concern, namely his fear that his spirituality is dead, that he needs to have the approval of the authority and that his rational self still restrains his 'subjective being' (as he puts it). His own interpretation of the dream was that the man in the white coat represents scientific authority and empirical knowledge which is rational and someone to look up to, because he is older. He says that he needs the stamp of authority, the stamp of scientific rationalism. But it is his non-rational self which first sees and *knows* the fish to be alive. The fact is that, apart from his spiritual needs, he also is deeply involved as a scientist in being objective and rational. As regards the fish, for him it is a creature that moves easily and without obstruction. It can swim at the surface or dive to the mysterious depths of the sea-bottom which may in some sense be representing the unconscious. Perhaps because of this, the dreamer says, he tends to be slightly afraid of fish. And yet, and this is something that I, when reacting to the dream, did not think about, was that the fish is a symbol of spirituality for this dreamer, for him it is the alpha X, the beginning. It is, of course, well known that, amongst the early Christians, the fish rather than the Cross, was the dominant symbol. Christ enjoined his disciples to become fishermen of people: for those open to his message this means that we should be like fish to be caught in the net cast by Him. It seems quite clear, however, that spirituality is here made evident not so much by the fish itself, but by the spatiality, the infinity of space in which the fish can move. As my young colleague himself put it, 'perhaps the infinity of the tank points to the boundlessness of spirituality'.

Whilst the spatial dimension is traced in spirituality in the above examples, this does not suggest that spirituality should be understood through this category only. Like all other aspects of being human, it involves all the other categories as well. Spirituality is a total process involving our being in all its relations.

Let us return to the theme of human ability to be with the thing to which we are relating. One's commitment clearly shows up, not as an inner structure but as an intense relatedness to those aspects of the world that are really salient to one's life, that really speak to one or in a sense demand one. Examples are not hard to get: the portrait artist will be very sensitive to the contours and colouring of the human face, the businessman will look at objects as possible merchandise, the mountain climber will immerse himself in the scalability of rock-faces, etc. However, very few people are able to describe their intense relatedness adequately – hence the following example. A talented young woman who had been in therapy for 18 months imparted, as one of her last themes in psychotherapy, a secret of hers to the therapist at which she had hinted quite a few times. Her therapist knew that she had a special relationship to trees – that these were by no manner or means mere objects to her. She then told him what now follows (on his request she wrote it out fully) and it is being used here with the express permission of both Mandy (a pseudonym) and the therapist:

The tree and I – by 'Mandy'.

'I sit in stillness and look at a tree. I study the colours and movement of its leaves, the texture of the bark, the shape of each branch, until finally I apprehend it as a whole, perfectly contained within itself. I concentrate fully on that apprehension and begin to lose awareness of my body and all that surrounds me and the tree. The senses by which I usually perceive the world are no longer distinct, they have become fluid, flowing into each other, and are gradually absorbed into the being of the tree. The awareness of Mandy – my single, separate identity – fades, and I merge with the life of the tree. I am contained within the tree. I experience a depth of stillness, yet there is also constant movement: energy runs like a stream of tiny gold beads through my entire being. My leaves are filled with it, and move endlessly in light and warmth, while my roots in darkness penetrate and are enfolded in damp, cold earth. I am everywhere – in light and warmth, in darkness and cold. I am everything – the sun and earth, air and moisture. I am life, and am contained within it.

'Time no longer exists. When I return to Mandy, I am simply there.

'This is only one experience, and contains the essential elements of my relation to trees at these moments; but each experience is different as so much depends on the state of being of both myself and the tree at the time. And the slightest breath of wind, or the shadow of a cloud, can affect the entire process almost as much as the time of day, the season, or the place where the tree is growing.

'In the garden of the house where we lived until I was four, there was an enormous old tree. From its lowest branch, my father had suspended part of an old tyre as a swing for me: it was big enough for me to sit or lie in, and I passed all the time I could there. I used to lie back looking up at the countless fluttering leaves against the sky, and the feeling of deep stillness at the centre of endless movement and shifting light was the same then as it is now, when I "become" a tree.

'I first realized the meaning that trees hold for me when my father, who had been cleaning his pistol, decided to shoot a bullet into the trunk of what I thought of as "My tree". I felt sick with horror, imagining that the tree would be killed and fall down in a mass of broken branches and torn leaves; I was also very afraid, as if I were being somehow threatened. My father, whom I had always regarded as warm and protecting, now appeared as a terrifying stranger capable of destroying me through the death of the tree. I cried and begged him not to do it; but not knowing how much I loved the tree, he could not consider my fear seriously. He shot at the tree and I closed my eyes, certain that the world would shatter around me. But nothing happened. I ran down and touched the tree with my hands, scarcely believing that it was still whole. Then I found the place where the bullet had entered the trunk, and wept when I saw the sap trickling slowly from the hole.

'For a long time after this, I was afraid of my father and began to realize that other people did not feel about trees as I did. I saw them all, especially adults, as potentially hostile and destructive, and knew that I must keep from them my awareness of the hidden sensitive life not only of trees, but of flowering plants, creepers, grass, moss and all growing things; and that I must hide from them also my part in that life.

'It was not long after this incident that I found I could deliberately enter the life of a tree whenever I was alone and still. I think that previously my merging with the life of something outside myself had been a "natural" process, that is, entered into without thought or intention: this happened, for example, when I lay in my swing beneath the tree in our garden. Trees were then, and have remained, the most accessible "form".

'Since then, these "moments" have come often. I have experienced myself in the life of many trees – solitary or in forests, firmly rooted and huge or delicately supple; in the life of grass and reeds, flowers, ferns, toadstools, and moss. My openness to the seasons, to sunlight and clouds, water, wind, shadow and the moon changes, is at these times so heightened that it spills something into my life as Mandy, but never with the same intensity.

'Thus, one morning I awoke very early, and walked through the garden. The grass, which was quite long, was still covered with dew, and I was fascinated to see it so brilliant and sparkling in the early morning sun, as if each blade were filled with light. It was very quiet, and I was alone. All at once, I felt strangely at peace there among the shining blades of grass: they welcomed me soundlessly, enveloping me passively in their life. I crouched down on my knees and touched the grass with my face, feeling the dew cold and soft on my skin. I entered the life of the grass. I felt my intricate roots, so still yet filled with movement, beneath the surface of the soil, interlaced with countless others, and my strong delicate blades stood firmly in the light with drops of dew moist upon them: yet all this contained in a wholeness of being in which separateness dissolved. When I became aware of myself as Mandy again, I knew that almost anything would be open to me when the right moment came, as it had that morning.

'I am, therefore, constantly aware of another state of being beyond my own, which I can reach in stillness. When I am depressed or confused, however, this "other life" is closed to me, and I remain locked within my self until something – like the sun's warmth in an old stone wall at evening – penetrates the greyness around me, and opens the way for me again.'

When we think of the world out there, we are inclined to resign the world to the discoveries, regularities and laws of physical science. We have a picture of the world as unidimensional in which things are just plain, brute, immutable facts or matter consisting of electrons, neutrons, atoms, molecules, etc. Although physics is no longer a monolithic mechanistic enterprise as it used to be, it still is an undertaking in which the nature of its reality is essentially and exclusively disclosed by measurement operations. Now, if we think of the experience of Mandy who suffered when her father shot at a tree but did not notice that the tree was bleeding, and if we uphold Mandy in her statement that she herself merges with or becomes the tree, then we shall certainly run into an argument as to the *reality* of this experience.

One can well understand Mandy's hesitation in telling her therapist about this experience: many psychologists and psychiatrists will regard her experience as pathological – even as a hallucination indicating severe pathology. Moreover, her experience with her father indicated to her that most people are unlikely to be able to share this experience – not because we others are incapable of having it, but because we tend to deny an experience such as this since it contradicts our socially validated 'consensus' – consciousness of reality.

In terms of our contemporary unilinear consciousness, we shall, in fact, dismiss the possibility that her merging with the tree is 'real'. We all know that a person is a person and a tree is a tree. It is all right to dream about things like that – the dream should be interpreted symbolically. But even in a dream of what could the tree be a symbol and why can it not stand for itself? As for an adult: belief in trees being the abode of fairies, we all know that there are no fairies in trees or anywhere else. A person who sees fairies in trees, or believes them to be there, must be suffering from hallucinations or delusions just as her belief that she can merge into a tree must also be some sort of hallucination, therefore such a person is probably mentally ill. However, the therapist may assure a sceptical friend that his client is in fact not mad, i.e. she has a fairly good if somewhat rebellious hold on socially validated reality as well; his friend will then argue that surely seeing herself as merging with the tree or spotting fairies in it is an example of *subjectivity*. To get hold of reality, we have to be objective and strip the tree of everything that is subjective – i.e. we must look at the tree as it is in itself and not as different people see it. In Cartesian terms the 'objective reality' of the tree is its extension which is measurable. We cannot, says the friend, go on people's experience (whatever that may mean, he adds sceptically) because we shall soon have a lot of conflicting and confused accounts. What we need is a method by which we can reach consensus and therefore the reality of the tree is to be sought by the methods of science in which one can check all one's observations and, provided the conditions are identical, come to the same conclusions every time. The same will hold if someone else makes the same observations. We can measure not only the height and circumference of the tree but also its chemical and physical composition, and these can all be checked provided we have the right instruments and facilities.

But how do we know that the tree will reveal its true nature through the measurement operations that seem to be all that you are doing, the therapist asks his scientist friend?

Well, now, you are in the area of philosophy. As a scientist I am only interested in what is tangible and measurable. What seems to be outside the realm of sciences today may well prove to be the next fortress that falls before the onslaught of our methods as even a casual acquaintance with the history of science will show you. As for trying to get to know the thing in itself – if you must speculate, let me refer you to Kant who argued that the thing in itself can never be known, or even to Plato's metaphor of the cave. As for me, I'm quite happy to leave those speculations to the philosophers. In spite of any philosophical objections, you cannot deny that science has saved millions of people from hunger and disease, has made it possible to put a man on the moon and has made motor cars and aeroplanes possible which you are perhaps using even more than I do.

There, then, the matter rests for the moment. The scientist does not claim that his hold on reality is total, but he suggests that science is an accumulative venture that systematically and securely expands our knowledge of reality step by step. Therefore, although we do not know everything and cannot know everything, we can at least be sure of what we know.

But is this method sufficient for getting to grips with human reality – which is after all what the enterprise of psychology is all about?

Let us go back to Mandy's experience of the tree. From her account it is clear that she experiences the tree in more than one way. Which experience is true or are they all true or all false? When the scientist says that these are not real (i.e. not objective) but only subjective, he means that the way we should look at the tree should be to strip the tree of man's presence. The way to understand the world in the physical sciences is to understand the world as it is uninfluenced by the observer. But is it possible to conceive of a world in which man is absent? Secondly, is it possible to conceive of an experimental situation in psychology where the human being who is the 'object' of observation is not affected by the situation of being observed? The answer to both these questions must be 'NO'.

Our scientist friend supposes that our best access to valid knowledge is by means of measurement operations. But many of us are inclined to forget that the measurement operations themselves depend on human consciousness in two ways:

(a) A metre is only a metre by virtue of the fact that we have agreed on a certain standard of what should constitute this measure. The metre is not found in nature.

(b) We are taught to believe in our eyes in some ways and not in others. (See figure 1.)

Figure 1

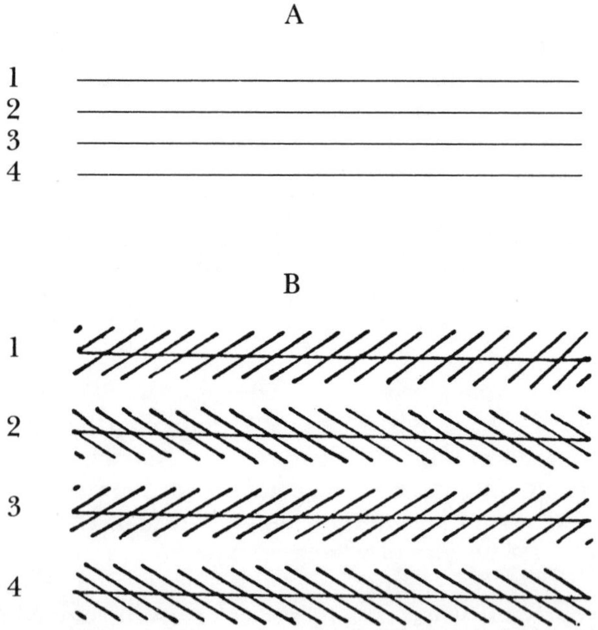

A

B

Thus the four lines are said to be parallel under both condition A as well as B. However, let us look at lines 1, 2, 3 and 4 under the second set of conditions. Obviously they are *not* parallel. On this basis we speak of the Zöllner illusion, i.e. we dare not believe our eyes. However, if we measure the distance between the end-point of lines 1 and 2 and 3, etc., we shall find that these distances are exactly the same. This time we *do* believe our eyes.

This means that in this specific case we can construe reality in two ways. (I realize, of course, that the argument can go much further than what I have taken it and, if we go on, we shall soon arrive at the question of the mutability or otherwise of matter, but that would take us too far afield. It may further be argued that the observations of the scientist are at a different level from ordinary experience and should therefore be treated as privileged and therefore be the only form of experience to enjoy scientific status. However, in view of the fact that psychology is basically a communicative science, this argument simply will not wash.) Following J. H. van den Berg (1969, p. 15) we speak of the first and second structures of reality, the first being our primary experience of the world out there, the second being the rational empirical measured reality composed by natural science. Following Erwin Straus, we can call the first (when we are talking of perception) pathic, the second gnostic sensing.

Phenomenology mainly moves in the first structure. In other words, phenomenology moves in the primary reality in which we live; it takes primary experience seriously and proposes to base the science of psychology on it, although this does not mean that the second (natural scientific, measured, objectifying) structure will be negated and not be used.

Cartesian philosophy and natural science look upon space as homogeneous extension, containing indifferent objects. The distances between these objects are measurable – the space between them being seen as homogeneous. We do not know whether the ashtray and the tea-cup experience themselves as being closer to one another than the coffee-cup and the sugar-bowl. We do know, however, that when we see a loved one across the street that person is much nearer to us than the bowl of flowers at which we had been looking a moment ago. If we are idealist philosophers, we can say that we only know our consciousness in which case space will be purely subjective. Space will therefore, in this mode of discourse, be within us. If we are natural–scientifically orientated, we will think of space as infinite and meaningless extension in which the earth, the plant and the sun are aimlessly drifting. However, in our primary experience, space is not in the subject neither is the world in space. Spatiality may rather be said to be in the world (Heidegger 1972, p. 111). Our existence manifests its spatiality in our intercourse with the things to which we relate in the world. The world in which things have their place and stand in meaningful relation to one another is the original form in which we are living. This is our primary spatiality from which is deduced the objective three-dimensional spatiality which we use when we practise the science of geometry or trigonometry or when we are planning a cupboard or a house. However, when we actually build a house, we find that the house has a physiognomy of which the blueprint tells us nothing. The interior of the house may be warm or cold, inviting or repellent; a landscape may be magnificent, threatening or monotonous. These spatial qualities or physiognomies of the world cannot be quantitatively assessed neither can they be adequately comprehended by an objective description of colours, forms, etc. (L. Cruse, p. 61). We do not observe things in terms of objective qualities; things speak to us as physiognomy of the world (L. Cruse, p. 65). The physiognomy of my world arises out of my relations to the world: although we all live in the same world, we all have personal landscapes. When we speak of a massive tower or a desolate landscape, we are talking of a tuned space. Our moods are embodied in the nearness and farness of things trusted and not trusted. People who are depressed or tortured by doubt see an empty and desolate landscape. In the emptiness of the heart the prototype of all emptiness is to be found, wrote Max Scheler (L. Cruse, p. 63).

Space as mood may also be reflected in the dream. Thus, Medard Boss (1974, p. 218) reports the dream of a man who was ambivalent and doubt-ridden in his love relations. He dreamt that he was with his girl-friend in a particularly small sitting-room in a rather depressing little hotel. Both he and his girl-friend were physically very small in this dream. Outside it was a very rainy and grey day. Suddenly, however, the sun was shining brightly in the room and at the same time he felt very much drawn to his girl-friend. He then noted that they had both changed into their normal sizes. Moreover, the sitting-room changed from a small depressing place to a gigantic, festive, richly festooned banqueting hall in a beautiful castle. However, when the dreamer's mood once again changed to indifferent, the room shrank again to a poor little sitting-room and the dreamer and his girl-friend became miniature people again.

In his exposition of the spatiality of love, Ludwig Binswanger points out that spatiality is not merely the possibility to be next to each other. If we see another person simply as an object we can occupy his position by forcibly removing him from where he stands (Binswanger 1964, p. 25). However, the spatiality of love is quite different – because love on the one hand and power of violence on the other are mutually exclusive. Similarly love and commercial exchange excludes each other. Once lovers start quarrelling over who has the right to this or that thing or 'position' they have ceased to be lovers. Lovers speak of their feelings in spatial terms. Thus William Shakespeare makes Juliet say:

My bounty is as boundless as the sea,
my love as deep; the more I give thee,
the more I have, for both are infinite.
(Shakespeare, *Romeo and Juliet*, 2.1)

In her *Sonnets from the Portuguese*, E. Barrett Browning writes:

Make thy love larger to enlarge my worth.

The overcoming of distance in love is clearly seen in Goethe's poem, *Nähe der Geliebten*:

Ich bin bei dir, du seist auch noch so ferne,
Du bist mir nah!
Die Sonne sinkt, bald leuchten mir die Sterne.
O wärst du da!

We have been talking so far about space as being a sort of spatial mood, in other words, space as apperceived in terms of our originary being-here. It is the foundational characteristic of the way in which we open the world up to ourselves.

However, in lived experience, space has mood as only one of its foundational aspects. The space of our everyday life is above all the space in which we are doing things, that is, we interact with things, we look at them, look for them in the sense that they are serviceable to us as tools. To quote Minkowski: 'we live and we act in space, and it is in space that our personal lives as well as the collective life of mankind unfold. Life extends space without properly speaking possessing geometrical expanse. In order to live we need expanse, perspective, horizon. Space is as necessary to the blossoming and development of life as is time' (L. Cruse, p. 33). We move ourselves, we move from one place to another. This movement as change of place in time means that our active space is also always a time-space, that is, it is structured in terms of time as well. Under this oriented space we may, following Bakker (1965, p. 40), understand the space of the individual as a structure in the midpoint of which I am always finding myself and of which the furthest boundary is the horizon. I do not wander around in an oriented space, on the contrary, I always take it with me. It is the most important characteristic of this oriented space that I am always constituting myself in this as a spatial structure and in this spatial structure, the body has a certain place. The place of the oriented space in which the body finds itself is of great importance. It is the absolute *here* in contrast to every *there*. Similarly, moving myself is something essentially different than the removal of two objects from one another (Cruse, p. 78).

I am always the centre of my world and the *here* of the body is always the absolute starting point from which space structures itself. Through this we can see that this space is inhomogeneous in contrast to the homogeneous spatiality of mathematics.

Behaviour space may be seen as being constituted by movements in specific directions and over specific distances to and from the things of the world. Action as goal-directed movement is only possible in an oriented space. Above and below, behind and in front, left and right are not something in our body or something in the things, but relations of our body in action on the relevant things. Observations and actions are possible only in a structured and oriented space.

Above and below

As we have seen under the discussion of bodiliness, the upright posture is very important for being human. The upright posture continually contests the force of gravity and therefore above is the direction of my use of my own strength whilst below is the direction in which gravity pulls me so that I fall or so that I have to bend. The prostrate posture is the posture of not only submission and desolation, but also of sexuality. However, even when I am lying down, the opposition of above and below remains stable. The orientation above and below is therefore not bound up with the position of the body neither is it bound up in the things. Above and below is determined by the activities of the bodily subject. For the orientation of the observed space it doesn't matter; what is important is not my body as it is factually or objectively, that is, as mere object in the objective space, but as a sytem of possible actions of which the phenomenal place is given by the task and the situation. As Merleau-Ponty has put it 'my body is there where it has something to do'.

While the up–down or high–low dimension is stable even when the position of the body changes, the right–left dimension is always taken with the body itself. Our culture is primarily structured for the comfort or convenience of people who are right-handed so that people who are left-handed more often than people who are right-handed meet things in their *obviousness* so that things that speak for themselves in for the right-hand person are more difficult for the person who is left-handed, for instance, the difficulties which people have with knives, scissors and telephone receivers.

Behind and in front – the dimension of depth

The space of our goal-directed action is the space in front of us. Our movement in action is forward and is therefore also oriented towards the future. Only in the classical dances (especially) the movement backwards is something that speaks for itself, it is spontaneous whilst in the action space movement backwards is only involuntary or reactive as retreat. When we speak of the observational space, then, it is exclusively a space in front of us.

Western man especially is very much oriented towards the conquest of space. In everyday life, however, we do not overcome the distance by simply moving forward. Nearness can always retain an element of farness. We can see that what is in linear terms very far can be very near. An important dimension of this is the at-handedness of things. The spectacles on my nose can be much further from me in this sense than from the cigarette lighter which is at hand.

The depth of space shows us that the human being as action-oriented being is always on the way to somewhere, to new aims. Man is *Homo viator*.

Let us return to Mandy's experience of the tree, but this time not as sceptical natural scientists or Cartesian philosophers who doubt the reality of human experience, but as phenomenological psychologists who adopt the naïve attitude – we believe people. We believe and trust our own experience and that of Mandy.

It seems that as a child Mandy's merging with the tree had been a natural and spontaneous experience. Children, it seems, do not set themselves off against the world as separate entities, perhaps because they have not yet been assimilated into our dominant world views. Perhaps if we could recapture our child-hood experiences, we would remember something similar. Perhaps we would remember that we could easily merge with what we are observing. It was only fortunate that Mandy realized at a pretty early age that such experiences were not part and parcel of the consensually validated reality and that one should keep this to oneself. Perhaps it was part of Mandy's isolation which later led her into the consulting-room of the psychotherapist that she had to keep large chunks of her experience to herself and avoid sharing these with others. Being neurotic means, *inter alia*, that there are large areas of one's experience that one cannot share with others.

However that may be, the fact remains that here we have a clear and explicated version of what observation can and does mean. Observation of the tree, our relationship to the tree does not mean that the tree is represented in our consciousness by an image but in fact that we move toward the tree, that we are with the tree and if our relationship with the tree is intense, we merge with it. If we generalize now to what it means to be a human being in the world of things, it means that observation is the process by which we sojourn in the world, in other words, when I look at the tree, I am with the tree, the tree is not represented by an image in consciousness. The tree is out there and I *ex*-ist with the tree, I am out there with the tree.

Mandy's experience also makes clear to us something to which we shall return later on, namely what the meaning is of interpersonal relations. I am at home with a person with whom I can share my world. The episode related by Mandy shows a turning point in her relationship to her father. She had always regarded him as warm and protective; now, however, he appears as a terrifying stranger capable of destroying her through the death of the tree. It shows also that sharing with others means being able to look at the world with them in terms of a common meaning structure.

Another aspect that is clearly shown to us is that when Mandy is depressed or confused, this 'other life' is closed to her and she remains locked within herself. From this, we see a clear illustration of how the various dimensions of being human are intertwined. Bodiliness, spatiality, being with others, time and life history, all these are facets of one reality and they are all present in all our experiences, as we may see in the next example too.

The world has an invitational character. On a sunny day, the sea invites me to swim, the sun and the sand invite me to bask. The mountain invites me to climb it and when I come into a room with people, the faces and postures of people invite me or do not invite me to make contact with them. In the waiting-room and elsewhere, the chair invites me to sit, the bed to lie, etc. Let us return to the young man mentioned in chapter I who had the problem that the chair was controlling him. This young man, in fact, was in a serious dilemma and he could easily have had the label schizophrenia applied to him. Now, how do we understand the nature of his experience? The therapist did not experience the chair controlling him, but accepted his statement that the chair and the desk were controlling him at face value. The chair invites one to sit, but one has the right to refuse. One is free, one can make choices, one experiences one's ability to make choices every day. So that if the invitational character of the world becomes tantamount to a command, one is distressed, anxious or experiences uncanny emotion. Should one stand at the top of a high building and look down, there is an invitation to jump, but most of us can easily refuse that invitation. It is when we experience the invitation as becoming a demand, when we are restricted in our freedom that this becomes an uncanny experience. It seems then that in the case of the aforementioned young man we do not need the concept of projection in order to understand his behaviour. What we must understand is that his relationship to the world has changed in such a way that the invitation from some things in the world has become tantamount to a command. The therapist could not experience being controlled by the chair because his relationship to the world was different from that of the client. He could, however, be with the client in his distress at this changed relationship with the world.

Through this relationship with a fellow man it was possible for the client to overcome, at least momentarily, the uncanniness of this other new relationship in his life.

BEING HUMAN AND TIME

Man always stands in relation to time, but what is time?

Our popular conception of time is that it is something that one reads from a clock or a wrist watch. However, this is measured time and measured time is a scientific, spatialized and secondary construction of time. Lived or anthropological time precedes measured time. It is important to realize that without man there would be no time. Man is not in time, we should rather say that time is in man; it characterizes his existence.

In measured time, time is conceived to be an infinite series of 'now' points, each of which can be initially located somewhere in the future, slipping past the human observing subject for one brief moment (the present) and then going into the past. According to this then, measured time can be spatially characterized but on an infinite scale.

In looking at our watch or clock, we may ask what the time is and see that it is half-past four. When we say that, we realize that it is *now* half-past four. In ten minutes time we may look again and find that it is twenty-to-five NOW. Every time we say 'now', we have the experience of something that we can share with others. However, the now that was then is no longer the same now as it is now. And yet, the time to us is real. Time then has a paradoxical character in that it *is* or is *real* in so far as it passes, as it vanishes.

Do you have time? When I use the word 'have' in this connection, it does not refer to something, as is usually the case, which is in my possession or which is my property. One may also ask: 'Will you have time tomorrow to lunch with me?' Here again we can see that we cannot have time in the way that we may possess an object such as a pen. When we speak of having time, we remain directed, not on time in itself or time as an object, but rather on what we have time for, i.e. we remain directed to what we want to do, what we are expecting or what we are waiting for. I have (or had) time, means that I am open to what is coming in the future but also that I can retain the lived time which was and which I am living *now*.

The foregoing should not be taken to mean that we can now slip back into a linear view of time. I am living in the future in such a way that I am being with and lingering with what is present to me now and at the same time I am also holding on to what was. This trifold way of being in time is the having of time for this or that and this 'simultaneous' standing out towards the three ecstasies of time is the true timeness of being human.

'Having time' may be compared with 'having anxiety'. Neither time nor anxiety can be 'had' as if they were objects. Having anxiety or the state of being anxious refers to a Dasein being attuned in a certain way. However, Medard Boss (1975, p. 268) (whom I am very closely following in this exposition) demonstrates that the having of time is a way of being human in a much more comprehensive sense than being anxious. The having of time always shows us, continues Boss, *that* and *how* a person *is* as a whole, namely that he exists in and as a fulfilment of one or other relationship to that which he encounters. In having time for this or another fulfilment of our behavioural possibilities, Dasein times itself in the sense of an unfolding and carrying out. Dasein uses its time and eventually 'uses up' its time in terms of death as the carrying out of the extreme, unrecoverable Daseins-possibility. Therefore, the having of time is the genuine timeness of being human in so far as it times his being-in-the-world or what we may call man's sojourning in the world.

Having time does not mean that time can be seen as an object which we can pass as we can in the case of the thing like a lamp-post, or can handle whenever we feel like it, e.g. a hammer. Our relationship to time, Boss continues (p. 269), carries our world-openness. Time, which we have or do not have, is time of which we can dispose in a certain way, which we can partial out or arrange in one way or another but *only* as time. In this way, we are always ordering the past, the present and that which we anticipate in one or other way and thus we are timing our dwelling and journeying in the world. In conclusion let us hold on to the idea that the three dimensions of time are equally originary so that we stand out towards all three ecstasies of time in the same way and contemporaneously.

Until recently psychology had very little to say about the future. In our primary experience we think much more often of the things that are to come than of the things that have passed, but psychology, especially under Freudian and behaviouristic influences, looks for schedules of reinforcement, complexes and determinations which means that we try to understand behaviour by searching in the past. One theorist who has broken with this is

George A. Kelly. His construct theory essentially states that man's psychological processes are channelized by the way in which he anticipates events (Kelly 1973, p. 218). However, we are not free from our life histories: the conditions for a decision are given by the past whilst the act itself originates from the future, from the expectance or wish or fear or desire (Van den Berg, p. 86).

This again parallels Kelly's construct that we anticipate events by construing their replications. This, at first sight, looks like an extension of a Freudian determination-by-the-past but Kelly points out that it is most unlikely that events really do repeat aspects of previous experiences. Although Kelly rightly denies that his theory is a phenomenological one, his conception of time seems remarkably like the foregoing exposition in that he states that 'the recurrent themes that made life seem so full of meaning are the original symphonic compositions of a man bent on finding the present in his past, and the future in his present' (Kelly p. 212).

Instead of developing a psychology of motivation on the basis of past happenings such as was done predominantly in psychoanalysis, we should rather think in terms of life projects; how our ways of behaviour and our choices are guided by the way we see our future.

The future is what is coming, as it is coming to us now. One does not go for a swim in the swimming-pool if one is not in the swimming-pool already. If one is on the point of taking a swim, the way one enters the water will be delineated by one's past experience. If one found water to be a congenial element, one would jump into or dive into the water with gusto. However, if water was not congenial, one would enter the water slowly and carefully. Thus, the past *meets* us out of the *future*. It means then that past and future does not touch each other in a zero point called 'present'. However, as we have seen in the example, all three dimensions or ecstasies of time are present in any single one act. The past is not something which lies behind us. The past is within the present which is the way it is appearing now. The future on the other hand is what is coming to us, it is *toekoms, a-venir* that which is coming to us as it is coming to us now. The present, say Van den Berg, is 'an invitation from out of the future to gain mastery over bygone times. Now it becomes clear why the neurotic (and often the psychotic) worries about his past, the past that seems chaos to him. *The future became inaccessible*, for an accessible future means a well-ordered past' (1972, p. 92).

Van den Berg quotes the example of a workman who falls from a ladder and breaks his leg (1972, pp. 92–4). He is taken to a hospital and the fracture is set. Eventually he is discharged as cured and has the prospect of returning to his work after further recuperating at home. However, when he does return to his work, he finds that his leg is very painful and so he goes to the doctor, who books him off for another week or two. Eventually it becomes clear that organically or structurally nothing wrong can be found with the leg and the doctor now starts thinking in terms of some sort of neurotic condition. In fact, his condition now becomes what is known as 'compensationitis', i.e. preferring to live on workmen's insurance payments rather than returning to the job.

Now what has happened in this case? Probably this particular workman did not have a happy relationship with his work. He probably did not like the work all that much, did not find his superiors sympathetic and his workmates congenial. He did not 'fit in'. This means that when he fell off the ladder he fell out of his problems. The future to him now is an invitation to the troubled existence that he had before his accident. It seems as if the patient made a choice. A future in the form of lameness and pain (because the patient really suffers) seems to him more inviting than a future trying to cope with the demands of his job, his supervisors and his fellow-workers. It means then that the re-habilitation of this workman will become possible only should he be able to find some new relationship to work or to the other contingencies of his existence from what it is now, in short, to find a more accessible future.

In Beckett's drama of the absurd, *Waiting for Godot*, all the persons in the play are characterized by being alienated people who relate to each other in a parataxic fashion and whose contact with each other and the world is deeply disturbed. Wladimir and Estragon talk to each other but most of the time they do not really hear each other. We see that the spatiality or the things of the world have become inaccessible to the two main characters, e.g. they find it hard to recognize the place where they are to meet Godot. However, the crux of the situation seems to be a disturbed time relationship in that the future has become inaccessible. Having once lost the accessible future, the past, too, becomes confused and shows practically nothing which could be of use in the present. The past seems to be as absurd and as aimless as the future. Estragon has to be reminded repeatedly that they have to remain at this particular place because they are waiting for Godot. However, what the nature of their previous contact with Godot was, apart from the fact that they put some sort of request to him, is not made clear. The nearest they come to an accessible future is where Wladimir says in the original French (left out in the English version) 'tonight we may possibly sleep with Him, warm and dry, with a full stomach, on straw. Then it will be rewarding for us to wait, not so?'

However, even in this passage, there is no secure hold on the future, there is no waiting for or anticipation of the future in the sense that the future is open to one as the sphere of one's life and action except in a very deprived fashion. The past can be an ordered past only if the future is accessible. Therefore, it is only appropriate that every time Godot's messenger comes it transpires that he does not know Wladimir. It is even said at one point by Wladimir that time has stopped. At the second meeting with Bozzo and Lucky, Wladimir says "we are no longer alone waiting for the night, waiting for Godot, waiting for . . . waiting. All evening we have struggled, unassisted. Now it's over, it is already tomorrow. . . . Time flows again already. The sun will set, the moon will rise, and we away . . . from here.' Earlier on Estragon had bewailed the fact that night doesn't fall and then it will be day again and then he says 'what will we do, what will we do?' Time is therefore seen as a meaningless passing of daylight followed by night, etc. And Wladimir says that putting on boots would be a good thing because it would pass the time. The emptiness of time, i.e. a deprived form of time in which the future is not accessible and the past not significant is then a mere question of passing the time. And so Estragon says quite logically, 'we always find something, eh Didi, to give us the impression we exist?' To which Wladimir answers impatiently, 'Yes, yes, we are magicians'.

It has already been pointed out that that spatiality or access to the world of things, interpersonal relations or being with one another, are disturbed. We see, however, a disturbed bodiliness as well. This is most clearly brought out in the fact that inexplicably the two other characters, Bozzo and Lucky, undergo a catastrophic change. Bozzo becomes blind and Lucky dumb. When Lucky and Bozzo fall, Wladimir and Estragon are unable to pick them up. Wladimir then falls and he is unable to get up and the same happens to Estragon. The tortured movement and lack of mobility of catatonic schizophrenics has been related to their experience that time no longer flows. Here we see again that time-loss is associated with inability to move. The body, too, ceases to move towards the horizon of the future. The immovable body then becomes nauseating, a mere object as we can see in the second meeting of the two main characters with Bozzo and Lucky.

HUMANNESS AS HISTORICITY

Although we shall later return to a consideration of memory, it will have to be briefly mentioned here, because of its intimate connection with one's life-history. Psychologists usually start with the (not necessarily articulated) assumption that intrapsychic *images* of the outer world are retained and recalled. Most psychologists and physiologists, moreover, would contend that memory is to be understood in terms of the trace or engramme theory according to which the perceptions that give rise to memory act on the brain, leaving a trace, which when reactivated, gives rise to a recall of what has been thus stored. That this is impossible will be demonstrated later on, but we may wonder at the ability of a trace to reactivate itself.

Phenomenology contends, however, that it is not an image that is retained, neither is memory understood by supposing that a trace is reactivated. What are retained are rather the events or the data as such. They are retained as meaningful presences, e.g. as something that happened at a certain time and place and shows itself to us as past within the openness of our existence. Boss (1975, p. 300) quotes St. Augustine, who writes in his confessions that the sounds which constitute his spoken words 'have been blown away with the echoes in the wind and they are no more. The things themselves, however, signified by those sounds, I did not grasp with a bodily sense, neither did I see them with my psyche somewhere and therefore I have retained them themselves and not their images in my memory.'

Memory means, then, that peculiar characteristic of Dasein of being able to retain a relationship with that to which one has related in one's life, to which one is in meaningful relation now and can be made present to one now (see section on time). As we have seen the past that is significant is the past as it shows itself to us now. We do not retain everything that we have experienced, but in the first place only those things to which we have had some relationship and, secondly, which has some significance to us in the present.

If one returns to a childhood scene in adulthood, one is usually in for surprises. Thus, in late adulthood, I returned to a farm where I had spent the first years of my life and which I had left at the age of ten. I remembered the house, the ditch, the fountain and the dam below the fountain as being a considerable distance from the house. To my surprise, I found that these were all in close proximity. Instead of the dam being a big, impressive pool of water, it turned out to be small and almost insignificant. The fact remains, however, that the way I saw the dam, fountain and the other things in my second visit, were hardly as they were in my childhood. The things in my childhood which had an influence on me were the things as they were *then*. The house really was far from the dam in terms of the length of my stride and the softness of my muscles. What was significant in my life was the things around the house as they appeared when I was a child. The things as they appeared when I was an adult did not have the same significance for me. The only significance they had for me was that I could see them through other eyes which were yet my own eyes.

Dasein is historical, in the special sense that one *is* one's whole life-history and one *is* one's lived time. One's life-history, and what one *is*, therefore include not only the past and the present, but the future as well. A life-history therefore always includes one's own death. Death is therefore always present to us even though, as will be seen later on, it may be in the form of an avoidance of this issue.

If this is so, then what is called identity is largely understood through historicity. One's identity can be traced to the fact that, although one changes, although one's existence is not the same from day to day, yet it is still the same existence. Martin Buber makes this point cogently in connection with guilt. Existential guilt, he says, occurs when someone injures an order of a human world whose foundations he knows and recognizes as those of his own existence, and of all common human existence (Green 1959, p. 1824). Buber goes on to describe the horror of this confrontation inasmuch as the person finds it difficult to identify himself *now* with the person that he was when he committed this betrayal, but at the same time, it is impossible for him to deny that he is that same person. 'What takes possession over again, has nothing to do with any parental or social reprimand . . . no court, no punishing power exists that can make him anxious. Here then rules the one penetrating insight – the one insight capable of penetrating into the impossibility of recovering the original point of departure and the irreparability of what has been done, and that means the real insight into the irreversibility of lived time, a fact that showed itself unmistakably in the starkest of all human perspectives, that concerning one's own death. From no standpoint is this so perceived as a torrent as from the vision of the self in guilt. Swept along in this torrent, the bearer of guilt is visited by the shudder of identity with himself. I, he, comes to know; I, who have become another, am the same.'

Freud's understanding of the human being is in the first place historical. Symptoms were meaningful: they were not (in most cases) indications of an underlying neurological dysfunction, neither were they evidence of malingering. They were real in the sense that they were consequences and manifestations of experiences and events in the life-*history* or biography of the individual. Initially, Freud looked for definite traumas in the life-history of neurotics but afterwards he had to abandon this hypothesis because he found most of the reports to have been false. He then sought the origin of the neurosis in the developmental history, i.e. in a fixation to the pre-genital stages. By this exclusive emphasis on the past Freud's biographical principle became a one-sided historicism. Adler countered this by stating that neurotics did not *suffer* from reminiscences but created them in order to sustain a false insight of themselves. The trauma, for Adler, is an alibi which the client uses to advance a plausible reason to account for why he has not succeeded in reaching his goal of power. The neurotic has an over-tense grip on the *future* in which he wants to be superior and powerful. However, Adler's criticism does not really overthrow Freud's basic principle that the biography of the individual which includes present, past and future is a basic framework for understanding the individual.

DEATH AND HUMAN MORTALITY

The one indisputable certainty that our life on earth holds is that it is finite; it must end. We speak of the mortality of the human being, but the same term can hardly be used for plants and things although they do not last for ever. Mortality is something specifically human in that the human being must, from an early age onwards, struggle with the fact that one day he must die. As far as we know, animals do not have this particular challenge so that we can say that, as far as we know, they are not mortal although their lives end.

Whereas in the latter part of the nineteenth century and the early part of this century, the great taboo in the Western world was sex, as of now, it is death. This, in fact, is a mighty taboo so that we do not speak about death or the certainty thereof or the concrete experience of dying in conventional circles. If it does happen, there is a certain embarrassment, a certain hidden or open anxiety. In medieval times in Europe, people saw each other die; in the time of the plagues they were dying in the houses, in the streets and in public squares. Thus, people were being confronted by death in everyday life. Contemporary Western man has medically well-equipped, sterilized, clinical hospitals and people no longer die at home, but in the midst of all sorts of apparatuses and medical technologies which postpone death to the last possible minute, and the funeral undertaker helps family members and friends to keep death at a distance by making the funeral an enterprise acceptable to the consumer orientation of contemporary society. On his death-bed, the dying person is usually surrounded by children, family members and friends who try to the last to reassure him that he will become better, etc. This means that the dying person is isolated and lonely, and cannot make contact with his fellow man who pretends that his condition is what it is not. Dying properly means to have an experience of great intensity, anxiety, meaningfulness and dignity but instead of that, we simply expire or end as mere organisms. By not confronting death we rob the experience of its dignity.

Medical technology is, in this instance, guilty of transgressing a boundary. The doctor, as medical technologist, should withdraw when it becomes clear that there is no chance for recovery and that the hour of death is near. The best place for a person to die is usually amongst family and friends who can help him to face this last challenge of his life consciously and with dignity. The doctor can still help with ameliorative medicines but mainly, and if possible, as fellow human being.

We can still observe conditions where dying is not taboo and is openly faced. I was once deeply impressed by a dying Xhosa herbalist who spoke freely, amongst others, about his coming death. At one stage he said that he did not want to talk to us too long because he is feeling very near to his ancestors and he knows that they are awaiting him. He made no attempt whatsoever to postpone death or to deny the reality of the experience that was awaiting him. It is also true that there are some people with an authentic faith who believe that being-in-the-world is not the totality of human existence, that human existence is not purely mundane, something that is locked up within itself. For people such as these, whether conventionally religious or not, death means not an ending but an entrance into an unknown, but none the less meaningful existence. However, for most contemporary Westernized people, this access to an authentic *yonder* is no longer available. For most people, death is simply a fact, the knowledge that one must die. But this is something that one can postpone. One may think that at some or other stage one has to die, but in the meantime it doesn't happen. The soldier may think that his comrades to the left and to the right of him will die but not he himself. We think of death as an event which is bound to come some day, but for the moment it doesn't. It is a hurdle which we shall come to some day but there is no point in bothering about it right now.

Attempts can be made to overcome this contemporary taboo, because a confrontation with death is necessary in order to achieve authenticity (Bugental 1973; Todres 1978). If one could get people involved in an imaginative encounter with death, it should be possible for them to overcome the orientation of death as being the death of another and instead come to a realization of the 'death of myself'. In his research Todres (1978, pp. 165–6) found that death can give meaning to life 'as constituting a finite existence which may be lived in terms of such an existential boundary'. However, it also appeared that the subjects were not able to clearly differentiate between 'death of myself' and 'death of another'. Todres concludes that people seem to live largely on the interface between these two structures. He goes on to say 'to the degree that the subjects authentically confronted death, did they realize the possibility and the necessity of reconstituting their life in the face of their death. They thus understood the value that death confrontation may have for life and, to this extent, the research situation may be seen as an initiation for them. The most natural and most validated approach to death seems to be "death of another" and it may be postulated that such a meaning structure is necessary for man's present mode of living. Any radical change to this meaning structure would have far-reaching effects throughout society.'

It seems then, that it is difficult to overcome our tendency to avoid death as an aspect of our existence. The fact that each of us does not come into the clear with that death which is specifically 'my death' is a correlate of the inauthenticity or fallenness of being human. As we shall see in the section on 'Being with Another' one easily 'falls' in the sense that one does not take upon oneself that life which is one's own, but rather lives one's life in terms of the tradition, the peer norms, and formulates one's view of life in terms of what other people think. One lives the way 'one is supposed to' or we do things 'the way people do'.

According to Heidegger, the unity of Dasein, which we are, can be understood from the perspective of one's own death. One's existence is always in front of itself and its final horizon is death. As long as we exist, we are always uncompleted and there are always still possibilities remaining open to us. This means that Dasein inescapably includes that we are always on our way to death. Death is therefore not just a mere ending, but a manner of being. The human being is old enough to die as soon as he is born. One is therefore from the very start oriented towards death and human Dasein is therefore a being-unto-death. It is thus the challenge that faces each one of us that we must discover our death and make it our own and thus come to an understanding of the radical finitude of our lives. Death is one's extreme possibility. Death is most distinctly one's own, absolute and not to be overcome possibility. By understanding death in this genuine fashion and by accepting it as one's own, Dasein breaks with inauthentic existence and throws itself on its own authentic possibilities (Preller 1977, p. 102).

I must therefore have the freedom to die. In other words, I must always be open for that death which is *mine*, which means that I am always in front of myself on the way towards death. With such freedom and the accompanying anxiety, I can release myself from the fallenness in the people-in-general and live authentically. Heidegger himself put it this way: 'Anticipation reveals to Dasein its lostness in the they-self, and brings it face-to-face with the possibility of being itself, primarily unsupported by concernful solicitude, but of being itself, rather in a impassioned *freedom towards death* – a freedom which has been released from the Illusions of the "they" and which is factical, certain of itself, and anxious' (Macquarrie's translation, p. 504).

Erik Erikson (1973, pp. 259–61) has dealt with our facing death as a last stage of human growth characterized as ego integrity *v.* despair. In his description ego integrity is essentially a post-narcissistic love of the human ego (not of self), the acceptance of one's one and only life-cycle as unrepeatable and as something that had to be like it was and as a readiness to defend his life-style. 'The style of integrity developed by his culture or civilization thus becomes the "patrimony of his soul", the seal of the moral paternity of himself. . . . In such final consolidation, death loses its sting.'

According to Erikson, then, one consolidates the previous growth stages and accepts responsibility for one's life-style. In a sense one, in looking back on one's life, becomes a responsible and loving parent to oneself and adopts an attitude of resignation to one's achievements, failures, triumphs and frustrations, to opportunities taken and missed, to experiences lived through and denied, to choices made and precluded.

On the other hand, according to Erikson, if the one and only life-cycle cannot be accepted in this resigned but positive manner there is a loss of ego integration and a fear of death. Despair arises in the knowledge that an alternate road has now become impossible. 'Disgust hides despair. . . .'

In Erikson's exposition we again meet our knowledge of death as lived time and the fear of death as the irreversibility of life-history. However, inasmuch as death is given to us as a possibility right from the start, one can hardly see it as being limited to a final stage of growth. Once a possibility of one's life becomes known to one, it is impossible for one *not* to relate to such a possibility, for it *not* to be relevant to one's behaviour. The 'if I had my life all over again' fantasies do not start in old age but are a defensive non-confrontation with one's mortality at any age. The same goes for the wish to have been born in another cultural era or place. An involved confrontation with death often commences when a person starts evaluating his life. It is true that such evaluations are more characteristic of the second part of life than the first and it is also true that younger people find denial of death easier as a defensive strategy than older ones. At the same time it is amply clear that psychologists should be prepared to help others come to grips with their finitude and it is fairly generally experienced that it is usually too late for this to be done when the person is already in a terminal illness. Moreover, if the psychologist is to be of assistance to his fellow man in being-with him in grappling with his finitude or 'living his dying' (Keleman,

1974) and if the psychologist himself is to live authentically, he should, by anticipation, resolutely encounter his own death.

EXISTENTIAL MOOD OR TUNEDNESS (DIE GESTIMMTHEIT).

As an open domain of being, human existence is always essentially and from the very beginning tuned or attuned to the world in some or other way. One's Dasein is always characterized by some basic mood. This is the basis of the fact that, as psychologists, we can describe in a person always some or other ontic mood. We must not think of Dasein as being somehow in a neutral mood into which we can project some or other mood or emotion or passion. We must not think of the mood as being caused to a neutral organism, on the contrary, Dasein is fundamentally co-constituted by mood.

Our being attuned in some way or another is a way of the openstandingness of our Dasein. Our predominating mood, our feelings, our passions, our emotions are this open condition in which Dasein finds itself and within the relation in which we stand towards the things, towards ourselves and to our fellow human beings (Boss, p. 291). We do come across people who are in a sense closed, who do not show emotion and who do not relate to their fellow human beings in a way disclosing their moods. However, we should see this as deprivation phenomenon of the fundamental openstandingness of being human. Our openstandingness can be characterized by a certain expansion or contraction, brightness or darkness and overtness or covertness of our existence.

It is important to differentiate in the first place between the fundamental moods, affects and passions. The fundamental mood, as already said, is our characteristic attunedness to the world. This diffused attunedness, however, can be differentiated further. Let us think of an *affect* or emotion like joy, rage. Closely related to rage is hate. Hate, however, cannot be seen as just another emotion but rather as a *passion*, although we call both forms of feeling. We can talk about a feeling of hate or a feeling of anger. However, there are essential differences. We do not plan to be angry, we are, in fact, suddenly overcome by anger. It is true that our hate can suddenly break out and in such a case we can usually point out that it has been building up for a long time and in fact we feed our hatred. On the other hand, although we can feel ourselves getting more and more angry, anger is not something that we feed or nourish, anger rather is something that suddenly overcomes us almost in the sense that when we are angry we are besides ourselves.

As far as hate or love is concerned, these are both passions which, in a sense, gather our whole Dasein together, collect it. In these passions we are 'together' persons; we are not besides ourselves as we are in anger, but in good measure we may be very perceptive as well as circumspect in both these passions. A person who passionately loves another one is extremely perceptive of any hidden good and beautiful characteristics and of the potential richness of the loved one. Also the person who has a strong passion of hate is very perceptive of the characteristics of the person that is hated. A good example of this is found in paranoid hate in which the person is remarkably perceptive in picking up the most subtle unfriendly or hostile nuances in his fellow human beings.

The openness of an existence which is passionately attuned in terms of hate or love remains of a limited openness for the perception of that which is present. The extensive perceptiveness occurring in both hate and love exists only in relation to particular domains of phenomena. It is therefore also possible to 'have' a blind love or hatred. Passionately hating people are not at all open for the 'good side' of people who are hated. Similarly a person who passionatly loves will tend to overlook the ugly or negative appeals of the existence of the loved person.

Boss (p. 295) says that only a state of being suffused with a mood of serenity: a pervasive letting-be-ness is a state of being in which all the significances and meaningful coherences of everything that is encountered is allowed to become clear. This serene letting-be-ness, however, is not indifference but a passionate devotion to or involvement with everything that shows itself to such a person as relevant to him. Inasmuch as this mood opens the human being to the widest possible responsivity it is at the same time happiness. Happiness then means a mood in which Dasein is attuned to the world in such a way that the carrying out of all its essential behavioural and relational possibilities stands open for it. Such a Dasein even is able to take the possibility of one's own death with a happy let-be-ness. In this attuning, dying as the most certain of all realities shows itself as a state of being brought before a void. But the nothingness does not show itself in the openness of letting-be as a nihilistic emptiness. On the contrary, this nothing is of such fullness that it appears to us as the void from which the things-that-are originally emerge (Boss 1975, p. 295).

A report of the LSD-experiences of dying people seems to confirm this. Thus, Grof and Halifax have indicated that: 'In a large group of transpersonal experiences, the extension of consciousness seems to go beyond the phenomenal world and the time-space continuum as we normally perceive it. . . . The ultimate of all experiences appear to be the Void, the mysterious primordial emptiness and nothingness that contains all existence in a germinal form' (Grof & Halifax 1977, p. 56).

This understanding and acceptance of death should be sharply distinguished from another basic attunedness of being human, namely our attunedness in anxiety. Anxiety is a paradoxical mood in which Dasein is open to but at the same time restricted to perceiving the possibility of losing its hold on all the things-that-are and is thrown back entirely upon itself as an existence which one completes on one's own and alone and is terminable. In this case, the 'object' of anxiety is death, i.e. the possibility of not being able to be in the world anymore, and therefore as a revelation of the negation of existence. In this sense, then, the object of anxiety turns out to be one's Dasein-possibilities. But not only the object or 'wherefore' of anxiety is one's own Dasein, but also the subject or 'why' of anxiety is Dasein because, to the extent that one's own Dasein gets involved in the possibilities of existence by that very same token, Dasein is always endangered. Since Dasein uses itself up in this existence, we invariably find that people who fear death most are also those who have the greatest anxiety for life (Boss 1975, p. 296).

In contemporary psychology we usually differentiate between an outward stimulus triggering anxiety in terms of whether it is fear or anxiety. Fear is supposed to be a rational response to an external danger, e.g. if one comes across a lion in the open veld, fear is a rational response and discretion will be the better part of valour! However, there are also 'irrational' fears, e.g. the fear that some people have for frogs or birds, as well as the state known as free-floating anxiety where the object of fear cannot be identified at all. Phenomenology looks at anxiety as presupposing the understanding of being endangered, being killed, i.e. in the last instance, death. Anxiety is grounded in the perception of phenomena as such. In the case of the fear of frogs or birds, there is a threatening reality in the frog or bird which is perceived. However, this reality is dominated entirely by the basic state of being which is a being-anxious. In such a case, what looks like something harmless to others can reveal itself to the perceiving person as something extremely threatening. Let us be quite clear on this point. All anxiety is fear of something threatening and in so-called free-floating anxiety it is the world itself that threatens one, in other words, it is a being that is dominated by the basic or foundational attunedness to the world as being fearful which means that Dasein itself is fearful (Boss 1975, p. 297).

A further example of a foundational attunedness or state of being is the mood of mourning. This mourning is not the same as the more pathological forms of depression. We speak of genuine mourning when in a Dasein there has been a break or schism in a relationship with another person to whom one is near and dear. This schism is, however, of this nature that the mourning person cannot simply rid himself of it. If, in fact, the being-with-the-person mourned was so broken and fragmented that it entirely destroyed this relationship, then it means that the absence of the person will vanish entirely out of the world of the remaining person and then there would be no question of mourning as such. However, in mourning the relationship with the absent person now becomes a very close one. This means that the break or schism relates only to the actualization possibilities of the relationship with the person mourned about. When one is in mourning, one realizes that the presence of the other person is now possible only in the sense of recalling. However, now that it is impossible for the person to be physically present to one, the bond with such a person in the sense of making that person present may become all the more intense. This means that one's Dasein may be broken for a time at least and this is the case where people lose somebody through death or through the breaking off of a genuine love relationship.

In the foregoing we see a serene letting-be-ness being clearly demarcated from the state-of-being anxious and of mourning. If a serene letting-be-ness is at the same time happiness, does this exclude suffering and mourning and can it really be contrasted with an attunedness of anxiety?

H. S. Sullivan has stated that the opposite of love is not hate but anxiety. Anxiety, according to Sullivan, is the great disjunctive force in human relations. Hate does not disjoin but rather relates, even binds people together. C. G. Jung has seen power, i.e. the need and propensity to control others, as the polar opposite of love. L. Binswanger, who saw love rather than Heidegger's care as the sein (being) of Dasein, has indicated that love on the one hand and power or violence on the other exclude each other (Binswanger 1964, p. 25). These serve as illustrations that the polar opposites of emotions, passions and moods should not be sought in grammar or language conventions but should be grounded in experience.

This leads me to the question of whether serenity as a mood of acceptant letting-be-ness thus constituting what Boss calls happiness should be opposed to the 'negative' moods of unhappiness, anguish or anxiety (*Angst*) and suffering. From the definition given by Boss, it is clear that a serene letting-be-ness (*gelassener Heiterkeit*) would be the predominant mood in authentic living, which, to me, means taking upon yourself that life which is *yours*. This means also, however, a being-unto-death involving freedom and therefore also anxiety. A Dasein which is serenely open for all its encountered possibilities must put itself at risk and therefore cannot be free of anxiety. Anxiety is part of the price to be paid for a refusal to conform for the sake of security, i.e. for the freedom that we realize (in the sense of making real use of it) in authentic living. Similarly a Dasein which is open and free for its encounter with the possibilities encompassed in its relations with the world cannot avoid suffering. It is hard to see how one can involve oneself in the possibilities open to one without being exposed to suffering. A parent, however serene, whose beloved child dies in (e.g.) a senseless accident will suffer deeply and severely. The parent's love for that child means that the parent was deeply involved in his encounter with the child and therefore also with the unfolding possibilities in the existence of such a child. However, if the parent is predominantly serenely attuned to the possibilities of his encounter with the world, it means that he has accepted from the birth of the child onwards that such a child may predecease him and it means therefore that the death of the child actualizes one of the possibilities given to him in his being-in-the-world. On this basis he accepts his suffering as actualizing one of the many possibilities of his Dasein and therefore suffering does not contradict his serenity.

The polar opposite of a serene letting-be-ness therefore is neither anguish nor suffering, but rather an attempt to avoid the genuine possibilities of Dasein. The opposite of serenity is non-involvement and denial of openness, i.e. a restriction of existence in such a way that one is not at risk, thus closing off not only one's possibilities for anxiety, suffering, humiliation and ridicule but also for genuine love, hate, anger and ecstasy. This one can do by conforming, by systematically and/or opportunistically striving for power, status, money, etc. One can in the words of K. Horney move towards people, move away from people and move against people, i.e. one's existence can be tuned predominantly in terms of love, anxiety or hate. One can, in the words of Rollo May (1959, p. 1358), succumb to the central preoccupation of contemporary Western culture which is 'that everyone should live in a calculated, technically well-managed way. Achieving this, the patient accepts his confined world without conflict, for now his world is identical with the culture.' All these as well as E. Fromm's non-productive orientations are ways of restricting the openness of our attunedness to the world and at the same time are indications of inauthentic living.

BEING-WITH-ONE-ANOTHER IN A COMMON WORLD

Our world is a world which we share with others of whom we have an originary knowledge of being in the world in the same way as we are. Being human means being in relation to others. Being human does not mean being born as a mere organism that then enters into object relations with other similar and non-similar objects or organisms or things. On the contrary being

human means relation to others right from the start. The baby
first reacts to mother as a diffused otherness and its first differentiated focus is mother's face. In the words of Bernd Jager,
mother's face invites the child into the world.

Neo-analysts such as Karen Horney and Harry Stack Sullivan
came very close to phenomenology in formulating an interpersonal psychiatry. Sullivan once defined personality as manifesting
itself in interpersonal relations and not otherwise. One can see
here that he moved away from the intrapsychic understanding of
the human person to an interpersonal understanding. However,
having defined personality in this way, Sullivan had to state how
this interpersonal contact was made possible. For this purpose he
used the term empathy, which first appears in his writing in
an article on *Archaic sexual Culture and Schizophrenia* which appeared in 1930 (Preller 1977, p. 38). Empathy, for Sullivan, was
a primitive exchange of emotional tone between mother and child.
It was the earliest form of communication whereby the child
came to realize something albeit in a non-verbalized manner.
Sullivan himself could not quite explain how empathy took place,
but said that we will just have to accept 'the one mystery of
empathy' (Preller, p. 38). Although Sullivan was the first to use
the term empathy, in the German-speaking world the term *Einfühlung* had been known since Theodore Lipps used it in 1908.
The concept was later taken over by Husserl and criticized by
Heidegger.

The characteristics of Sullivan's empathy may be summarized
as follows:

1. Empathy is a non-verbal matter and as such takes place
   non-verbally and on the emotional level. In later life, it is akin
   to what is sometimes called telepathy or intuition. Sullivan
   further says that it may be connected with mediumistic or
   hypnotic phenomena.
2. Empathy plays a role throughout life.
3. Although empathy is to Sullivan a mystery, in his later writings it gets a causal mechanistic colour in that empathic
   experiences in early life may be the primitive root of later traits
   of personality. The concept of empathy is an ineradicable
   aspect of interpersonal relations. It lays the necessary primitive bases of interpersonal communication (Preller, p. 151).

However, Sullivan did not really succeed in overcoming the
subject/object dichotomy by this concept. Empathy is an attempt
to articulate what goes on *between* people. This between, as
Sullivan himself has to admit, remains mysterious. Sullivan
realized that we are not, as it has been poetically put, like ships

which pass each other in the night, but he was not fully able to overcome the sylopsistic, encapsulated conception of the isolated person. He said in another of his writings that the unique individuality of the person need not concern us *scientifically*, which means that he did not really overcome the sylopsism but bracketed it.

In criticizing Husserl's concept of *Einfühlung* Heidegger said that *Einfühlung* is not a primary characteristic of our originary existence but is only possible because there is already an originary being with each other or Mitsein. In Heidegger's own words: 'Einfühlung does not constitute Mitsein, but is only possible on the basis of Mitsein' (1972, p. 125).

Elsewhere I have pointed out that Xhosa diviners see no difficulty in making statements like 'I know what the other person is suffering from, because I can feel it in my own body' or 'when I touch the other person I feel his sickness in myself' or 'my ancestors come to me in the shape of my animals and tell me what is wrong with the other person'. Diviners even aver that they dream of what is wrong with their patients. These statements are possible only if the diviners work on the assumption that the reality of the other is open to one, which means that, given the right conditions, and given the necessary personal growth on the part of the diviner, the articulation of the accessibility of human beings to each other is not problematic.

What then is the meaning of Mitsein or being with one another? We know that people can be lonely, but the phenomenon of loneliness would hardly be possible if people did not fundamentally tend to be with one another. Of an object we can say only that it is the only one of its kind in a certain area. We do not, however, speak of an object as lonely. We do know that animals sometimes move in packs and sometimes alone. Since it is clear that an animal is not confined to his own skin, and lives in relation to a world that presumably has meaning for him, it is possible perhaps that an animal may be lonely. However, since we cannot communicate with the animal, he cannot tell us what it is like for him to be the only one of his kind in a certain area and so we can hardly establish and articulate the phenomenon of loneliness as far as the animal is concerned. However, being lonely is part of the primary experience of every single human being.

The indisputable phenomenon of being with one another once again shows that the conception of man as an encapsulated subject is untenable. Although psychologists, if pressed, say of the perception of the subject of people and object that the 'inner' images we form of the 'outer' world and other people are immediately projected back to a perceived object and human being, nobody has ever been able to demonstrate convincingly that or how this takes place. On the other hand, our primary experience clearly shows that we are in touch with others, that we communicate with each other and that we feel upset when we are unable to communicate with another person. Saying that we cannot understand another person and saying that we cannot communicate with him usually means one and the same thing.

In the following illustrations, an attempt is made to give a representation of the two modes of viewing relations between two people and how they share the world. The example is taken from the salient work by Medard Boss. He first shows how a consistent adherence to Cartesian dualism would be represented (Figure 2), while the second shows how the matter is viewed phenomenologically (Figure 3).

The sketch illustrates a chance meeting down-town between two lovers (let us call them Joan and Peter). Joan saw Peter on the opposite side of a busy street and seeing him was enough to fill her with joy. Impulsively she ran across the street, embraced and kissed him. They started talking about the happy time they were hoping to have together. They discussed their forthcoming vacation in the Canary Islands, and, as they walked hand-in-hand up the street, this prospect became more 'real' to them than the street in which they were walking. They both knew the hotel where they were going to stay in the Canary Islands, imagining (which means a making present of the hotel and its environments, not in their heads but of it, there where it stood in the Canary Islands) all the details of swimming, lying in the sun, etc., of their anticipated vacation.

Figure 2.

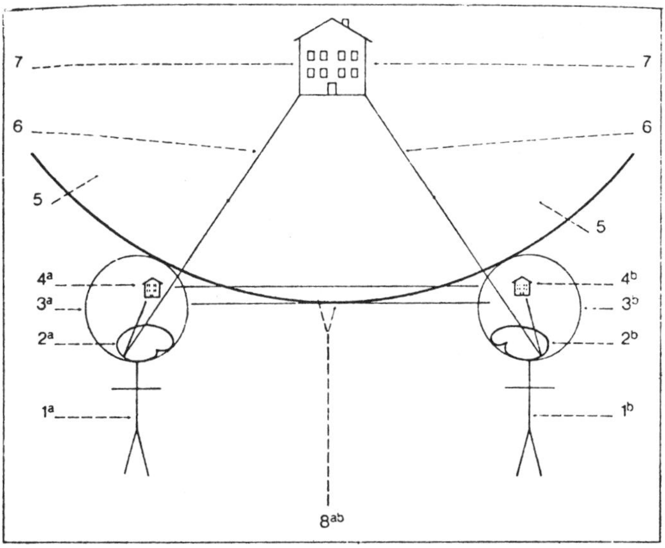

The intrapsychic view of interpersonal 'dialogue'

1a & b: Bodies of Joan and Peter.
2a & b: The brains of Joan and Peter.
3a & b: The psyches of Joan and Peter.
4a & b: The two lovers having intra-psychic images of the hotel out there (each having her/his own image).
5.   The world out there.
6.   Light stimuli of the objects in the world out there.
7.   Object in the outer world.
8a & b: The talking to and fro (dia-logue) of Joan and Peter each with reference to her/his intrapsychic image of the hotel in the outer world.

Source: Medard Boss (1975) *Grundriss der Medizin und der Psychologie,* H. Huber, Bern, p. 288.

Figure 3.

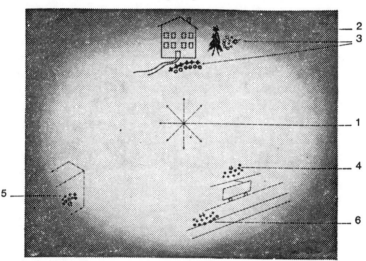

Existence as being with others

Co-human existence as primary being-with-each-other with the same things in a common world.

1. The Dasein of Joan and Peter as an illuminated sphere of world openness in which the two with-each-other stand out in the mode of perceiving and responding, to the things revealed in the world in their spatially defined presence.
2. Hiddenness (darkness).
3. Thematic sojourning of the two lovers at their holiday hotel in the mode of a perceiving 'making present' (concrete imagining) of this locale.
4, 5, 6. The being with one another 'at the same time' of the two lovers with the sensorily present passing tram, with the façade of a house on the opposite side of the street and with the sidewalk in the mode of not specially extending to these tending towards quite unrelated themes.
oooo pointers to Joan's ek-static sojourning in the world in the sense of an openstanding, perceiving, being-with-the-things encountered.
++++ Same for Peter.

Source: Medard Boss, op. cit., p. 289.

Being with one another means being able to share the things of this world, i.e., as the above example makes clear, to be in a certain world openness standing out towards the things that can be encountered there together. To be at home with another person, to be really a friend of another, means that we can let our bodies and the things of the world be for each other. I have asked first-year students to note how they experience a conversation with someone whom they liked or did not like. The following were typical reports, of students' experiences of talking to someone they like: (a) Ease in looking at the person *and* in not looking at her/him. (b) Body inclines towards person. (c) One sits comfortably, slumps, etc. (d) Body relaxed. (e) Felt less pain of injury. (f) Free to take in more of physical environment or to take in less. (g) Uses slang. Conversation flows. (h) Able to concentrate. (i) Wanted to stay in situation. (j) Uses gestures freely. (k) Nice bubbly feeling in stomach.

In the case where the other person was not liked students reported wanting to escape by leaving physically or changing the subject; feeling sick, e.g. headache or shivers; sitting rigidly upright, body feeling tense; conversation and body shifted; feeling threatened; becomes fidgety, hands become big and cannot use them; has saliva in mouth; sweats; throat and stomach contract.

It is a well-known fact that when people are not at ease with each other they start talking a physical language, i.e. they talk about things like weather, the condition of the road, the vagaries of buses, trains, aeroplanes; the facilities available, etc., etc. When you are with someone with whom you cannot communicate, you become restless in your chair, or your body becomes tense; you feel unable to enter into subjects that you would easily broach with someone else. In other words, if you have a good relationship with someone, you are at home in your body and in the world. The other 'allows' you to let your body be and to let the world be for you.

Van den Berg (1972) gives a beautiful example of a Jewish girl and her mother, characters in a Dutch novel by Corry van Bruggen. On the morning of the Sabbath, mother takes the daily red and black cloth from the table and replaces it with a gleaming white one. Always 'there is one undertermined moment when "it" happens, a moment one always missed' (Van den Berg 1972, p. 6). When the tablecloth is changed mother suddenly has a new face and all the furniture looks different too. The physiognomy of the world changes in accordance with our relationship to fellow-man. Van den Berg (pp. 65–6) summarizes: 'A word, a look or a gesture can brighten things or make them gloomy. The person with us is not another isolated individual, next to us, who throws words in our ear and who remains foreign to the object around us.

He is the person who is either with us or not with us and who makes the degree of togetherness or distance visible in objects, concretely and in reality. Togetherness is no mere idea. Togetherness and distance appear within the physiognomy of the world.'

A true encounter between two people is a letting-be-ness of the things-that-are as they present themselves to the person in a shared world, allowing the other person to express freely what he or she is. A real encounter is one in which both partners can reveal themselves without fear. A client, Sara, who said that her experience of psychotherapy had been good and successful, said that being in therapy means 'having somebody with whom you can confront your life, somebody who has faith in the fact that I will overcome, and somebody who understands my situation totally. So I can open myself totally to that situation, sort of take stock of it. And I can say "this is a situation, this is what I've got to fight the situation".'

On another occasion, she also said that being in therapy is not like having a friend. She goes on to say 'it's far superior to merely having a friend, because – I think that's why it is important not to have social contact with your therapist. I mean if X had, if we had had outside contact, I would have been ashamed to say to him, say certain things to him, because as a friend I would then be disappointing our relationship. But as a therapist I could say anything to him because he had no right to say that someone I was talking about was his friend and how can I (Sara) then say such and such about him.'

As will be shown later on, psychotherapy is a true encounter or it is nothing. Within this true encounter, the client gradually builds up the courage to be completely herself. Sara was troubled by psychosomatic disorders like asthma, an ulcerated stomach and other symptoms and then one day she realized that she had in fact been using these psychosomatics in order to be able to avoid certain types of contacts and responsibilities. She says, 'admitting this to myself was terrible; the worst thing was having to go to my therapist and say "I've got to admit to you and I have admitted to myself, but I've got to admit to you as well, that, you know, I've been a bad girl".' She further continues: 'I was so nervous to go to X you know, I knew that I had to say to him as well, because it's no use just admitting it to myself, because I can just bury it again. But once I had said it to X, I had freed myself and it was fantastic afterwards.' (See Eppel 1978.)

We find striking confirmation of Boss's statement (1975, p. 314) that people nowadays are lonelier than ever before when we look at our therapeutic case histories and find that so many people do not have friends with whom they can be completely open and with whom they can share. The aim of therapy then must be for human beings to be able to be themselves, to find someone with whom they can relate and with whom they can be completely open, or at the very least, to be so open that they need not hide things from others and from themselves as well. This last is characteristic of what is called neurosis or psychological dis-ease.

This does not, however, mean that the 'normal', average, i.e. conformistic, person lives the encounters in his being-with-others. Our Mitdasein always implies the invitation of a true encounter, but this invitation is mostly refused because the 'ownness' or authenticity of Dasein gets lost in that we structure our individual existence not in terms of those facets of the world that truly exercise an appeal on us but rather in terms of how we see our fellow men responding. We therefore structure our lives in terms of how others live. In this way we 'foreclose' on the unique possibilities offered to each of us in our specific set of relatedness to the world. Our Dasein therefore becomes lost in the being-with-others so that we tend to have inauthentic encounters with the things and fellow man to whom we respond, not in terms of their own unique possibilities but in terms of stereotypes or roles.

The tendency to loose ourselves in the structure of 'people-in-general' ('das man' as Heidegger calls it) means that our lives easily become 'other-directed' as Riesman has called it. Other-directedness characterizes the life of most contemporary people. The lostness in 'das man' also means a limitation on freedom of choice. It is in Erich Fromm's terms a flight from freedom or a 'living in bad faith' (Sartre). Most of us then do not take upon ourselves the life that is ours but rather structure our lives in such a way that we fit in and avoid anxiety, involvement, loneliness and suffering as far as possible but also serenity, ecstasy and transpersonal experiences.

Being Human and Being Free

The basic characteristics of the various dimensions of being human are co-originary. Taken together, we can see their deployment as a freedom of the autonomous person. They are equally originary in that they belong to a unitary coherence. This unity is characteristic of our existence. Being human basically means an open standing towards, an ex-isting. All the possibilities of our being human – bodiliness, being with others, etc. – are of this nature (Boss 1975, p. 314).

We should guard against reifying the open-standingness of human existence. We should not look at a human being as an 'opening' in the physical sense on the one hand to be contrasted to the things-that-are on the other. Boss suggests that the open-standingness of human existence should rather be described as a constant perceiving openness and taking-into-account of the world as it appears to us; it is a letting be of the things-that-are as they present themselves (Boss, p. 315).

Now it is this very letting be of the things-that-are as they reveal themselves that constitute a precondition of the possibility that man is free. Letting be does not mean indifference. On the contrary, it means being involved in that which is encountered in such a manner that these can unfold to their full presence. Because of the ability to let things be, the human being finds himself challenged to choose and to decide, i.e., to exercise his freedom. The fact that we utilize the possibility to choose is part of our everyday experience. Our freedom is therefore a primary indisputable fact.

The indisputable phenomenon of human freedom of choice and decision is basic to the phenomenon of responsibility and guilt. If there was no freedom of choice or decision, nobody could have been held responsible for or deemed guilty of anything. Neither would any therapeutic procedure to relieve people of neurotic or earned guilt feelings have any point. The very fact that we try to persuade people to another point of view, or that we allow them to overcome their feelings of guilt, or that we hold them responsible for something, or that we allow people to let their responsibility for things unfold, means that we perceive freedom as a basic existential.

It must not be thought, however, that the aforegoing argues that human freedom is unlimited. If I was born as a tribesman in Pondoland, it could hardly be expected of me to be able to generate an ideal to become a philosopher or a specialist in surgery or an entertainer in a night-club. However, as a tribesman in Pondoland, I am free within a certain situation. I am free in that situation which is mine.

We also have to understand a certain helplessness of man vis-à-vis being born as what-we-are in a certain situation – Heidegger calls this initial helplessness *Geworfenheit*. We are 'thrown' into the world. The situation into which we are born, i.e. the nature of the culture, family situation, etc., as well as the nature of our bodiliness, the characteristics of the historical period, etc., is entirely out of control. However, we take our life situation upon ourselves as being ours; we participate in the society and in the world and thus, although we are shaped by the world, we in our turn take part in shaping the world. Even should we, in the extreme case of total withdrawal, indicate to others and to ourselves that we do not want to have a further part in shaping the world, we are by that very action giving shape to the world; by our very withdrawal, we are actively shaping the world in which we live.

The above is not an attempt to afford a scientific proof for human freedom. No such proof is called for because it is part of our primary experience that we are free, that we participate in life, that we are responsible and that we can experience guilt as well as acceptance and freedom. Neither should human freedom be seen as a mere exception to the rule of determinism. Human freedom falls outside the entire cause–effect schema as constructed by natural science. Being human means being free. As Frankl has pointed out, even in the extreme case where we are threatened with a set of circumstances over which we have no control whatsoever, e.g. the gallows, we still have freedom in that, although we can no longer choose our actions, we can still choose our attitude towards what is going to happen to us. Thus, these extreme situations should not be seen as exceptions to our choices, but rather as deprived and limited forms of human freedom.

A poignant example of freedom of choice in extremity, which at the same time illustrates an acceptance of death in a mood of serene let-be-ness is the death of the German theologian, Dietrich Bonhoeffer, who took part in the internal German resistance movement against Hitler's National-Socialist regime. Bonhoeffer was found guilty by a people's court and executed at Flossenbürg in April 1945. According to an eyewitness, he remained cheerful and in good contact with his comrades even when he knew that his position was hopeless. When he was called to what he knew was going to end in his execution, he said that this was, for him, the end but also the beginning, and sent a message to a friend reaffirming his belief in a universal Christian brotherhood which rises above all national interests – the cause for which he was dying. He prayed at the foot of the gallows and then mounted the steps steadily and courageously (Bethge 1970, pp. 1037–8).

Strict determinists would argue that man's behaviour, like that of any other natural object, is governed by strict laws, yet to be discovered. Motivation then, is the main road along which human determinism is to be elaborated. However, as we have seen, in the hundred years since Wundt's 1879 initiative no laws have been formulated and psychology remains a post-dictive rather than a predictive science. Most current psychologies of motivation have shown a profound weakness in that they cannot accommodate the future as future and, as we have seen, human motivation essentially involves a living towards the future and not simply a living out of the past. It is therefore a futile endeavour to try to erect the structure of the psychology of motivation on the natural scientific model by endeavouring to isolate cause and effect sequences. It seems much more promising to study how people live *out of* their potentials and *towards* meaningful goals as part of their life projects, whether articulated or not.

CHAPTER III

Three Topics in Contemporary Psychology

1. VISUAL PERCEPTION

Van den Berg (1972 a) points out that there are two ways of comprehending visual perception. One is the psychology of explaining (*Verklärung*) and the other is the psychology of understanding (*Verstehen*). Both psychologies have a right to examine the field of perception, but in textbooks on psychology it is only the psychology of explaining that has priority, whilst an understanding psychology is rarely, if ever, discussed in standard textbooks. A psychology of understanding which leads us to a phenomenology of visual perception belongs to human existence as such and the psychologist who wishes to participate in the existence of others will have to use this psychology – even to give it priority over the other methods – because of its direct, non-artificial nature.

Although the natural scientific psychology which tries to explain seeing in scientific terms has developed over the centuries it nevertheless goes back, in spite of its sophistication, to the fundamental ideas of Descartes, who announced his theory of visual perception in 1637 (Van den Berg o.c., p. 12). In terms of this theory, it is necessary to understand the structure of the eye and the fact that there are certain light stimuli in the environment. If one buys an eye from the butcher and removes some of the membranes from the back of the eye without harming the inner membrane, i.e. the retina, one can then turn the eye towards the light and by looking inside the eye, one will see a whole panorama reflected in inverted form on the retina. According to Descartes, what one does then as observer is exactly what is done by the soul which Descartes located in the midbrain, i.e. inside the pineal gland.

There is, in fact, a rather difficult problem in this connection: once the process of perception has been explained in this manner, one would want to know where the perceiver is. The process of explanation, however, having explained the whole perceptual process in terms of physical stimuli and physiological actions, cannot then tell us how this is translated into consciousness. Is there another observer that observes the image in the retina? We shall, in a moment, examine later and more sophisticated theories and see that this difficulty is not overcome. Another important point to remember is that we are told that what we see is not the world out there, but a representation of the world on the retina conveyed to the brain and further we are told that what we see is essentially a picture formed in the visual cortex. However, this does not overcome the problem as to how this becomes conscious. The basis then of the natural scientific paradigm can be outlined as follows:

1. Perception is inactive. The subject (i.e. the homunculus inside the brain) passively waits for the information or stimuli coming into the brain. He has to accept them all.
2. Perception is receptive. In other words, to observe is to allow stimuli to enter.
3. Observation is a mechanical process. Everything happening in this process must happen in accordance with the laws of physics and chemistry. The eye, the connecting nervous tissue, the brain; all these form a complex apparatus. It was, in fact, the conviction of Descartes that perception, like any other process in the human body, is, in principle, a mechanical process. In other words, what we would call observation in everyday life – seeing and hearing events – is not accounted for in the theory of Descartes and the perceiving subject is not considered; in fact, cannot be considered.
4. Perception is solitary. The homunculus or soul or mind in the brain who performs the observation or, in any case, completes it is alone. He is not relating to anyone and in the cells of the brain he is alone.
5. It is easy to narrate this explanation of the process of visual perception. It is certainly a matter of elementary scientific thinking to make it clear to everybody that the object emits stimuli which thus depicts itself as a photo on the retina, that these stimuli are led along the path of the eye-nerve to the brain and that the stimuli somehow are translated into consciousness. However, what is missing in this, is the real 'observation by the soul' or the real process of how this becomes conscious? This remains a metaphysical leap. Most contemporary theorists simply do not discuss this and restrict themselves to the observable psychology and physiology of visual perception. Through all this, it seems then that contemporary visual perception theory deals with every aspect of the process but avoids getting to grips with the seeing of the seeing person, i.e. with perception or observation as such.

However, on the other hand, looked at from the point of view of a psychology of understanding, seeing or visual perception is active, evasive or volatilely moving, selective, communicative, and not easily narratable. In order to understand seeing, one has to be able to put oneself into the position of the seeing person. One has to take his place in the landscape and try to look at the world through his eyes.

Mark McConville (1978) points out that in the classical natural science of perception, psychologists recognize the two most general components of all perception as being the perceived and the perceiver. When we speak of the perceived, we usually speak of distal stimuli which refer to the objective, physical world which surrounds the perceiver and reflects energy – such as light – towards him. In this we can clearly see that, for the purposes of the psychology of perception, the natural scientific picture of the world as a system of physical facts is accepted. On the other hand, the perceiver is often conceptualized, not as subject, but rather as being composed, for the purposes of perception, of proximal stimuli and this refers to the effects and processes which result from the impingement of physical energy upon the sense organs. According to the summary by Mark McConville, the impingement 'creates a new pattern of stimulation, a proximal (and essentially physiological) one, which is the immediate cause of our perceptual experience. The retinal image, or pattern of light-activated neurons across the retina is one good example of proximal stimulation' (p. 95).

A more sophisticated variation of the Cartesian theory has been the subject of some debate and disagreement. However, according to Mark McConville (p. 96) the subject has commonly been conceptualized as a reactive physiological information processing organism. Light energy strikes the retina and depending on certain characteristics such as wave-length, and certain sensory characteristics of the neuron, this energy is transformed into a neural form. Thus, neurons react to light by firing impulses along the optic nerve which then pass through the sub-cortical thalamus to a small area of the occipital lobe known as the striate cortex. Here the raw neural information is further processed and related to the neighbouring visual cortex and from there to other areas of the brain. At the striate cortex level, the information is raw and consists of relatively pure visual sensations; in the visual association areas, it is interpreted and given some immediate perceptual meaning. At the final stage, perception is integrated with non-perceptual functions such as thinking, memory, etc. Julian Hochberg (McConville, p. 97) restates the representational theory as follows: 'in short, we do not see objects directly, nor do we "see" the retinal image, nor do we "see" the excitation of the optic nerve. At most we can say that what we "see" is a final effect on the projection area of the cerebral cortex.' It should be noted that Hochberg does not succeed in bringing the perceiver back into perception, but only translates the experience of seeing into the language of physiology.

One of the weaknesses of this two-stage theory is that meaning can only be conceptualized as a somewhat mysterious process taking place right at the end of the process of visual perception itself. However, there is nothing in the experimental literature to show how this is done and, in fact, it is quite clear that the metaphysical leap cannot be taken this way.

According to McConville, one theorist who has attempted to overcome the separation between sensory stimulation on the one hand and meaning on the other is J. J. Gibson (1966). Gibson (McConville, p. 101) attempts to solve this problem by introducing the idea that the sensory events are to be understood in terms of the physical world itself. Instead of talking of stimuli as emerging from points, he states that stimulus units are contours, shapes and surfaces. Stimuli, then, are defined by Gibson in global terms so that perceptual meaning is not something that is deduced or inferred by non-perceptual secondary operations, but is directly caused by the external world of molar stimulus patterns. Thus, all the qualities of surfaces, edges, slopes and shapes are in fact stimuli and all qualities of motion, action and causality are also stimuli and the same would go for the qualities of persons, institutions, words and symbols, etc. However, this still does not overcome the difficulty of the passivity of the subject, namely, that perception is defined as a unidirectional relationship of cause and effect from the visible world to the perceiver. Therefore, even in Gibson's theory, the perceptual process is still something in which the perceiver himself remains passive. Gibson's role in the psychology of perception, then, according to McConville, is similar to that of Skinner in the psychology of behaviour. It is as if Gibson, like Skinner, declaring himself uninterested in events going on inside the skin, tries to deduce the nature of perceptual behaviour entirely and unidirectionally from the relations between the organism and the environment. The environment provides the conditions controlling the organism and what is not given in the environment cannot be reacted to and therefore cannot be the cause of anything.

J. H. van den Berg, in his seminal contribution to the understanding of visual perception, mentions the case of a blind woman who worked as a social worker. As an adult, she became blind and never recovered. However, she was able to complete her training as a social worker and to perform her work as well as most seeing persons. She had no difficulty in travelling from place to place and in walking the crowded streets of Dutch cities. Her task was to visit blind people, especially those who had recently become blind and to help them. She usually introduced them to Braille reading amongst other things.

Braille, however, is not the only language accessible to blind people. In the middle of the last century William Moon developed an alternative method. What he did was to use a modified form of ordinary writing in upper-case letters in which the letters are given in relief, omitting all unnecessary details. For instance, A becomes an inverted V; only the cross-bar is left out. Similarly, the vertical bar of the B is omitted and so on. Most blind people only learn Braille but in some cases it is necessary to teach them the Moon variation. This is the case when elderly people become blind and find it difficult to learn Braille which is entirely different from ordinary writing. Older people will obviously find Moon's system easier to learn. The social worker very seldom came across people who had need of being taught the Moon system. However, on a certain occasion she was asked to visit a person who had need of this and because she had not used Moon for quite some time, she decided that she needed to practise. She thereafter tried to read a few pages of Moon-writing but after several minutes she had to stop because of pain in her eyes.

This is most surprising. How on earth could blind eyes become painful because of reading? After all, she reads with her fingers and what have fingers, which touch and feel shapes by moving over them, to do with one's eyes? When she consulted Van den Berg, he asked her to read a portion of Braille and then a portion of Moon for him. He found an interesting difference. When reading Braille, her blind eyes looked towards an undefined horizon. When it came to the Moon writing, however, she directed her eyes on to the paper. Van den Berg noted a second difference. With Braille writing, her fingers flowed obliquely and evenly over the points. When she was reading Moon, her fingers stood vertically on the page. With this information, the difficulty became clear.

When she was reading Moon, she was trying to *see*. She held her eyes directly focused on to the book and she put her fingers vertically on the pages. One can say that she tried to remember how visible letters must have been. But that trying was, and had to be, a *seeking* with her *eyes*. If one ventures outdoors to try to see how the various constellations of stars look when it is not evening, one forces one's eyes. In the words of Van den Berg 'his visual memory is situated there on the expands. Visual memory lies around us, in the visual world around us, when we try to remember how an object or a thing looks which is far away. When you are trying in Amsterdam to remind yourself how many stories the Eifel tower has, you are seeking with your eyes in Paris'. (Van den Berg, o.c., p. 4). In the case of the social worker, she was seeking with her eyes in a visual void. It was not only her fingers which glided over the reliefs of the Moon writing, but over and above everything, her blind eyes. But she could not see. That does not mean, however, that the visual world was lost to her. If she ascended the stairs of a client, she could feel whether the house was properly looked after or not. She could smell the homeliness of a house. There are blind people who can 'hear' whether a person who wears spectacles actually has them on his nose. There are many blind people who can hear if the speaker is turning his head away when he is talking. In other words, the world of the blind person is richly supplied with heard, touched and smelt visuality. When she was trying to read the Moon writing, she was trying to reinstate the original seen visuality; i.e. the activity of her eyes, into the reliefs. Her eyes did not allow that. In doing this, she was violently trying to overcome the limits of her existence imposed by the fact that she had gone blind.

Even from within the natural scientific orientation there are indications that perception is not a passive process. Thus, E. D. Adrian as long ago as 1928 noted that visual perception is possible only when the eye, and with that, of course, the image on the retina, *moves*. Later on the Russian researcher, A. L. Yarbus, showed that eye-movements which include movements of the retinal image were mandatory for visual perception.

From a wider phenomenological perspective both the above findings can be easily understood. To be able to see one looks. Perception is one of the ways in which we intentionally relate to the world.

The natural scientific approach to perception has always been embarrassed by the problem of meaning. By concentrating on the camera conception of visual perception, it could only end up as a study of physiological processes on the one hand with stimuli on the other. The research done by Gibson locates meaning in the environment, but still leaves out the perceiving person. Research into the brain processes involved, whilst generating a great amount of information, has always stopped short of the metaphysical leap needed in order to bring physiology and physics back into the world of everyday experience. In this world where we see, hear and smell we bypass the eye, the ear and the nose. Our perception always refers to something meaningful out there in the world. It is an act whereby a meaningful world appears to us.

We are not trying to suggest the world in itself is a meaningful world – it is not meaningful *'en soi'*; we can speak only of a world as it appears to us, i.e. as it shows itself to us as perceiving subjects. Neither do we suggest that the subject *confers* meaning on what he observes. The subject has a unique relationship with the world and within the openness of his standing out towards the world, he finds those meanings which are particularly significant for him. This means that the world as it is *present* to us in our perception is already a meaningful structure inviting our behaviour.

Studies of perception on the camera model presuppose a clear, highly articulated conscious experience of an object or an array of stimuli. However, our conscious contact with the world is definitely not always of such a definable nature. E. Straus (see McConville, p. 104; Van den Berg 1972 *b*, p. 44) has delineated two different levels of sensing which he called the pathic and gnostic modes. In the first mode our sensing is physiognomic, giving us an immediate, concrete, but undifferentiated intercourse with the things which, however, can be articulated. Thus, J. H. van den Berg describes how, expecting a visit from a friend, he prepared his room for the occasion, putting out a bottle of Medoc, cigarettes, etc. However, his friend rang to say that he could not come. Later having immersed himself in a book, he looked up again, saw the bottle of Medoc and, in seeing the bottle, *he saw* his friend's absence (Van den Berg 1972 *b*, pp. 33–4). The bottle of Medoc is not simply an object which, at closer inspection, turns out to be of a particular colour, to have a label advertising its contents, to have a peculiar type of cork, etc. – the bottle in the first pathic sensing reveals the physiognomy of the perceiver's world, reveals to the subject the landscape of his lonely evening. On closer inspection, the bottle will become accessible to a gnostic perception – its shape, label, colour, etc. The bottle then is extracted from its landscape in the first structure of reality and becomes a differentiated object from which a clear distance is maintained and this permits a judgment and reflective analysis. In the first pathic sense, the bottle reveals itself primarily as part of Van den Berg's being with another who is a friend whilst the second could already betray his membership of a scientific, technological or consumer community.

This pathic-gnostic integrate of perception is further exemplified by the case of Mandy. Mandy, in recounting her earlier life, says that after the incident of her father shooting a revolver bullet into a tree 'I found I could deliberately enter the life of a tree whenever I was alone and still'. She also thinks that previously her merging with the life of something outside herself had been a 'natural' process, which was entered into without thought or intention and that this happened sometimes when she lay in her swing beneath the tree in their garden. It seems, then, that Mandy is one of those rare people who has been able to keep the pathic sensing from her childhood possibly in view of her disturbed interpersonal relations so that the tree offered her a refuge where she could be paradoxically herself and at the same time be not herself by flowing into the life of a tree. It seems, then, that although pathic sensing precedes the gnostic one, one is able to do it the other way around as well. Thus, at the beginning of her report, Mandy states that she can start by looking at a tree, studying the colours and movement of its leaves, the texture of the bark, the shape of each branch, until she apprehends it as a whole, perfectly contained within itself. When she concentrates fully on that apprehension, she begins to lose awareness of her body and all that surrounds her and the trees. In other words, Mandy now loses the distance which characterizes this gnostic sensing and her senses become fluid, flowing into each other and being gradually absorbed into the being of the tree. With that, her awareness of herself as a single separate identity, separate from the tree, fades, and she merges with the life of the tree. She then experiences herself as if she is a tree, as if she is encompassed by the tree. In this pathic sensing she recovers an almost pre-conscious experience of the tree and this, one supposes, is the nearest one can come to what life is like before one starts reflecting upon it.

Perception, according to Merleau-Ponty, is faith that there is a world (Bakker 1965, p. 58). It is this initiation which comprises our involvement with the world and which is prior to every reflective orientation. Since this faith does not constitute knowledge, it can always be threatened by disbelief. Truth and untruth are two ways of existing on the level of the same reality. It is possible for me to observe something in the distance which does not correspond with reality as later assessed. For instance, I could see what looks like a pool of water in the road, but which is in reality (on closer inspection) caused by the play of light. However, the correct perception, namely, the play of light, and the incorrect perception, namely, pool of water, are not distinguished from each other in the same way as a complete absolute thought will distinguish itself from an incomplete thought. I am able to perceive correctly only when my body has an accurate grasp of the observed, but this does not mean that my grasp will ever be total. That is impossible in principle. However, I can only correct my impression as a result of my trusting the world. It means too that a defective perception is never absolute because it is oriented towards a horizon of verifiability and so I am never entirely shut out from the truth.

Perception realizes itself in the first place on the pre-reflective, pre-personal level. This means that perception is a phenomenon that may remain to a large degree inaccessible to conscious reflection. We have seen that it is only in rare cases such as Mandy's in which a portion of the original pathic perception has remained through her barring it against contamination. Perception, as Van den Berg said, cannot be easily narrated and, in the words of Merleau-Ponty, perception participates in the ambiguity of human existence.

Perception precedes reflective consciousness and therefore it is impossible for us to obtain full clarity concerning the sources of our existence and conscious life. Merleau-Ponty describes, as we have seen, consciousness as faith in the world, but faith is no absolute knowledge. It may therefore be that we alternately live in a world of illusion which is repeatedly in contact with reality. Illusion and reality, truth and falsehood are inseparably bound up with each other on the moving level of the original perceptive existence. In the original experience both of these can exist next to each other without difficulty. However, as soon as we absolutize and bring these experiences onto the level of reality and oppose them to each other, they destroy each other and leave us in confusion (Bakker 1965, p. 65).

I have a certain reservation about the conception of reality reflected in the previous exposition of Merleau-Ponty's thinking. On what basis are we to say that some perceptions are real and others not? Obviously a perception which cannot be integrated into our lives would usually be one which does not correspond to a socially defined and validated reality. But is this the only reality? Let us postpone a further discussion of this till a later chapter.

How then should we understand perception? It seems to me that the best would be to discuss this question and to consider perception in relation to certain categories which we have already discussed, namely spatiality, bodiliness and time.

PERCEPTION AND SPATIALITY

It is true that our perception never achieves a total grasping of the perceived. According to Husserl (Bakker, p. 65) we perceive '*Abschattungen*', adumbrations. This means we always see things within certain perspectives and the object or thing perceived can never be totally grasped in a single perception. It can, however, be seen successively or alternatively in different perspectives. If we look at a house, we see only one or two sides, at the same time. However, when we see the front side of the house as front, it implies that the hind-side is implicated at the same time. We can also say that we see the other side of the house as the not yet seen other side. One perspective implicates and anticipates another. This means that we never have a perception-in-itself, but always a perception within a certain horizon, i.e. everything I perceive is perceived from the perspective of a wider coherence of meaning. When I focus on one object, i.e. I bring it forward into my perception, the other objects within my perceptual field fall back. However, they do not vanish, but remain in a certain background-edness and as such they constitute the permanent horizon of my perception. According to Merleau-Ponty (Bakker, p. 66), seeing is stepping into a universe of things-that-are which show themselves and they would not be able to show themselves to me if they could not be in obscurity behind each other or behind me. When I look at an object or thing, I put myself in the position of that object and in that way I 'dwell' in the thing perceived. McConville (p. 109) gives the following descriptive example of a visual experience: 'From a roadside view the stately Georgian mansion stands behind the coarse and rusted iron gate, far beyond the roadside pines, nestled among the green of its guardian elms.'

In this example, we see that the mansion stands *behind* the rusted gates *among* the elms and *beyond* the other trees. This description, however, cannot possibly imply that the term behind, among, and beyond refer to a purely objective arrangement. If these things had not been perceived by an observer, there would be no sense in the words behind, beyond and among. In nature, says McConville, 'these terms – behind, beside and so on – do not differentiate themselves. If we pretend to imagine a subjectless natural world, these terms all mean the same thing, but if we think of space being for a perceiving subject, and specifically a bodily behaving subject, then the sense and meaning of different spatial arrangements is restored.' It means then that we cannot see human spatiality without considering our bodiliness. In a previous example, I mentioned that when I revisited the place where I had spent my first years, I found to my surprise that the fountain and the dam were quite near to the house and that they were small. This difference in size does not only indicate a time relation but also a body relation as well because space as it unfolded itself to me as a child was apprehended not only by my senses (in an 'objective' sense), but also in a bodily sense considering the shortness of my stride and the softness of my muscles at that time.

It seems then that we have to consider bodiliness as well.

PERCEPTION AND BODILINESS

In 1540, the reformer and theologian Phillip Melanchton wrote a book called *De Anima* in which the passive nature of perception was expounded for the first time. Melanchton had earlier attacked the 'Galenic' emission theory of the senses according to which the senses and in particular the eyes are active, that is, they send out rays. From his time onwards, the idea of the passivity of perception took root in psychology. However, the discredited emission theory of the senses nevertheless still corresponds with everyday truisms preserved in the language such as 'throw his gaze' or 'he looks through me' or 'his gaze struck me in my heart'. Van den Berg (1973, p. 12) points out that, simultaneously with Melanchton's writings, the humanist Juan Luis Vives pointed out that our senses receive and do not *do* anything. This was in the same period of time, early in the Renaissance, when Vesalius wrote a book called *De Humani Corporus Fabrica* where the human body is given its first physiological description. At the same time Copernicus' major work on the heliocentric system was published. With these two contributions the natural sciences triumphantly entered the domain of the human body and the domain of the universe so that both the inside and outside of man's life were taken over by natural science. Thus, man gave up his incarnated worldly existence. Descartes apparently, then, was logical in setting the soul apart and lodging it in the pineal gland in the mid-brain isolated from world and the body. Certainly, we cannot plead for the ancient doctrine of the emission of the senses, but most certainly we can try to achieve a psychology of perception which includes the active subject perceiving and behaving in a humanly meaningful universe of discourse.

McConville (p. 110) reports two experiments which demonstrate the link between bodiliness specifically with regard to activity and movement – and the spatiality of existence. In the first experiment, Held & Hine (1963) studied the visual learning experience of baby kittens. These kittens were brought up in darkness except for a limited time each day when they lived in normal light. The amount of visual stimulation was thus the same for all the kittens, but some were carried in a small gondola while others were permitted to walk. The researchers then found that the kittens who were carried around in the light were perceptually retarded, having failed to develop normal depth and distance perception. However, those kittens who had moved around did better on the subsequent tests of depth and distance perception.

In another experiment this time with human beings, the two subjects, one of whom remained in a wheelchair with the other pushing him, were required to wear lenses which turned the visual world upside down. In previous experiments with these lenses, the well-known 'adaptation phenomenon' had been demonstrated repeatedly, namely, that after a while, the inverted world again appears right side up. In the present experiment the adaptation phenomenon occurred only in the case of the subject who was pushing the wheelchair whilst for the subject who spent his time in the wheelchair the adaptation did not occur and the spatial world remained jumbled and confusing. McConville concludes: 'both of these experiments demonstrated that the perceptually meaningful structure of the spatial world is not something passively registered on the retinas, but something actively solicited by a body which moves through space and engages the world.'

Perception, Merleau-Ponty says, is a bodily event (Bakker, p. 70); we perceive through our body and the body is the subject of

perception. Our body is never an object in space in the same way as things are objects in space. As we have already seen, the abstract geometric space always takes the body as its point of departure. Our body is not a thing which is enclosed within itself, not something of which one can enumerate the characteristics. The body is our point of view of the world.

It should be understood that in talking about perception in particular and phenomenology in general, the body is the lived human body, not the body of physiology. The body known by physiology is a dead, dissected body. The body of physiology has an inside but not an outside. It is an entity closed in upon itself and does not permit us to look at its inter-relations with the world except in so far as this is reflected in structural precipitates, for example, if the person had been a victim of malnutrition. But even then, the relation of the body with the world is not described. As we have already seen, the body of physiology is the body that one has, but not the body that one is. To understand perception, we must deal with the body as a living, experiential, active body. Mark McConville (p. 108) gives a good example. As one writes one usually does not feel the pressure of one's fingers against the pen although physiologically these pressure sensations are true and can be observed if one looks for them, but usually one's tactile experience locates itself in the tip of the pen – one feels it scraping or gliding across the paper. The living body therefore goes beyond the boundary of the skin and incorporates the pen as part of its structure in this instance. Similarly, when one is looking at the tree outside, the lived body has its boundary in what one is looking at. It is not necessary to teach the meaning of hardness, softness, motherliness, at-homeness, etc., except verbally, because these experiences have already been encountered by one, pre-verbally, with one's living body. It is therefore part of our pre-verbal encounter with the world and these meanings are already given, i.e. incarnated in what is perceived.

In our discussion of bodiliness in chapter II, we have already seen that, according to Erwin Straus, the human face is a seeing face and so it is not strange that sight should happen to be our most important perceptual category. Perception, says Merleau-Ponty, is not a specialized thing, it is a common act of all our motoric and affective functions and not only of our sensory functions. Let us return to Mandy. Mandy relates that as a child she awoke early one morning and walked through the garden. 'The grass which was quite long, was still covered with dew and I was fascinated to see it so brilliant and sparkling in the early morning sun as if each blade were filled with light. It was very quiet and I was alone. All at once I felt strangely at peace there among the shining blades of grass: they welcomed me soundlessly enveloping me passively in their lives. I crouched down on my knees and touched the grass with my face, feeling the dew cold and soft on my skin. I entered the life of the grass . . .'

Vision is lived as the gaze. Since gaze is an activity rather than a passive receiving of stimuli it shares in the structure of the body's behavioural engagements as we have seen in Mandy's description. An interesting issue has been raised by J. H. van den Berg in that he sees a difference between the male and the female gaze. The female seems to have a less penetrating gaze and she seems better able than the male to let her gaze rest on the contours of the thing. The male, on the other hand, seems to have a more penetrating gaze and in looking at women he seems to 'undress' them. (Van den Berg 1959, p. 224).

PERCEPTION AND TIME

We see that each percept takes place within a spatial horizon. However, there is also a temporal horizon, for instance, the house that I saw yesterday, I can see again today. Every perception in the present also includes the no-longer actually perceived dimension of the past as well as the not-yet of the future. Thus, every moment has its protentions and retentions. Every object, every event, is surrounded by a temporal horizon, according to Bakker (p. 68). For instance, if I see somebody walking past my window, this walking is meaningful within a certain temporal horizon. He doesn't just suddenly appear before my window coming from somewhere or going somewhere. If I think about the incident, it could be that I will say to myself that he must have passed my neighbour to the left of me previously and in a few moments he will also pass my neighbour on the right. However, people whose lives have become problematic in the sense that they see things as referring to them in a secretive or suspicious manner would see this differently. Such a person would be shocked by the sudden appearance of someone passing his window, perhaps glancing up casually with a seemingly hidden intent and then disappearing again. In such a case it means that the temporal dimension of this person's life has been disturbed and, if that is so, then his suspicion of this person who suddenly appears in front of his window, and then again goes, becomes something uncanny. He may realize that his suspicions are unfounded but it none the less remains an uncanny event for him.

As we have seen in the section on Being Human and Time, man lives ecstatically in all three time dimensions at once. In the moment of perception, then, one holds the horizon of both past and future as part of the present experience. If we have this temporal horizon, we will see that it is impossible to look at time as a series of ever new moments of the present. By the same token we have to give up the conception of perception as a thing in itself. By the protentions and retentions which root me in a milieu, my perception does not take its point of departure from an ego but in the field of my perception itself in which present, past and future form an ecstatic whole.

The fact that the percept takes place within a temporal horizon, as already made clear by Bakker, is further articulated by McConville, who refers to the familiar expression 'do you read me?' McConville says that one can read the expression on a friend's face telling one whether he is upset and whether one should brace oneself for the impending confrontation. Similarly, one walks into a room and senses the relations between the participants. You 'read' the situation. We are also fond of using the term 'I could see what was going to happen'. This means that one should actually take this literally. One sees in the sense that the unfolding drama already includes the future. McConville says, 'my reading of an unfolding play is a visual act which both predicates and is predicated upon (an ambiguity intrinsic to perception) my behavioural response to the visual scene'.

In conclusion, we have seen that perception is not accessible to consciousness in clear ways. If we prefer to *think* of perception instead of being led by our primary experience and then test our ideas on the subject in the laboratory, we shall be restricted to a science of explanation, in other words, we shall be restricted to what Van den Berg has called 'the second structure of reality'. The alternative to this is to approach perception as an explorer of vaguely familiar but uncharted territory. We may have seen that Mandy's perception of the tree does not make sense in terms of a natural scientific model; it certainly cannot be taken as real in any sense whatsoever if we stick to the camera model of perception. McConville (p. 117) aptly says, 'one is reminded of Fritz Perls' frequent exhortations to his psychotherapy patients that they shall "loose their minds, and come to their senses". This is very much the same advice which phenomenology offers contemporary psychology.'

2. THE STUDY OF MEMORY

THE ENGRAM THEORY

Psychology and neurophysiology have been deeply influenced by the idea that memory has to be understood in terms of the storage capacity of the brain and a concomitant process of recognition or recall, nowadays called information retrieval. All current theories of physiology and psychology can be traced back to this position, namely, that perceptions make an imprint on the plastic material of the brain which then, at the moment of recall or recognition reproduces itself. This is the engram or trace theory. In a seminal essay on this subject, Erwin Straus (1966) points out that the simile of the trace is already present in Aristotle's treatise on memory according to which one must look at memory as at a portrait. 'For the act of perceiving imprints, so to speak, a schema (typos) of the perceived, as if one seals it with a signet ring' (Straus 1966, p. 76). Most contemporary physiologists, Straus continues, would probably agree with Fessard's definition of memory:

> 'Any conscious experience is at the beginning of a memnonic recording, and any trace left by a conscious state is capable of engendering it anew. Thus, it seems difficult to suppose that the ultimate basis of "experience" in the physical world could be of another nature than that admitted for the storage of memories, i.e. a more or less durable modification imprinted on a plastic ultra-structure of the neurone" (Fessard 1954, p. 234; see Straus 1966, p. 76).

It seems somehow ironic that Fessard should put the word 'experience' in quotation marks whilst speaking of the trace as if it is a concrete observable happening. One wonders how Fessard came to any conclusions in his research, or how he was able to do research at all if he was unable to use his own experience of what was going on in the experiments designed and observations made by him.

Straus points out that, underlying these views, 'is a naïve conviction that the trace, understood purely as a physical or physiological structure, could explain the phenomenon of memory' (1966, p. 76). However, the question as to what a trace is, is seldom asked by researchers in this field.

More recently, Holger Hyden (Pribram 1969) studied the role of ribonucleic acid (RNA) and the stable substance DNA in the mechanisms of genetic 'memory' which offers a possibility that RNA could also be involved in what is called neural memory.

Pribram suggests that there is a strong possibility that RNA production by nerve cells is in some way involved in memory consolidation, a process required in order to fix memory traces in the brain.

Contemporary neuro-chemical and psycho-physiological research proceeds on the basis that memory is a very intricate form of storage of traces of not only previous perceptions, but of other events as well. Memory must thus include genetic events amongst others. Memory can be even more inclusively defined. For instance, some scientists have suggested that linseed oil has a 'memory' because if it is briefly exposed to sunlight, it changes slightly and repeated exposure changes the substance entirely, which means that the linseed oil in the process of change does not have to start from the beginning again, but 'remembers' the changes previously made. This serves to remind us how easily concepts such as memory can be extended into a loss of its original meaning by physicalistic thinking. Memory is briefly defined by Pribram as 'any set of events that makes available to an organism something of the situation after that situation no longer obtains' (Pribram 1969, p. 54). One sees that Pribram at least restricts memory to an organism. Hyden suggests that engram function takes place through a change in the sequence of the four bases of the RNA molecule. In terms of this theory, then, we may also speak of molecular memory.

Although a lot of research has been done on the chemistry and neurology of memory, much remains mysterious, e.g. how is a selection made from all the possibilities in the chemical and electrical process that involve millions of nerve cells? (Boss 1975, p. 83).

Robert Sardello (1978, p. 136) states that contemporary theories of memory revolve around the notions of short-term memory, long-term memory and retrieval. Such a theory requires first that a stimulus has to be perceived and processed through short-term memory where forgetting occurs extremely rapidly, but if the stimulus or information is rehearsed, retention is prolonged and short-term memory then transfers itself to the long-term memory category where items can be retained for longer periods. The acquisition and storage of information thus acquired can afterwards be followed by retrieval processes, namely, those of recognition and recall. Most theories clearly state that long-term memory is linked to physical properties of the brain. The storage of information is related to the growth of connections at the synapses of neurons and is accompanied by chemical or molecular changes in the nervous system. Some permanent impression has thus been made upon the brain. Memory is then the reactivation of this trace. Forgetting is explained in that the physical trace in the brain is said to decay through a process of time.

Thirdly, contemporary memory theory puts forward the concept of information retrieval. The two ways of retrieval are recognition and recall. We speak of recognition when we form a judgement that something or somebody has been perceived before. It is possible for us to recognize a person or object without being able to recall any details about such person or object. Recall, however, means that the form and content connected with the recognition can be regenerated.

Sardello summarizes the current understanding of memory as follows: '. . . we could say that the psychology of memory is concerned with the acquisition, storage and retrieval of perceived information. Different conceptual models are employed to study memory. The acquisition phase of memory is dominated by functional and computer models. Functional models are concerned with establishing functional relationships of the form $x = f(y)$. Thus, for example, acquisition time is a function of the meaningfulness of the material. Acquisition is also understood in terms of "input", when a computer analogy is employed. Memory storage is dominated by physiological and computer models. The theory of the trace is dominant in the understanding of storage, but storage is also referred to in terms of storage of bits of information. Memory retrieval is dominated by computer and signal detection metaphors. Retrieval is output and processes which interfere with output are conceived within the fantasy of computers. The metaphors of false detection, false recognition, and misses are taken from signal detection theory, a model borrowed from the study of sensory processes' (Sardello 1978, p. 138). Sardello goes on to comment that whilst metaphorical language is being used in trying to understand memory so that we could understand it as if memory is a computer or as if it were a physiological mechanism, in the actual research itself these metaphors are discarded and become literal fact. Sardello also feels that contemporary psychology has contributed a great deal to the understanding of the thing-like properties of memory. However, the most significant thing about memory is exactly the non-thing quality of memory as lived.

Lashley's extensive research on the cerebral localization of memory did not yield any definite results. He could not establish any memory traces in the brain itself. He then developed the concept of equipotentiality according to which the trace of memory image is not fixed in a definite brain state but is held through a total diffuse brain process. Other theorists, however, have not given up the search for memory localization and do not necessarily agree with Lashley that memory traces cannot be found.

Apart from the fact that the basis of these theories is a trace simile, we see also how deeply these theories are rooted in positivisitic, empiricistic assumptions: A psychic process must necessarily be rooted in some physical process to make memory understandable, the methods and conceptions of natural science must be used and will ultimately solve the problem. Although these researchers are by no means uncritical of their findings, they see the solution as something that has so far eluded them, but that they will, or should, eventually succeed. To them the ultimate solution is a matter of overcoming limitations in present techniques and concepts, and the problem, to them, remains in principle soluble by new discoveries and technical refinements in terms of the paradigm of natural science biology. The possibility that an understanding of memory as such is, in *principle*, impossible by research along these lines will, however, have to be considered by the phenomenologist.

Secondly, the over-inclusiveness of definition of memory by many researchers in this field is striking. Terms such as molecule memory, neural memory and genetic memory and statements like 'DNA has memory' are examples of these and make one wonder what is left of that peculiar human ability to give continuity to life, to experience joy when seeing a long-lost friend or recite a poem of deeply felt significance.

Most important, however, is the fact that the basis of all this research, namely, the engram theory, is mostly not questioned. Significant in all the views is the conviction that the trace understood as a neurological structure of some sort would explain memory. Although Lashley was compelled to conclude that it was not possible for him to locate a memory trace anywhere in the nervous system, natural science ideologists would argue that this in itself proves nothing. If ultimate reality is to be sought in that which is physically measurable (which is the assumption of natural scientific oriented physiologists and psychologists) then it follows that the answer must somehow be prised out of the human body with the central nervous system as the obvious place to look for it. In contradistinction to this, phenomenology has to question the pre-suppositions which guide our thinking, research and experimentation on memory. Erwin Straus holds that the memory trace as such cannot, in principle, contribute to our understanding of memory as we know it in primary experience.

Let us take the example of a trace such as those caused by an ox walking in newly ploughed ground. If we look at the tracks made by the ox, we can certainly, if we know what an ox is, recognize these as reflecting the passing of this animal, but the traces themselves cannot possibly reproduce the form of the ox. We, as independent observers, have to do this by virtue of the fact that we know what an ox looks like or what sort of tracks he makes, let us say, compared to a sheep or a dog. The fact that traces can be read by an independent observer does not, however, argue for their permanence. The traces made by the ox will only be permanent on the supposition that there will be no climate changes, that the growth of plants in the newly ploughed soil will not disturb the traces or by the supposition that the land will never be ploughed again. If, as it is stated, a stimulus can make some sort of impression upon the brain, what guarantee have we that such an impression will be lasting? Moreover, if there is no independent observer (physiology cannot posit the soul as an independent observer trying to make sense out of neurological material), then how is the trace reactivated?

If a trace is a more or less lasting modification of brain tissue, then a reactivation of a trace is impossible. A trace cannot possibly return to the starting position by itself.

Straus suggests that the present position of memory-theorizing with the trace at the basis 'takes place at the end of a long chain of misinterpretation of the physical and physiological happenings, which occurred in the following stages:

1. Perceiving is reduced to a perception image which appears in the consciousness of the perceiver.
2. The reduction, however, is not complete. The observer reserves to himself a privileged position. He remains in the natural attitude. From the environment accessible to his sight, he selects some visible objects which he relates to another object – the body of a man.
3. In progressive reduction, the objects, which are visible to the observer, are reinterpreted as stimuli in relation to another individual.
4. The invisible stimuli produce in the retina photo-chemical and photo-electric reactions which, after conduction through the afferent system, are followed by demonstrable electric effects in the brain cortex.
5. This effect in the cortex is thought to be accompanied in consciousness by a perception image.
6. As perceiving is reduced to an image of perception, remembering is reduced to an image of recollection.
7. It is assumed that perception image and memory image are alike as, for example, the first print and a later print from the same photographic plate. According to the present-day theory, the memory image is more similar to an over-print of several different plates.
8. The analogy demands the reactivation of the inactive engram' (Straus 1966, pp. 97–8).

We should clearly distinguish between thinking and memory. To think is to let the world appear. Thinking then, is an ever new relating and going into that which appears in the openness of one's world. This includes natural scientific thinking, which is also nothing other than a letting things appear but in such a way that their possible causal coherences may be shown.

One does not remember everything that one encounters in the world. First of all, our being in the world is a series of encounters within certain limits. Not all the things-that-are will actually enter one's horizon so memory only becomes relevant in respect of those aspects which we have actually encountered. Something which appears on our horizon, but to which we do not relate at all, is not remembered, e.g. one does not remember the number of cars that one has passed on the road or their colours except when one's world is so constituted that colour or the number of cars on the route from home to work is a matter of special interest in one's world.

Most of what we encounter does not remain thematically present, but does constitute a background unthematically. Even such a presence is something which can speak to us, i.e. it is a relevant presence of some or other meaningful thing or datum in our world.

Medard Boss (1975, p. 302) suggests that a clear distinction be made between a thematic presencing of a datum that was unthematically present and a reminding of oneself of earlier events and experiences. Let us go back to the example of Peter and Joan in order to make this clear. When Peter and Joan were walking down the street talking about their forthcoming vacation in the Canary Islands, they were making the holiday hotel thematically present to themselves. However, this is not memory in the strict sense. It is simply making the hotel present as it is now; there in the Canary Islands. This is imagination. However, if they remember the last time they were there and the actual act of signing the register for instance or what the receptionist said and so on, then this is a making present thematically of something in the past as *past*, i.e. as something that took place *then*. Memory in this strict sense then is reactivating the past *as* past, the past as it was then but as it appears *now*.

What then is forgetting? Do we really forget, or are psychoanalysts correct in holding that all memories are somehow retained but are simply repressed into the unconscious under certain circumstances. If we look at the word 'forgetting' itself, then we note that the prefix 'for' could be regarded as a negative and forgetting would then mean something that we 'did not get'. But is this really what forgetting is about?

Let us look at various examples of forgetting. I go to a friend and I leave my pipe there. This cannot be regarded as forgetting in the sense that my pipe now falls entirely out of the totality of things present in my world. In fact, for me to be conscious of my 'forgetting', I have to have a certainty that this pipe still belongs to me, i.e. I am still in a relationship to this particular pipe as being part of my existence.

I could only have forgotten my pipe if in the time of parting I was still 'body and soul' with my friend and with the theme of our conversation. As a result of this thematic being-with-another, the pipe came to be at such a distance from me that a thinking of its objective presence did not form part of my world at the moment of parting. In this case, one cannot speak of forgetting in the strict sense of the term but only in the sense that something escapes one's attention, i.e. disappeared as a thematic presencing in my relationship to it. The psychoanalyst would, however, have explained this 'forgetting' in terms of repression. This they would see as part of the psychopathology of everyday life. It could have some phallic significance and there could have been some reason why I repressed any thought of the pipe in the situation which I had with this friend.

However, Medard Boss suggests that my forgetting of the pipe cannot have its cause in repression as postulated by psychoanalytic theory, i.e. a repression of my image of the pipe into the unconscious. In order to be able to repress something into some sort of region, one must be in some sort of actual relation with it. However, when I leave my friend, I am not in relation to my pipe, but in relation to my friend.

Another type of forgetting is when I recognize a face but forget the name of the person involved. Such a failure in being able to recall means that, in this case, the datum itself has escaped me. The name that has fallen away for me, however, remains present to me as something which is hidden from me. This is properly called forgetting. Medard Boss puts it this way: 'in this "knowing about", i.e. in the revealing to me of the hiddenness of the name, I know about the forgetting of something. It is possible that I do not even have this knowledge of forgetting, in other words, that I do not know for certain that I once knew the person's name' (p. 306).

Forgetting something always means a bit of self forgetting. Because, whatever falls away from me, means that a part of my relationship to the thing forgotten has fallen away. In the case of the person whose face is known to me, some part of my relationship has fallen away and does not exist anymore. Should I succeed in revealing to myself the name of the person, then it means that some part of the relationship, which had fallen away, is thematically reinstated.

Both remembering and forgetting concern themselves with the data of the world as such. These data always remain the lost name, the person or the thing itself as they showed themselves in my world-openness which I can retain or which falls away. Forgetting is not a matter of the retention of something which exists merely in an intrapsychic manner and/or the reactivation of a trace which is the materialistic variant of the intrapsychic theory. Fundamentally, memory is to be understood from the characteristic openness of human existence. This openness is, in contrast to the openness of a lifeless thing, essentially an openness *for* something, for the perception of something which makes some sort of appeal to us. The openness of human Dasein therefore holds the possibility for perceiving the presence of those things which can show themselves. It is, however, by the same token a concern for these in such a manner that something that shows itself in some or other way is responded to as presence. Dasein is also openness for that which was, for something which was observed at some time. What *was* does not become for Dasein something that has totally vanished or that has been exhausted. That which was, is kept in the openness of human Dasein in such a manner that it is constantly present and constantly speaking to us in such a way that it is relevant for present behaviour. In this way then, the past lives on in the future (Boss, p. 307).

Memory should be clearly distinguished from learning. Sardello (1978, p. 145) reminds us that learning and memory have often been confused, but that these should be clearly distinguished. He says 'effects carried forward from the past do not have anything to do with memory. One learns to write but does not remember the past as past in the act of writing.'

Remembering is bitemporal in the sense that we have a past and a present. For instance, I slept or I worked. Here again, the identity brought about by time should be kept in mind. The 'I' who is working now is the same 'I' who worked yesterday. But yet, one is not entirely the same. Sardello puts it this way: 'The I that speaks from the present is the actual I. But the actual I is actual only against the background of its possibilities. The present is expressed through the act of speaking, the past is expressed through the content of the spoken' (p. 145).

We have seen that memory is a making present of the past as past. However, this past is made present as a possibility because if the past is made present in its actuality and its entirety it means that an accurate memory would take as much time as the actual event which is remembered. Such a memory would be valueless. We live in time as life history; the fact that there is biographical time makes it possible for us to have a temporal order of events and experiences. We have also seen that we do not remember everything, but we remember those things which we somehow take upon ourselves, to which we relate. Usually that to which we relate and which we remember is the remarkable, i.e. things must be different as well as important. When I see a person and remember this person, it means that such a person has in some way become important so that he or she finds a relation to one's individual past and future.

MEMORY AND IMAGINATION

We have seen that memory is a possibility, i.e. it is a making present of the past as a possibility. However, the total context of possibility includes imagination. In this sense then, memory relates to the context as that which was in so far as it lives on in the present and keeps on living as possibility. Sardello, drawing on Gaston Bachelard, states that as the slope of memory is descended imagination is discovered. This is something that was brought home to Freud when he required patients to report earlier and earlier memories of childhood traumas. He later found that in many cases these memories could not be trusted. In pressing people for memories, Freud in a sense forced his patients to imagine the past, i.e. make present a past that could have been.

A good example of the relationship between memory and imagination is to be found in the reverie. This is like memory, except that the bitemporal tension which exists between the present and the past is loosened and there tends to be an identification of the past with the present. Thus, a reverie is typically a reliving of a past situation as if it is taking place now.

MEMORY AND PSYCHOTHERAPY

Why do some clients have difficulty in recounting past events? In short the answer is: that the past that already embraces the possibilities for the future, the past that meets one out of the future, is the past that is accessible to one. The 'neurotic' or 'psychotic' is a person who has found great difficulty in the unfolding of his potentialities. This means that his future is not readily accessible. In the case where the client has no difficulty in talking, it is perhaps because he has already accepted, albeit unwillingly, the fact that his future will be an uninviting one and his coming into therapy means that he tries to overcome this set of possibilities. In other words, he is trying to struggle with his fate as it would have been if he had remained set in his ways. It is clear from clinical experience that people who go into psychotherapy are not ultra-conformistic people, i.e. not people who simply orient themselves to the everyday construction of their life situation, but who have some conviction that this could be different.

To reiterate: the past that meets us out of the future is the past that can be recalled, because such a past already holds within itself the possibilities for the future. If, in the past, the person's attempts towards unfolding his potentials had been uniformly or largely unsuccessful, then much of his past will be barred from him. However, it is unlikely that anybody is completely unaware of certain sets of happenings that had been meaningful to him sometime or other. Let me make this clear with an example. A young man in therapy had great difficulty in talking about his past. It became clear that his family situation had been quite a catastrophic one in that there was very little communication in the family. In an interview with the client and his parents it became clear that it was difficult for them to appreciate their children as individuals with their own unfolding possibilities so that the children were often told what they should experience rather than having the parents respond to what the children actually experienced. This is what is called invalidation in the writings of Laing and others. This particular young man tried to tell me about certain things he had done of which he was ashamed. One of these was the fact that he had arrived very late for the funeral of a friend, because he had been smoking grass with others before the funeral. He said he would never forgive himself for this and he found great difficulty in talking about this. However, since the event is past, and since this event in itself did not close off any possibilities for him to unfold his potential, one may well ask why. The reason should be obvious. The difficulty in telling this event was the recognition by the client that this represented the structure of his existence and thus telling about this was difficult because the same set of life circumstances under which this unforgiveable (in his own eyes) happening took place would present itself again during his lifetime. More concretely put, it was difficult for him to talk about his mistakes because he sees himself as a sort of person who is likely to make similar ones again. Moreover, since he felt crushed by invalidation and disapproval in the past he can see himself being crushed again in similar situations.

One can now see why a dialogue therapy could be a good therapy. The reason is that talking about past events, or talking about things which happened yesterday or the day before – that is, talking about the past whether this is a recent past or a remote one – always holds within itself some of the same sets of possibilities as the future. It would be wrong, therefore, to characterize Freud's approach as lending itself to an understanding of the past of the client only. Freud's patients did not get better simply through gaining insight into their past behaviour. As the client opens the landscape of past and present the possibilities for the future also become evident to him. Some therapies use this as a short-cut, e.g. in the reality therapy of Glasser and integrity therapy of O. H. Mowrer (1964) the person is encouraged to report what he actually did wrong and then to make restitution for past violations to correct irresponsibility. A dialogue therapy would not, however, approach the matter in this manner, but would rather leave it to the client to select for himself (i.e. without direction from the therapist) those possibilities which he feels he can actualize in the future. A successful conclusion to therapy would therefore mean that the client, in the process of uncovering his personal history, i.e. opening up the landscape of his world, discovers for himself those sets of possibilities which he can actualize, i.e. take upon himself, and those sets of possibilities that he will no longer try to actualize.

3. A NOTE ON THE UNCONSCIOUS

Freud's psychology is a depth psychology which means that the inner life of the person consists of layers. The deepest layer is the unconscious and about this deep layer, the following may be said: firstly, that it is unconscious which means that the person concerned does not know what is going on in this sphere of his mental life. Secondly, the unconscious has a character of its own; the laws governing the unconscious are dissimilar from those of the manifest, known and superficial layer which we call the conscious. Thirdly, there is a tense relationship between the unconscious and the conscious. Van den Berg (1971, p. 10) calls the unconscious an anti-ego. Furthermore, the unconscious is said to represent the authentic and true man, i.e. what man is in reality when you strip off layers of conventions and man's conscious image of himself. From this it follows that what is conscious is in the last instance to be explained from the unconscious. The authentic drives of the individual human existence are to be found in the unconscious.

In the interest of clarity, the above may be paraphrased and amplified by the following. The unconscious is that aspect of our inner life which cannot be brought to consciousness by ordinary introspective methods. Secondly, the unconscious is the area of primary process thinking. According to McIntyre, Ernst Jones has called the primary process 'the kernel of the unconscious proper' (McIntyre 1976, p. 30). In the third place, the concept of the unconscious is closely tied up with the concept of repression. Initially, it appeared as if Freud thought the conscious was entirely built up from repression but later on it transpired that there would have to be contents which had never been conscious at all. In the fourth place, the unconscious, in Freud's psychology, links infancy with adult life. The concept of infantile sexuality, libido, the subsequent form of unconscious wishes and the effect of all these on adult life are all comprehensible in terms of the unconscious. In the fifth place, the unconscious is always a background to our conscious and overt mental life. It exerts a continual causal influence upon conscious thought or behaviour. It may be seen, at this juncture then, that the unconscious seems to be characterized by causality. This point should be made clearer. As is well known, Freud's understanding of the neurosis started out as a theory of meaning. More recently Rycroft (1966) has pleaded that psychoanalysis should retransform itself into a semantic theory, i.e. a theory of meaning, and should not operate with causes at all. However, the fact remains that Freud himself and most of his followers stick to the theory of psychic determinism and causality. The unconscious can therefore be said to operate in a causal manner. Whilst at first Freud used the term unconscious in the adjectival sense, a switch came in that he moved away from the descriptive use of the term to a substantative use in that he talked about a dynamic unconscious. It seems, then, that the adjectival use was characteristic of the descriptive phase of Freud's development of his theory, but as soon as he moved into a causal account of human behaviour, he also conceived of the unconscious as some sort of entity.

For Freud (McIntyre, p. 33) the unconscious was the name of a system of mental acts. The justification for holding this view is, firstly, that we are then able to account for behaviour which cannot be accounted for in terms of conscious intentions and, secondly, if one assumes in psychoanalytic practice the resistance of an unconscious, the analyst is able to bring into consciousness contents of which the client is unaware.

As contents of the unconscious Freud specifies in the first place instincts. However, this is said in a 'loose sense' because 'instinctual impulses could never become conscious except in the form of something not themselves, that is, in the form of ideas and emotions and because even in the unconscious, it is in the form of ideas (as the bearers of impulses) that the instinct take effect' (ibid.). Apart from this, emotions are contained in the unconscious. If an emotion is repressed from consciousness, it results in an unconscious disposition to give expression to such feeling although the form of that expression will not be the same from one person to another. Moreover, it is conceived that as a result of repression an emotional impulse may be transferred from one idea to another or it may be simply dammed up awaiting a release when a suitable circumstance arises. Now it is obvious that in making these statements Freud is in one sense completely at odds with Descartes and in another sense completely at one with him. The Cartesian cogito means that whatever is real is what one can form a clear idea of. It means therefore that the mind is capable of knowing itself through and through. Freud clearly opposes this point of view: to speak of the unconscious is to say that the mind cannot possibly know its whole extent. However, Freud retains the idea of the mind as something distinct and separate, i.e. some sort of container which is filled with entities such as ideas, instincts and emotions. These are non-physical entities or substances which again corresponds with the Cartesian idea. However, it seems now that the Cartesian idea of the isolated self has been further compounded by adding another isolated entity, namely the unconscious.

If the concept of the unconscious is to be retained as a *substantive* term, one could demand, as F. B. Skinner does, that its spatial characteristics be demonstrated. Its reality would then be shown by the ordinary processes of positivistic scientific proof adductions. However, it is interesting that this is what Freud attempted in 1895. He set out to write a systematic account of psychology in terms of neurology. McIntyre says: 'it is a delightful and ingenuous *tour de force* in which the contemporary dis-coveries of neurophysiology are skilfully blended with the pre-conceptions of that 19th Century materialism which took the schematism of Newtonian mechanics as the archetype of all authentic scientific explanations' (pp. 16–7). In this project Freud set out a conception of mental phenomena in terms of material states of affairs whose changes were susceptible to mea-surement and subject to the laws of motion. The mind, therefore, would be just another billiard ball in the universe of Newtonian mechanics. The neurons in Freud's project are bearers of excita-tion which is derived either from external stimuli or from stimuli within the body. Individual neurons discharge excitation along certain nerve fibres. The total amount of excitation tends to remain constant. We can see already here the move to homeo-stasis, i.e. of excitation seeking an equilibrium.

It is also evident that Freud was not trying to develop neurol-ogy as such, but to write up a neurology in psychological terms. McIntyre remarks that Freud sometimes wrote as though the subjective aspect of life was indeed a neurological event (p. 20). Furthermore, in this fundamental project, which Freud never published, the basic instinctual stimuli, a set of which Freud called *wishes*, result in excitation which would sometimes flow freely and sometimes would be inhibited by that organization of neurons which Freud called the *ego*. Freud considered that this inhibition by ego-neurons prevents some instinctual stimuli pro-ducing images indistinguishable from the end products of stimuli from the external world. In other words, this sort of inhibition prevented hallucinations. He called this free flow of excitation 'primary process' and the inhibited redirected flow 'secondary process' (p. 21). Primary processes worked for the satisfaction of the personality and Freud identified this with pleasure. Secondary processes are those which give rise to the distinction between external and internal or instinctual stimuli. The correspondence between the project and his later structural theory of the 'psychic personality' is striking. It seems clear that Freud, although he gave up this project, seeing the impossibility of describing psychological events in neurological terms, arrived at a working model of the mind as a piece of machinery. This model of the psyche as being an organization working on the same principle as the Newtonian universe is something that Freud never gave up.

It has already been made clear that neither a psychic 'Ding-an-sich' such as Freud sometimes conceptualizes the substantive unconscious to be nor an unconscious conceived in neurological terms can be justified. (See chapter I.) The question then is whether psychology, conceived of as a human science, has need of the second concept, namely, the unconscious as a hypothesis not indicating any particular entity but merely serving as a theoretical concept to explain phenomena. In order to understand this question, let us take an example from Sara's experience of psychotherapy. She told the researcher: 'I think that's another thing about my experience of therapy and that is that it has made me look at myself and made me be totally honest about myself. . . . I don't have any illusions about myself. I can't lie to myself which is difficult. It's hard to live with yourself if you can't lie to yourself anymore. I feel that there is something that I shied away from in that first year of therapy, this facing up to pain, the hurting of yourself. Because it is inflicting pain upon yourself to be able to say "you're a shit; you lie to yourself; you've been conning everybody; you've been using your body as a little shield". You know, I've just remembered that, that was another, another big, big insight was that, ja, it was after that year, it was after I went back to X, I'm not very clear on the times and things like that. . . . Well, I was hassled by psychosomatics after that and I've started living with David. And one day, it was almost a year later actually, and I went back to X, I've been back to X and then I came home and I felt awful and I realized that I had to admit to myself that I've been using all this psychosomatics, that I've been a big fraud and that I've been play-acting all the time and that I've been wanting people to feel sorry for me. And admitting that to myself was terrible . . . And I'd freed myself and it was fantastic afterwards.'

It seems that Sara had limited her involvement with and openness to the world in terms of her lived bodiliness. The body shapes itself in accordance with its task in the world. In her case, the body clearly shaped itself as a sick organism that could not enter freely into the spirit of social life, could not give herself in sexual intercourse, and could not face the intrusiveness of her fellow human being. The Freudian doctrine of the unconscious would have us believe that her inner conflicts – which should, in Freudian terms, have been traced back to her relationship with her parents with an emphasis on the Oedipus complex – should be seen in terms of a split-off set of ideas and emotions which are then converted into somatic symptoms. We have already discussed the impossibility of this in terms of how we meet the human being and in terms of the fact that such conversion is inexplicable in experiential terms. No one has ever had an experience of converting a psychic conflict into a bodily symptom. The strong version would have us understand not only that Sara was unconscious of what she was doing, but it would have us understand too that she did not know what the purpose was of what she was doing. The doctrine of psychic determinism would have us believe that Sara was not actually *doing* this, but rather that this was *happening* to her. In other words, if we are strictly to remain within a causal account of human behaviour, we would have to say that Sara was not using her psychosomatics in order to avoid contact with other people, but that psychosomatics were using Sara in this way, that the forces determining Sara's existence were shaping her this way. However, this causal account must collapse in terms of the first person account that Sara herself gives us because she says (p. 98) 'that I had to admit to myself that I've been using all this psychosomatics, that I've been a big fraud and that I've been play-acting all the time and that I've been wanting people to feel sorry for me'. Sara is saying that those symptoms are under her control and had been used by her in a purposeful manner. What she does not say, however, is that she had been conscious of it all the time. In fact, Sara had not been conscious of the fact that she was using this *modus operandi*. People around her, and especially her therapist, might have been conscious of her using her psychosomatics in this way. But Sara herself only came to realize that this was the case after she had achieved that particular insight. In some way, Sara came to learn that her psychosomatics were a way of being in the world, she might have understood that, whenever problematic situations arose, she was prevented from participating in these situations because of asthma or her peptic ulcer. Sara herself repeatedly told the therapist that she found it very difficult to face people at parties, in shops, and so forth. Sara did not then see the connection between her psychosomatics and these problematic situations. So, in a sense, we can say that Sara was conscious of her actions but, and this is the important point, she did not see what the *significance* of those actions were. She came to see the significance of those actions only when she achieved this insight. By achieving this insight, she was sharing a level of consciousness that was already present in some people around her, notably her therapist. What was 'unconscious' in the life of Sara was conscious in the life of people with whom she was interacting. In other words, there was a sense in which people realized that Sara was reacting to stresses and strains by means of psychosomatic disorders. There is a sense in which a husband knows that when his wife is complaining of a headache, there is something wrong in the relationship between the two of them, or there is something wrong in the relationship between his wife and his friends, etc. The wife knows this too but she does not know in what way this is so. She realizes that her actions are a reaction to her total life situation but she does not know in what way. Inasmuch as this is usually quite clear to the therapist, the unconscious of the client may be said, following on from Van den Berg, to be located, not inside the client, but in the world openness characterized by the relationship between the client and the therapist or between the client and significant others. Psychotherapy then may be said to be the process by which what is not thematically present and open in the life of the client becomes so for that client to the extent that she now shares the consciousness of herself which was always available to the therapist. When she has her life in hand to the extent that she can look at it in as open a way as the therapist does, then she has achieved communicative equality with the therapist and there is no point in continuing with that particular therapy. At the very least, then, one can say that what is 'unconscious' is dependent of the context in which the client is sojourning. What is conscious in one context can be 'unconscious' in another and vice versa.

Slips of the tongue or the pen and of unwilled forgetting are often cited as proofs of the unconscious. A famous and amusing example of a slip that took place in 1936 is cited by J. H. van den Berg (1971, pp. 234–6). In that year, Freud became 80 years old and S. E. Jelliffe, a prominent American neurologist, organized a meeting to honour him and he himself read a paper *Freud as a neurologist* in which he mentioned Freud's work in the laboratory of Meynert. Other workers in the laboratory were Allan Starr and Gabriel Anton, both being well known to the American audience. After this lecture, the neurologist Bernard Sachs, another member of Meynert's laboratory, spoke. Amongst others, he mentioned how well he remembered the days in the laboratory of Professor Meynert. Yes, he said, there I was with three others, Starr, Anton, myself and . . . a fourth man. 'Who was that fourth man? Who was that other fellow?'

The fourth man was Freud, who at this meeting was the 'first man' and who was being honoured by the presence of Sachs, Jelliffe and the meeting of an august body. This was a *faux pas* of enormous dimensions. Now, should this be seen as an unconscious manifestation? Certainly, if Sachs did not really like Freud, he could not have chosen a worse moment to show his dislike. However, reflection will show that he chose exactly the right moment. What better time to show that he did not like Freud than at a meeting chosen to honour Freud? At the moment when Freud had to be the first for everyone, Sachs shows that, for him, Freud could not be the first, not even the fourth person in his life.

Van den Berg demonstrates how this can be understood without recourse to a substantive concept of the unconscious. In terms of Sullivan's parataxia we are not constant entities. We reveal different aspects of our Dasein to different people to whom we relate. In a sense, I am 'Al' when relating to my wife, 'A2' when relating to my neighbour, 'A3' when relating to a colleague at work, etc. If I have my neighbour, my wife and my colleague in the same room and if my relationship to each of these persons differs appreciably, then I shall be in a conflict situation and such a parataxic contact will be characterized by being uncomfortable, i.e. by not being able to be my bodily self and will also be characterized by forgetfulness. I shall have difficulty in recalling what we were talking about. (See section on Being-with-one-another in a shared world.) Contemporary society is of such a nature that it is possible for me to belong to a multiplicity of groups. There is no strongly integrated coherent community in which I can be a constant self. I am therefore, in a sense, a divided self. One's existence is fragmented. Bernard Sachs's *faux pas* is an instance of how one's existence can be fragmented. He belongs to a group of people who are present at a meeting in the form of their belongingness to the American Neurological Society. Sachs is, moreover, an important member. He is important in the sense that he is a leading neurologist and also in the sense that he shared some of Freud's life as a neurologist. At the same time, Sachs is a man who does not really like Freud. However, this is not supposed to interfere with his life as a scientist. Therefore, he belongs to this group of scientists and he also belongs to another group who do not want to have anything to do with Freud. Sachs proves the presence of separation. At the moment of making this slip, he was with the others, but yet not with the others – to such an extent that he was even antagonistic to them. None the less, he stood amongst the others and spoke to them. He was communicating in a manner in which he proved that he was at the same time belonging to the group and yet not belonging to this group (Van den Berg, p. 236).

This means that Freud's discovery of unconscious factors in everyday life is a discovery related to the psychological history of Western man. The 'unconscious', J. H. van den Berg (1963, 1971a, 1971b) argues, is not an invariant constituent of man's life but only of a specific epoch. The hidden sector of life became strongly accentuated in the nineteenth century and therefore it could only be discovered then. It was discovered by many but Freud was the first to try to delineate it in a systematic fashion as a dynamic unconscious.

Van den Berg shows that it clearly was not always so. Locke, for instance, wrote that Descartes' conviction that the soul perpetually thinks cannot possibly be true because he conceived it to be impossible to deny that one can have a dream at night without having a recollection of the dream next morning. He argued that, if that were possible, namely, that if after sleeping the soul would have no recollection of a really dreamt dream – that is, a form of thought according to Descartes and Locke – then he would have to say that Socrates asleep and Socrates awake are not the same person, and such a conclusion is not acceptable. He argues therefore that we are one and indivisible, in other words, that we are always identical with ourselves. Early in the seventeenth century there is, therefore, no sign of the divided existence, which becomes so clear in the writings of later thinkers and writers.

One of the first examples of a divided existence may be noted towards the end of the eighteenth century, when J. W. von Goethe made mention of 'the two souls in his breast'. Later on we have the work of Gotthilf Heinrich von Schubert who in 1814 published his famous *Symbolik des Traumes*, in which he already speaks about the fact that the dreamer in us, is both more intelligent and more poetical than can be deduced from our everyday existence but at the same time worse, more evil than we are able to suppose. He further stated that this dark figure that one is when one is dreaming turns against the self. Here the conception of a duplicity in our existence is already brought out very clearly. At about the same time, a whole Doppelgänger literature arose in Germany so that there is the novel of Jean Paul's *Unsichtbare Loge* and also his *Siebenkäs*. Then there is E. T. A. Hoffman's *Elixier des Teufels* of 1814 and 1815. In 1886 the plurality in our existence is brought out only too clearly in R. L. Stephenson's famous novel of Dr. Jekyll and Mr. Hyde. This is the same time as Freud and Breuer's discovery of the unconscious. In 1888 already in the Netherlands, Frederick W. van Eeden had independently published a treatise on *Our Double Ego*. Most important of all, in 1891 in the *Principles of Psychology* James said, in a paragraph under the heading *The Constituents of the Self*, that our self or ego is not indivisible but falls apart into at least three components which are separate, almost autonomous elements and he distinguishes between the spiritual self, the material self and the social self. He also said that we do not have one social self but many: 'a man has as many social selves as there are individuals who recognize him.' However, since individuals belong to classes or groups of equal-minded persons, the number of social selves of everyone is not, in fact, as large as the number of people that we know but considerably less.

This divided existence, which gave rise to the unconscious or obliterated parts of our lives, as it occurred in a striking manner in the historical cases which came to psychiatrists and neurologists in the latter part of the nineteenth century and in the earlier part of the twentieth century is a passing historical phenomenon. Whereas in Victorian times vitality, in the form of sexuality, had to be blotted out of the existence of respectable people this no longer applies in our time. Very few people nowadays have dreams in which sexuality is represented in disguised form. In fact, in contemporary society there is very little or nothing that prevents us from having sexual dreams. Our lives have opened up: our existence has made the sexual sphere fully accessible to us. On the other hand, it is also clear that we tend to close off our existence from the spiritual and this is one of the roots of the fact that death has become a tabooed subject in most circles of contemporary society.

'The unconscious' is not something that is part of us, it is an ability to hide from ourselves and others; this hiddenness is part of the social structure. In a technological, highly organized society the spiritual, the finiteness of human existence, the ever-present possibility of death simply does not fit in because technological society is built on continuity of performances and this presupposes a life without shadows, a life which is conducted in a rational, organized, technically well-adapted fashion.

CHAPTER IV

Research: Toward a Phenomenological Praxis

'A phenomenological psychology worthy of its name has to face up to a very special kind of challenge and it is this: the challenge of being able to offer a constructive alternative in terms of praxis to the psychology we now have.' Giorgi (1970) continues that the problem to date has been '. . . that even those who understand the phenomenological approach have not been able to translate it into praxis in a systematic and sustained way' (p. 77). This is the task of the present chapter.

Phenomenology is a method; more properly it is an attitude but not that of a technician with his bag of tools and methods ready to repair a poorly functioning machine. Rather, it is one of wonder and of respect as one attempts a dialogue with the world – to get the world to disclose itself to one in all its manifestness and complexity. The phenomenological psychologist is identified not by the subject-matter with which he deals, but by the way in which he attempts to understand and describe his environment. He is obsessed by the concrete; his primary aim being to observe, to comprehend, then to render explicit what was initially seen vaguely in the first comprehension (Van Kaam, 1958). Yet he is wary of theoretical observations and accepted opinions lest, prejudging that which has yet to be fully known, he fails to be faithful to the phenomena as they appear. 'This is the basic principle of all phenomenology: the investigator remains true to the facts as they are happening' (Van den Berg 1972, p. 64). In other words, the phenomenological psychologist can no longer insist prior to beginning his research that his final description and understanding conform to a particular theory nor that they comply to the requirements laid down by other disciplines, nor that they support the commonly accepted conceptions of man's niche in the universe (Moustgaard 1975).

This certainly does not mean that the phenomenological psychologist has no presuppositions about what he has set about to understand. Clearly, anyone setting out to systematically and rigorously investigate any phenomenon is, from the beginning, guided by what he already understands about the phenomenon. Since the phenomenological psychologist acknowledges that his research and the results obtained are – to a certain degree – guided or determined by his approach, he raises the issue of objectivity and grasps the fact that the results of research are inextricably bound to the perspective of the method used (Brandt & Brandt 1974; Kracklauer 1972). To cite from Giorgi (1970),

113

'All facts are selected . . . by the activity of our consciousness, and hence they are always interpreted facts.' '. . . the fact of perspectivity thus rules out . . . the possibility of an absolute stance – and this applies to a phenomenological perspective as well' (p. 162). Thus one of the ways in which phenomenology has enriched psychological praxis is that it has taught psychologists to begin research by describing the phenomena as they are, before establishing theories and hypotheses, and thereby place above all else a 'respect for the phenomena' (Husserl).

A major difficulty, however, is in deciding what phenomena are relevant and proper for a psychology conceived as a human science. 'For it makes a difference whether the psychologist proceeds according to the schema of a "rat in a maze" or according to the fundamental thought of encounter. It is not irrelevant whether the researcher, in interviewing someone, thinks that by means of sounds he has to provoke reaction from a strange organism or believes that he should have a conversation which is meaningful both for him and for the interviewed person' (Strasser 1963, p. 311). The crucial difference between these two schools of thought in research is their approach, i.e. the basic philosophical underpinnings according to which they view the world. Thus, if it is believed, for example, that experience is an epiphenomenon of a more concrete reality – that of behaviour – then the researcher may be tempted to describe a man fleeing from an angry crowd in terms of the movement (behaviour) of two points A (the man) and B (the angry crowd) through space per unit time. That is, the subject matter of his research is the spatial behaviour of the man and the crowd. In other words, the content of his research is locomotion, which one can adequately investigate within a natural science paradigm. However, the situation of a crowd-pursuing-a-fleeing man is essentially different from that of the wind-chasing-a-paper. It is true that both can be studied and understood in terms of locomotion yet the former situation is different by virtue of the intentionalities of the persons involved. To omit terms such as anger and fear because they are 'subjective' is to leave out of this situation those characteristics which are uniquely human. The content of research with man-as-man rather than with man-as-thing must be, by definition, that characteristic which is peculiar to man – his existence as an experiential being. Thus, the human scientist will accept as evidence – and hence as the content of his research – the man's experience of being-afraid and the crowd's experience of being-angry. Consequently, the method he employs to explicate the structures of these experiences will be that which yields most fruitfully an understanding of the situation of a man-being-chased-by-a-crowd as opposed to a paper-being-chased-by-the-wind.

It is imperative for the human scientist to avoid an approach where '. . . reality is pressed into a system of ideas in which the human elements as such disappear [for] it follows that this system is unsuitable for the scientific purposes which he pursues. Motion, for example, can be described in a way that is equally applicable to an electron and to a human being. Such a description is useful for a man of science who is interested in 'locomotion' but it is meaningless with respect to a man fleeing from a pursuing crowd' (Strasser 1963, p. 161). It is perhaps instructive at this point to see what Strasser has to say about the meaning of the term 'method'. 'According to the original meaning of the Greek term, 'method' means the road to be taken if one wants to reach the desired goal. In other words, the purpose determines which road should be taken. If, therefore, the aim pursued by human sciences differs from that of physical sciences, different methods have to be used in them' (p. 22).

The upshot of what has been said is that any explicit method carries with it an approach, either explicitly or implicitly, and defines the content of research by virtue of the nature of the questions it poses. The essential point to be noted here is that it is not possible to separate either the method or the content from the approach. The psychophysical parallelist, for example, believing that experience, emotions and cognitions are paralleled by brain-wave patterns (his approach) will not develop methods to study these phenomena *per se* (the content) since he sees no need. They are – as far as he is concerned – only epiphenomena of various brain states and so are most adequately studied by investigating these brain states (the content) which can be described quantitatively. The human scientist, believing that experience is an irreducible phenomenon (Beshai 1971 *inter alia*) will set about to study experience as it appears.

It is frequently maintained that in order to be rigorous, one must quantify the data (Blasius 1976; Johnson & Solso 1971). This is true to a great extent in the natural sciences where, for example, it is meaningful to ask with what velocity a stone falls through space. However, if the subject of our inquiry is not a falling stone (nor man-as-thing) but rather a falling man then is it not equally meaningful, if not more so, to ask about the experience of falling? As Strasser points out, '. . . any methodic principle is merely an *attempt* to comprehend the inexhaustible wealth of forms in which human life manifests itself' (p. 133). Since then, it would seem possible to be rigorous without quantifying the data (as shall be shown later) – providing the data are examined in a manner that is relevant to the phenomenon under investigation – we would, in the case above, accept as legitimate subject-matter for scientific research the experience (not speed) of falling. The important point is that there are different ways (methods) of being rigorous depending upon the content – which is inseparable from the approach – of our investigation. Being rigorous or 'objective' is actually an '. . . intellectual attitude of someone who pursues his study in an unprejudiced fashion and allows his judgement to be determined by that which really presents itself' (Strasser 1963, p. 59). It is certainly legitimate to quantify the data if we are looking at *Homo natura* (Binswanger) – man-as-a-thing – while man-as-an-intentional-being requires that qualitative data be accepted as evidence for our investigation (Romanyshyn 1975).

It is felt by many (Johnson & Solso 1971) that experience is not valid subject-matter for a rigorous discipline because it is considered to be 'subjective' and therefore unreliable. However, even within the natural sciences – which pride themselves in being rigorous disciplines – data is ultimately arrived at via the investigator's experience. For example, the researcher observes readings on a calibrated measuring instrument (which incidentally was calibrated without the exclusion of experience), designs an experimental paradigm, selects equipment for measuring certain aspects of the phenomenon because he feels them to be important and so forth. In the words of Merleau-Ponty (1962) '. . . all my knowledge of the world, even my scientific knowledge, is gained from my own particular point of view, or from some experience of the world without which the symbols of science would be meaningless. The whole universe of science is built up upon the world as directly experienced . . .' (p. viii). Although it is not possible to separate the experimental situation from the scientist's experience, the entire situation is nevertheless considered to be rigorous. Why? Because his experience of the situation can be verified by a body of like-minded scientists. In other words, his investigation is considered rigorous because his experience of the subject being investigated agrees with that of other scientists. That is, they agree on sharing the same experience – there is consensus or intersubjective validation (Moustgaard 1975).

When conducting research in psychology conceived as a human science, it is imperative to realize that the design is not centred around a subject–object relationship but rather a subject–subject relationship (Barrell & Barrell 1975; Brandt & Brandt 1974; Giorgi 1974; Kvale 1973; L'Ecuyer 1975; Lyons 1970; Strasser 1963, pp. 143 ff.). That is, the 'object' of research is an experiential being who is present to the research situation. As such, he brings with him his past and intended future: human temporality being experiential, each moment tends toward a future not being simply an extended present. Each future-intending moment is one filled with '. . . possibilities, anticipations, anxieties, and questions which have as their natural frame of reference his behaviour in the present moment of the experiment' (Romanyshyn 1971, p. 101). Thus, the subject's present behaviour – that is, behaviour occurring within the quantitative boundaries of the experimental situation – intends some future and incorporates various aspects of his past '. . . even if only vaguely sensed by the subject and ignored by the experimenter' (Romanyshyn 1971, p. 102). Furthermore, the paradigm of an independent observer is no longer viable, it being important to recognize that all experimental situations comprise a convergence of two sets of intentions, those of the researcher as manifested in the research design and those of the subjects as they behave in and experience that particular experimental situation. In addition, as Strasser (1963) points out – extra-experimental meaning is always brought into the research of man-as-man, since ' . . . the one who makes the encounter possible, who prepares and organizes it, is man as pursuing science, and the one who allows himself to be encountered, either directly or by way of documents, cultural products, statistics and test results, is simply man. For this reason the situation will always have a different meaning for the former than for the latter. The difference is an essential aspect of the research situation' (pp. 147–8).

That there is no guarantee of the subject experiencing the experimental situation as the investigator intends him to experience it is clearly demonstrated by a study which set about to ascertain whether persons blind from birth were able to perform a given task more efficiently (more rapidly) than people with sight but blindfolded. The initial results showed that the blind subjects performed more efficiently than the blindfolded subjects. At this point, a phenomenological psychologist would ask the following question: 'How do these subjects experience the situation which they are in?' The answer would be forthcoming that in the above situation, the blind subjects experienced the task as being easy because they were in their normal mode of relating to the world. The blindfolded subjects, on the other hand, experienced the task as difficult, because this was not their normal mode of relating. In the traditional psychological experiment, the researcher would determine the boundaries of that situation while the subject would merely participate in it without being allowed to at least contribute to the definition of that situation in terms of how he experienced it. In other words, from the point of view of research orientated towards the natural sciences, the subjects were matched; both groups were deprived of visual sensory data. However, from a phenomenological viewpoint, the two groups were not equally matched since they did not experience the situations similarly. A truly rigorous design would have utilized a task or possibly different tasks such that both groups reported that their mode of relating to the task or tasks was either normal or not.

In a second experiment (Cloonan 1974), subjects were randomly assigned to one of two conditions, operationally defined as either a non-communicative situation or a communicative situation. However, when, at a later stage, the subjects were asked about their experience of the situation in which they found themselves, it was discovered that their experience of that situation did not necessarily coincide with the operational definition of the situation in question. Thus, the above experiment would have been better conducted by having the two situations experientially defined. That is, rather than randomly assigning subjects to one of the above conditions, they should have been asked how they experienced the situation and then assigned a non-communicative or communicative condition to the subjects according to the nature of their experience.

In any form of research, the human element is present even in the most mechanized, automated designs, without mention of the interpretation and discussion of results. Further, it must be remembered that 'objective' (gnostic) knowledge is a derived and secondary way of knowing the world, which is dependent upon the way in which the world appears to us in a primary and pre-objective, pre-reflective (pathic) way (La-Pointe 1972; Romanyshyn 1973). Hence any scientific (rigorous) investigation entails a formalized, 'objective' study of that which was always already known in a pre-scientific, pre-objective, pre-articulative manner. We know it by virtue of our being-in-the-world. Thus, in order to be truly rigorous in the investigation of any given phenomenon, the researcher should specify the way in which he is present to that which he is studying. That is, the approach of the investigator should be made explicit. This is essential, for as De Waelhens (1967) saliently notes 'At every given moment of our lives we carry with us, we are, a certain perspective — insurmountable in the instant where it appears — *from which basis* everything begins to present itself to us. It is true that I can change this perspective — but that will be substituting this for another . . . it is not possible to escape the necessity of a perspective' (pp. 159-60). Thus, it would be a profound illusion to suppose that one can undertake an inquiry and yet maintain an attitude of uninvolvement — one is involved by virtue of being-in-the-world which one is investigating. The knowledge derived from such a procedure should be intersubjectively valid, providing the judges adopt the same perspective (approach) as the initial investigator. The approach of a phenomenological investigator is characterized by the attitude of openness for whatever is significant for the adequate understanding of a phenomenon. Hence, the student of phenomenological investigation should not prejudge any particular phenomenon nor see it through any given perspective merely because of previous knowledge about that phenomenon. His method would involve the processes of intuition, reflection and description. In other words, the researcher should firstly concentrate on what is actually given, and only thereafter should he put specific questions to the phenomenon. The essential point of the above is that only after the researcher has concerned himself with the phenomenon as directly experienced should he systematically manipulate variables to ascertain whether his ideas about the phenomenon before him are valid. Concurring with the above mode of research, Van Kaam (1969) 'defines the mode of existence of the phenomenological psychologist as one in which he seeks a comprehensive understanding of the phenomenon '. . . as it manifests itself, with the least possible imposition of psychological theory or method, personal and cultural prejudice or need, and language habit' (p. 243).

The operative word in phenomenological research is 'describe'. The researcher aims at describing as accurately as possible the phenomenon as it appears, rather than indulging in attempts to explain it within a pre-given framework. Scientific explanation has its usefulness, but it too often becomes so involved in explaining that it loses sight of the original data altogether (Merleau-Ponty 1962). Furthermore, explanation shifts the focus of attention from the phenomenon under investigation to the description of phenomena antecedent to the phenomenon in question – the antecedent being assumed to have causal links with that which it precedes (Beshai 1971; Giorgi 1970; Moustgaard 1975). In other words, in such a case, the researcher is no longer concerned with *what* is given but rather with the *why* of what is before him which is a failure to remain faithful to the data as it occurs. To reiterate, phenomenology recognizes that the way to study experience is not necessarily the same way to study physical or biological realities. As Van den Berg (1972) expresses it, 'The psychologist can expect no greater results from the tools of the physicist than a painter can from the tools of a blacksmith' (p. 127). Romanyshyn (1971) is of the same opinion, asserting that 'It is the unique demands of the problem which indicate the method rather than the method which limits the problem . . . When the problem changes then the method must also change, or at least its inappropriateness for the problem as it then presents itself must be recognized' (p. 107).

Since the method must be relevant to the subject-matter, a phenomenological viewpoint recognizes the possibility of both measurement and meaning perspectives; some phenomena such as visual thresholds are best understood by means of quantification, while others such as the experience of shame or love are more fully comprehended by ascertaining what they mean to the person who feels ashamed or the person who is in love.

Having outlined the orientation of a phenomenological researcher, it is felt necessary at this point to present briefly a number of studies which make use of phenomenological approach. It is hoped that this will serve to clarify for the student of a human scientific psychology what is meant by a phenomenological orientation before we move on to a step-by-step description of a method for explicating experiential data.

BRIEF OVERVIEW OF SOME PHENOMENOLOGICALLY
INSPIRED STUDIES

The majority of studies on visual perception using the Necker cube have focused on obtaining quantitative data. For example, the difference in the rate of reversals per unit time between introverts and extraverts, or the degree of change in the rate of reversals of the Necker cube over a period of time, would be considered appropriate subject-matter. Wong (1975) hoped that by approaching the phenomenon of perception from an empirical as well as from a phenomenological perspective, the lived-experience in its totality might be further explicated. A pilot study revealed that as subjects visually perceived the cube 'rising' and 'falling', they correspondingly felt the cube turning in their hands when instructed to hold the cube. On being instructed to manually resist the reversal, they reported that visually the cube also appeared to reverse less rapidly. On the basis of these preliminary observations, Wong proceeded to develop an elaborate experimental design, although for our purposes we need only concern ourselves with one particular phase; when the subjects were instructed to hold the Necker cube and simultaneously to visually oscillate positions. This phase of research comprised four conditions; firstly, a verbal condition in which the subjects gave a description of their experiences during the actual process of perceiving the cube and, secondly, a non-verbal condition in which the subjects reported their experiences only after the perceptual phase was complete. The interviews concentrated on the relationship between visual and tactile experience. Each of the above conditions took place in a bright and a dim light condition, controlling for the degree of visibility.

The interviews concerning the subject's perceptual experiences were tape-recorded (this ensured an ease of 'catching' everything said). The transcriptions of these interviews were interpreted and scored according to three criteria. Firstly, the frequency with which recurring descriptions appeared. Secondly, the emphasis that subjects placed on particular items, and thirdly, the position of expressive components.

The results of the above revealed that there is a correspondence between visual and tactile perception. This is in accordance with Merleau-Ponty's (1962) contention that the lived-body must be viewed holistically and that one cannot justifiably speak about one perceptual mode without incorporating other modes of perception. It was also found that verbalization interfered with both the rate of oscillation as well as the degree of correspondence between the two perceptual modes. In addition, the degree of visibility was found to affect perception, such that as the degree of visibility increased so also did the rate of oscillation together with the degree of correspondence between the visual and tactile modalities.

Wong's aim was not only to empirically validate Merleau-Ponty's theory of perception but also in her own words: 'This project is an initial attempt to approach psychology from both empirical and phenomenological perspectives. As such, it is also experimentation in methodology. The experiment itself developed from questions raised by results obtained as each stage of the project opened possibilities for further investigation. Therefore, the conclusions presented are open-ended' (p. 87).

A second exemplary study is that by Giorgi (1971), who conducted research into the problem of meaning and serial learning. He made use of a design that initially satisfied all the traditional criteria for experimentation within a natural scientific paradigm, but at a later stage introduced a non-interfering (phenomenological) modification. This supplementation made it possible to ascertain whether the additional data inspired by the phenomenological modification enhanced the understanding of the subject-matter. Interviews from a preliminary pilot study revealed that subjects experienced learning a non-pronounceable nonsense syllable list more difficult than learning a list of ordinary words. It transpired that the list of ordinary words was experienced as being shorter than a list of trigrams, since each letter of each trigram was experienced as not-fitting-in-with the other two letters, unlike the letters of an ordinary word. Thus, it became important to control for this variable otherwise the subjects would be learning lists that were not experientially equal. (This, of course, already points to the flaw in many studies on verbal learning where subjects have been given lists of trigrams which were treated as single items because they were considered to be such by the investigator (Postman & Keppel 1969 *inter alia*).) These lists could be equated, for example, by presenting 12 pronounceable monosyllabic words (12 items) together with 4 trigrams (12 items) or by presenting two lists each with 12 words or 12 letters. (It was this latter procedure that was adopted by Giorgi.)

The items were presented tachistoscopically to 27 undergraduate students and the learning of letters and words was counterbalanced. The performance criterion adopted was two consecutive trials of serial anticipation without error. Having completed the learning phase of the experiment, the subjects were asked to state whether one of the lists had been easier to learn and, if so, they were to explain why. It was this particular phase that represented the phenomenological modification.

In brief, the quantitative results indicated that there was no statistically significant difference between the number of presentations of each list before criterion performance was attained. From this data on its own two conclusions are possible; that the words and letters are equally easy to learn or that the same number of subjects find the words easier to learn than the letters as those who find it easier to learn letters. The qualitative modification, however, suggested that the second conclusion is more valid. Furthermore, this phenomenological phase also revealed the reasons for experiencing one list as easier to learn than the other. These are interesting because not only do they reflect the methods whereby the subjects learned the lists, but also they showed that frequently an identical reason for finding one list easier was applied to either type of list. For example, eleven subjects considered the letters easier to learn because they could be associated more easily, while five subjects felt that the words were more easily learned for the same reason. Similarly, five subjects maintained that the words were easier since they already had a meaning while six other subjects explicitly claimed that it was precisely this already-given meaning of the words that hindered their learning process. It transpired that these latter subjects learned by imposing a meaning on the items in each list. Since their imposed meaning did not always coincide with the already-given meaning of the words, they found learning more difficult.

Giorgi continues with a most thought-provoking discussion of the results, but for our present purposes it is sufficient to note that the '. . . quantitative analysis revealed the *fact* that there was not a statistically significant difference in the number of trials required to learn the list of letters and the list of words. However, the sheer establishment of the fact does not reveal its meaning, because two interpretations of the fact remain possible. In order to ascertain the correct 'interpretation another fact was required, and this other fact depended upon the analysis of how the subjects experience the situation . . .' (Giorgi 1971, p. 92). The exclusion of experiential data in traditional experimental psychology is unfortunate since it eliminates some of the more important analyses from psychology such as the elucidation of the relationship between experience and behaviour. With traditional approaches it is only possible to infer from the person's behaviour how he experienced a particular situation. Finally, Giorgi's motivation for conducting the above research was not only '. . . a desire for a rapprochement between phenomenological and empirical perspectives, but also to try to demonstrate that on the one hand, the science of psychology can benefit from phenomenological insights, and on the other that phenomenology and experimentation are not as far apart as is generally supposed' (p. 99).

Let us now proceed to look briefly at Colaizzi's study (1971) on the experiential aspects of learning. A large majority of studies on learning have concentrated on the performance of subjects within or over a given period of time. Few studies, however, have concerned themselves with the experience of the material being learned, yet one of the tenets of phenomenology is that in order to know any object the human subject must allow that object to reveal itself to him, and that any object will only emerge according to its concrete spatial and temporal relatedness to the human subjects. In other words, applying the above to a learning task, a phenomenological orientation would assert that each learning moment discloses different and changing phenomenal aspects of the material being learned.

Colaizzi was able to validate the above assertions empirically by explicating the perceptual experience of material at various phases in the learning process. By adhering to a phenomenologically inspired rigorous design, he was able to show that the learner's experience of the material did indeed change as he became more familiar with the material.

The essential point to be grasped from the above is that additional information relevant to man's experience can be yielded by phenomenologially based research. Purely quantitative research on the learning of material serves only to supply information about the learner's performance. True, we can infer his experience from his behaviour, but such a procedure is open to criticism since not only does it fail to be rigorous with respect to experience *qua* experience, but it impoverishes our understanding of fellow man.

In agreement with the points emerging from the preceding pages, Graumann (1970) asserts that not only should the method of phenomenological psychology supplement psychological research paradigms but also that it '. . . should precede any other empirical procedure. Experimentation should not be the first step, but rather the description of individuals in their natural settings . . .' (p. 58).

PHENOMENOLOGICAL PSYCHOLOGY RESEARCH: A METHOD

Having briefly presented a few representative studies conducted along phenomenological lines, it is felt necessary now to give a detailed step-by-step exposition of how the student of phenomenological research should set about his task. Methodology in psychology conceived as a human science is concerned with the rigorous description of a phenomenon while at the same time remaining faithful to its context in the *Lebenswelt*. The rigorous procedure of explicitation must be made publicly explicit so that the research may be replicated by another researcher if so desired. The validity and reliability of the research will not depend upon the replicability of results but rather on the reappearance of various essential themes which initially led to a greater intersubjective understanding of the phenomenon concerned (Munro 1975).

At the outset it is imperative to be cognizant of the fact that the method below is not the only way to conduct research if one wishes to be a human scientist. To the contrary, it is but one method of many. It should be borne in mind that the method must dialogue with the content (Beshai 1975; Giorgi 1970, 1974; Kracklauer 1972; Thines 1970; Van Kaam 1966) and that the method presented below is subject to modification depending upon the nature of the subject-matter to be investigated. We cannot reduce a phenomenon so that it will fit into a pre-existing method. As Kullman & Taylor (1966) point out, there is a danger in prematurely fixing the categories of the world and the methods used to elucidate such categories, since it '. . . precludes the development, discovery, and invention of new modes of "expliciting" and predicating that which is encountered in the pre-predicative "flux" of experience' (p. 126). Confirming what has already been said about the dialectical nature of the development of a phenomenological research methodology, Giorgi (1971) points out that "It is phenomenologically unsound to establish a method that must be used that is prior to and independent of the phenomenon to be investigated. The problem of methodology cannot be considered in isolation, but only within the context of the phenomenon to be investigated and the problem aspect of that phenomenon' (p. 11). Hence the '. . . interesting thing is that phenomenological method is reflexive in nature and intent: phenomenological method is itself phenomenologically derived' (Natanson 1966, p. 11).

The method outlined below must not be viewed as a method *per se* but rather as a guideline for the further development of a more specific methodology in relation to a particular identified phenomenon in various areas of psychological research. The specific steps to be followed constitute specifically applicable procedures which are examples of general principles in phenomenological research. Such general principles embody procedures which allow the emergence of an essential description of the phenomenon without distorting the essential meaning of the original data.

A. THE CHOICE OF A SUBJECT OR SUBJECTS

In choosing subjects the following conditions have to be met:

(a) The researcher should preferably have the same or, at least, be fluent in the home-language of all the subjects. This aids in obviating information loss due to interpretation from one language into another (Levy 1973 *inter alia*).

(b) The average subject should express a willingness to discuss matters freely and openly with others.

(c) The subjects should preferably be naïve with respect to psychological theory. Their being untrained would increase the probability of their verbalizing the data of their awareness without undue interference from implicit philosophies of various schools of psychological thought. In the words of Kullman *et al.*, 'In describing our "original" experience of the world, we must not let ourselves be influenced by any empirical or philosophical theory of perception, any hypotheses concerning its nature, causes, or physiological or other underlying processes involved' (p. 117).

Furthermore, rapport should exist between the researcher and the subjects, and it is important that the researcher create a situation in which the subject can feel relaxed, unthreatened and where he has time to spend with the interviewer. Arrangements for the interviews should also be made so as to accommodate the subjects: the researcher emphasizing that the subject should choose a time and place (this condition cannot be easily met where laboratory facilities are to be utilized) where he would feel relaxed and be able to devote his full attention to the interview or experimental situation.

The research design may solely comprise the interview material or the interview may serve as an adjunct to a design aimed at yielding quantitative data.

B. NATURE OF THE INTERVIEW

It is suggested that at the start of the interview session the subjects complete Personal Data Forms so that the researcher has biographical information should such data be required at a later stage. If the subjects are not required to put any personal identification on the forms they may be afforded greater ease in expressing their true feelings.

Having completed this form – if it is to be administered – the interview proper should start. Since it has been found that questionnaire-completion type interviews tend to result in responses of a distant and highly reflective nature (Stevick 1971), it is probably best to put questions to the subjects in tape-recorded interview sessions. Furthermore, it has been found that the spoken interview allows the subjects to be as near as possible to their lived-experience (Beshai 1975; Dublin 1972; Parker 1977; Romanyshyn 1975; Stevick 1971). 'In effect, when I speak, I am my speaking; I become one with my words. Certainly . . . to speak puts me at a certain distance from that of which I speak. But between my consciousness and my speech there is no distance at all: I am in union with the language I use' (Dufrenne 1967, p. 215).

It is imperative that the researcher has previously considered carefully the nature of the question or questions he wishes to put to the subject so as to be sure of anticipating a yield of fruitful data. (However, the researcher must be mindful to remain faithful to his original objective no matter how great the wealth of data.) If the subject appears not to fully understand the question put to him, it should be repeated in such a fashion that he is clear as to the meaning of the investigator's enquiry.

The open-ended interview should be conducted in an informal, non-directive manner, the interviewer attempting to influence the subject as little as possible. As Markson & Gognalons-Caillard (1971) point out, the great advantage of a semi-structured or non-directive interview is its flexibility, allowing the investigator to grasp more fully the subject's experience than would be possible in a more rigid methodological technique. They forcefully note that 'Structured interviews . . . are impregnated with subjectivity in the form of working . . . assumptions made by the researcher [and hence] they are likely to yield little understanding of the experiential world of the [subject]' (p. 206). If the researcher fails to understand a particular point made by the subject, then he should ask for clarification. The interviewer must, however, avoid at all costs asking questions that could be construed as leading the subject.

The duration of each interview should be self-determining; once the subject has pre-scientifically explicated all that he – the subject – feels is related to his personal experience of the situation being researched (cf. Giorgi 1970 *inter alia*) the interview ends. The interviews, of course, may vary in duration from a few minutes to over an hour.

Having finished the interview, a useful data-gathering procedure is to ask the subject to complete a form which makes the following request: 'Please write down your experience of the interview which you have just had. You could, for example, state your attitude and feelings towards the interviewer and the interview-situation, as well as any other feelings you have towards the situation you have just been participating in.' This technique aims at receiving feed-back concerning the subject's experience of the interview itself, from which the researcher could decide whether to accept or reject a given interview for use in the study.

The taped interviews can then be transcribed and the scientific phase of the explication can begin.

It is inevitable that many, if not all, of the descriptions by the subjects of their experience will be incomplete or imperfect. Lack of skill in expression, forgetfulness, poor vocabulary and the inability to express oneself clearly could all be contributing factors (Van Kaam 1958, p. 61). These imperfect descriptions would certainly not invalidate the subject's experience but may fail to reflect an essential part. This problem can largely be overcome by the use of more than one subject. By making use of a variety of subjects, the possibility of finding underlying constants or themes in the many forms of expression the experience takes is greatly increased (Munro 1975). Thus, the problem of certain aspects being omitted is minimized and those aspects which are most important should appear most frequently, assuming – and not unjustly so – that those aspects which are most important are least likely to be forgotten. Similarly, a subect may concentrate on one particular area and fail to describe other aspects of his experience. This does not necessarily imply that this is all there is to his experience – merely that he has not explicitly described other aspects. Thus, the explicit areas of concern mentioned by other subjects may be implicit in his descriptive expressions. At least, they should be compatible. If not, then it is incumbent upon the researcher to make mention of this in the *Extended Descriptions*.

C. SCIENTIFIC PHASE OF THE EXPLICITATION

This phase of the research comprises six sub-phases to be dealt with below. These sub-phases are based on an understanding of phenomenological research as represented by the work (Colaizzi 1968; Giorgi 1971, 1975; Stevick 1971; Van Kaam 1958 *inter alia*) conducted at Duquesne University. These sub-phases should not be seen as operating independently and mostly overlap with one another. As Van Kaam (1958) points out, 'They form partly a set of ordered abstractions describing the complicated mental process that the phenomenological scientist experiences as a natural totality' (p. 28).

At intermittent stages throughout the scientific explicitation, the researcher may wish to consult various persons also involved in phenomenological research concerning doubts about the validity of a given sub-phase or aspect of a sub-phase. In addition, he may also wish to seek consensual agreement concerning, for example, the delimitation of a *Natural Meaning Unit* and its reduction.

1. An intuitive holistic grasp of the data

Since phenomenological research is engaged research, involving the researcher in an interpersonal situation, the researcher's mode of involvement in the scientific phase of the explicitation is crucial. In his initial reading of the protocols the researcher should bracket his own preconceptions and judgements and to the extent that he is able he remains faithful to the data. After achieving a holistic sense of the data, the protocols are read again (if necessary repeatedly) – with a more reflective attitude – in order to prepare the researcher for the further phases in which a more particular and exacting analysis is stipulated. In addition, the repeated reading of the protocols in this early phase assists the researcher in retaining a sense of the wholeness of the data despite its dissection in the subsequent phases.

2. Spontaneous emergence of Natural Meaning Units (NMUs)

The data are broken down into naturally occurring units – each conveying a particular meaning – which emerge spontaneously from the data. This unit, termed a *Natural Meaning Unit* (NMU) may be defined as '. . . a statement made by S [the subject] which is self-definable and self-delimiting in the expression of a single, recognized aspect of S [the subject's] experience' (Cloonan 1971, p. 117).

In the example below, each NMU is separated from other NMUs by a diagonal and denoted by a number. '. . . Well, I had a very sort of, normal family background/(1) I hated school – (laughs) – it was lousy, I didn't like it at all. The two years that I did enjoy were nine and Matric/(2). Before that, I was very normal in my school life, you know, nothing outstanding, nothing spectacular – very ordinary./(3). My family was a very normal one. There were four children; three daughters, I'm the only son, I'm the second child. My father, you know, I would say, we're a middle class family,/(4) they're very staid people, not very good church-goers to begin with,/(5) but then, those are the years when I developed/(6). . . .'

The intention conveyed by each NMU is then expressed in a reduced form as concisely and as accurately as possible. For example:

1. Had a normal family background.
2. Disliked school, except for the last two years.
3. Was an average student.

4. Comes from a normal middle-class family.
5. Critical of family.
6. These were the years of his development.

.
.
.

N.

Wherever possible, the subjects' own terminology and phraseology – his linguistic style – should be adhered to in order that the data may 'speak for itself'. However, the shared nature of our lived-world suggests that we are able to understand fellow-man's meanings and as such the researcher may articulate the central themes (reductions of the NMUs) in words other than those used by the subjects so as to clearly express the intended meaning. The· task of this phase is an '. . . articulation of the central themes that characterized the respective unfolding scenes of each protocol' (Fischer 1974, p. 414). In this manner the richness of the data is exposed for further explicitation in the phases to follow. It is essential to be aware that each meaning unit exists in the context of the other inter-related meanings of a protocol. This implies that regardless of how clearly meanings are differentiated from each other conceptually through the questioning of the data, there is nevertheless an inseparable relatedness of all these meaning units.

3. Constituent Profile Description

Having listed all the reductions of the NMUs, the researcher then proceeds to eliminate those units which are repeated, that is, which convey an identical intention or meaning. Having done so, the next step is to eliminate any irrelevant units. To ensure rigor, only those units which are very obviously irrelevant to the question being researched are eliminated at this stage. The remaining units are considered tentatively to be non-repetitive and relevant descriptive statements concerning the experience being investigated. This is termed the *First Order Profile*. This *First Order Profile* is then converted into a *Constituent Profile Description*, in brief, a condensed summary of the original data, containing the essence of what the subject expressed.

4. Second Order Profile

The *Second Order Profile* results from a repeat of phases one through to three, but performed on the *Constituent Profile Description*. The elements emerging from this procedure are then listed and numbered. This repetition aims at ensuring that the raw data have been fully but not overly reduced. Over-reduction should not occur at this stage because the development of the *Constituent*

Profile Description enables the researcher to systematically check that this description does indeed contain all the constituents necessary to be able to fully identify the original data. The final elimination procedure performed on the *Constituent Profile Description* aims at removing any redundant constituents. This, as has already been stated, is termed the *Second Order Profile*.

At this stage in the scientific explicitation of the data, two paths, so as to speak, may be taken. If the study is ideographic, then the researcher carefully develops – from the *Second Order Profile* – an *Essential Description* of the raw data. An *Essential Description* is a succinct description emerging from the process of explicitation – the making explicit that which is implicit in the raw data – and containing all the essential elements in the structure of the phenomenon under investigation.

Parker (1977), for example, by following a phenomenologically inspired method of explicitation (different from the above method yet not dissimilar) was able to express the essential elements of a 65-page interview concerning a bisexual individual's experience of being bisexual in the following form: 'Bisexuality is the experience of a wider range of emotions than are traditionally acceptable as appropriate to a one gender-linked role. The emotions related to the expression of dominance, self-sufficiency and efficiency, are fulfilled in relation to women – interpersonally and sexually. The emotions related to the expression of passivity, coyness, and the need to be taken care of, are fulfilled in relation to men – interpersonally and sexually' (p. 191).

For research making use of more than one individual, the other path taken is to repeat, for each subject, the first four sub-phases previously outlined.

5. Hierarchical Categorization

Having repeated the above four sub-phases on the protocols of each and every subject (in the case where N > 1), the researcher proceeds to the fifth stage of gathering those descriptive statements with similar, though not identical, meanings into clusters which are termed *Categories*. Any given *Category* may contain elements from only one subject or from possibly all the subjects. These *Categories* are then arranged in a hierarchical fashion in order to facilitate the next stage of the scientific phase of the explicitation.

6. Extended Description

Taking the first few clusters of *Categories* (containing thematic elements), the researcher writes an *Extended Description* of what these *Categories* tell him about the overall question being investigated. He then adds to this description the next *Category* in the hierarchy and so either extends the description or modifies it in the light of the new information in the additional *Category*.

This procedure is repeated until further addition of *Categories* is rendered superfluous since the essence of the data is already contained in the *Extended Description*.

Following this, the researcher systematically and carefully checks the remaining *Categories*, ensuring that they are compatible with the *Extended Description*. Those thematic elements (contained in the *Categories*) which are not compatible are described and, when possible, the researcher shows that these elements are only apparently incompatible.

D. RIGOR OF EXPLICITATION BY THE USE OF INTERSUBJECTIVE JUDGEMENT

Since the hallmark of any scientific endeavour is that there should be consensual validation of the outcome, a panel of judges (other than the author) may be used to determine whether the *Essential Descriptions* (in the case of ideographic data) or the *Extended Descriptions* (in the case of nomothetic studies) are true to the data.

The criterion for validity is not whether another researcher (or a judge) would use exactly the same words or arrive at an identical description of the data. Rather validity is indicated by whether such differences in wording may be intersubjectively understood to reflect an identical meaning or indicate similar essential themes to those which emerged from the data as explicitated by the original researcher. In summary, it is essential that any form of phenomenologically inspired research fulfil at least the following criteria:

1. The research/interview situation should entail a description of experience or meaning-structure, i.e. the phenomenon, in its lived-world context.
2. Essential themes should be extracted in their varying manifestations.
3. Explicitation of the protocols should be concerned with the meaning of the data from the participant perspective.
4. The dialectic between approach, method and content should be maintained. That is, the method and content of the phenomenological approach should reflect its understanding of the human condition.

Although this type of research is still in its infancy, research has and is being conducted in the Department of Psychology at Rhodes University. Todres (1975), the first to produce a project with a phenomenologically inspired methodology, worked on Transcendental Meditation (TM). He used a total of nine subjects, ranging in age from 19 to 45; the criterion used for their acceptance as subjects being not only that they be willing to share their experience of meditation, but also that they had to have been meditating for at least seven months prior to the start of the research. The interviews, which lasted from 30 minutes to 90 minutes, enquired into the following two areas; the experience of TM in terms of Van den Berg's (1972) categories of bodiliness, self, fellow man, world and time, as well as the *mantra* (a sacred utterance – syllable, word, or verse – considered to possess mystical or spiritual efficacy –. *Encyclopaedia Britannica*, vol. VI, 1975, p. 582) and secondly the subject's everyday experience of 'body', 'self', 'world', 'time', and 'life-project'. Apart from these general guidelines, Todres conducted the interviews in a fairly unstructured, non-directive manner.

The data resulting from each interview were explicitated according to three phases. Phase one aimed at 'letting the data speak for itself'. In other words, the meaning of what was said was *intuited* and from this a fundamental description of the meaning structures of the data was arrived at. Phase two involved a *reflection* upon this description so arriving at '. . . an elaborated and explanatory expression of each subject's meditative modality of being as well as his life-world and project for life' (p. 30). In order to avoid undue repetition of similar data, Todres extracted '. . . different possibilities or potentialities of similar themes in different subjects in varying degrees of depth' (p. 31).

The two phases described above correspond with, although are not identical to, the first four sub-phases presented earlier. The third phase of the explicitation of TM was concerned with an *Essential Description* of the meditative mode of being, together with the elucidation of any common themes making up the *Lebenswelt* of the subjects.

Perhaps the crucial question at this point is concerned with whether Todres derived any benefit from using a phenomenological approach. The answer quite simply is 'Yes'. Previous studies on TM had largely focused on the physiological correlates associated with the practice of TM. The danger of such a one-sided approach is that it increases the probability of TM being conceptualized in a dualistic framework, that is, in terms of the bodily or physiological responses and also in terms of the awareness developed by this state. However, because the natural scientific view is concerned chiefly with the measurable bodily changes, the awareness aspects of the practice of TM tend to be neglected if not relegated to the realm of epiphenomenal. However, as Merleau-Ponty and others have so repeatedly pointed out, the whole person must be seen as living a situation – one cannot justifiably split man into his constituent parts and hope that an explanation or description of each will be describing the total person. Todres, by using a phenomenologically inspired methodology, was able to show that '. . . TM is a response of the whole person to a situation which is lived before it is reflected upon, and bodily is part of the way the subject lives the experience' (p. 76). (After Stevick 1971, p. 145.) This non-dualistic conclusion follows directly from his *Essential Description* of TM which exposed the dynamic lived-experience of TM: 'Transcendental Meditation is the pre-reflective and progressive experience of the world, body, self and *mantra* moving towards the dissolution of their mutually interdependent boundaries.

'The body moves from functional body, as being-operational-in-the-world to pre-reflectively losing body/world boundary in terms of defining space. Self-as-agent-of-action is transformed into pre-reflective Self/body/world experiential unity. This occurs in terms of the dissolution of actor/acted boundaries with the emergent, "*mantra*-as-happening". *Mantra*, as a definable word, becomes less structured both spatially and temporally and briefly loses its definable distinctions. Temporality loses its quality of succession-as-strictly-structured to a more durative modality' (p. 74).

In researching the significance that our *own* death holds for our lives as individuals, Todres (1978) argues that 'man as relationship' is a fundamental tenet of phenomenological-existentialism, and so he chose to re-search man's temporality as a dimension of his *Lebenswelt*. Since temporality is bounded by birth and death, man's awareness of his particular individual death gives rise to the awareness of finite temporality. Taking his cue from Heidegger, Todres asserts that to make a person more aware of the imminence of his own death, is to make him more aware of his own life. In other words, just as one has to do one's own dying, so, too, must one do one's own living; death is an integral part of life, the two are inextricable. A literature survey revealed that many terminal patients and aged people who had not yet come to terms with their own finitude were unable to do so at this late stage owing to more immediate concerns such as coping with acute and chronic physical ailments, loneliness and other debilitating aspects of being old and/or dying. As Todres points out, there is a great difference between 'receding from life' and 'confrontation with death'.

Todres aimed at elucidating man's finitude by engaging in phenomenological praxis. He posed the following questions: firstly, can people relatively early in life experience their finitude more fully and, secondly, if so, what is their experience of finitude? He developed a series of experiential procedures allowing the subjects to consider their lives in the face of their own deaths in an interpersonal, temporal and bodily context. In this way it was felt that each of the subjects may come closer to an experience of confronting his own finitude than by reflection alone. The six subjects were chosen according to the criteria outlined earlier in addition to the criterion that the subjects express interest in enquiring into the dimensions of their own existence and a commitment to self-understanding. They were thus not 'naïve' subjects and all admitted that they had reflected on the nature of death in the past. Since Todres's concern was to clarify the phenomenon of confronting one's own finitude, such past reflecting by the subjects was considered to be of assistance in his task. Data was derived from two sources. The subjects were asked both before and after the series of procedures to write a short essay entitled: 'What my own death means to me', followed by a comma and their own name, in order to bring home the impact of the situation and, secondly, they were then required to record in writing – not verbally – the immediacy of their experience directly after each procedure. The data were analysed following a method similar to that of his first study (Todres 1975) as well as incorporating phases five and six of the method outlined earlier. (It is important to remember that the method must be in dialogue with the data to be explicitated.)

In addition to the above procedures, Todres aimed at elucidating the individual's *Lebenswelt* at any given stage of confrontation with his finitude as well as a developmental history of the individual's progressive confrontation with his own death. Todres hoped by this procedure to delineate the structure of more fully becoming and being a finite existence.

The question as to whether his phenomenologically-inspired research – being as time-consuming as it is – achieved anything different from what a traditional psychometric approach would have achieved must be answered in the affirmative. Firstly, a questionnaire expressly concerned with man's experience of his finitude (not merely temporality) has yet to be developed and, secondly, even if such a questionnaire were to be developed, it would then force the subject into a particular mode. That is, the structure of finitude explicitly or even implicitly conveyed by the questionnaire may not be true to the subject's particular awareness of lived-finitude with the result that the data derived from such a questionnaire may not reflect faithfully the phenomenon of his finitude. Another objection to the traditional approach in researching this particular area of concern is that such a questionnaire could be developed only *after* the researcher had explicitly delineated the structure and significance of man's awareness of his finitude; in other words phenomenology is prop-aedeutic to any form of scientific psychological research.

Phenomenological research at Rhodes University Psychology Department has not been solely orientated towards traditional psychological content but also towards transcultural concerns. Schweitzer (1977), for example, conducted research over a period of three years into the categories of experience amongst the Xhosa. The study placed great emphasis upon an in-depth ideo-graphic explicitation of each of the various categories of divination within a Xhosa cosmology. Schweitzer maintains that it is im-perative to pay attention to the actions, thoughts, feelings, memories and dreams of the subjects, as the only guide to an adequate interpretation of divination is the experiential reality of the subject himself. In this sense, he draws upon phenomenologi-cal tenets and so is able to assert with confidence that the '. . . most "scientific" findings in this field have generally reflected not the characteristics of the phenomena being studied, but the con-ceptual framework and biases of the respective authors' (p. 3). Schweitzer determined to suspend as far as possible various 'conceptual schemas' in an effort to understand 'the experiential reality of the particular category' of experience. Concurring with a phenomenological orientation, he points out that the interpreta-tions presented in and arguments developed by his research are tentative and subject to continual review.

The study chose to use an ideographic mode of data collection, since it was believed that development of a meaningful relation-ship with one central 'informant' would yield more pregnant data than would a nomothetic approach. Furthermore, such an ap-proach is probably more efficacious than one continually referring to already established categories of experience (within the West-ern traditional framework) which may not necessarily be con-gruent with those of the Xhosa cosmology. In any case, one can ascertain whether there is, in fact, congruence between the two cosmologies only after one has fully grasped the underlying mean-ings and meaning relationships of each cosmology. Schweitzer continues that 'The categories of experience to be explicated are . . . not primarily viewed as constituting psychopathologies (that is, with reference to Western psychiatric diagnostic schemata), but as the expression of affectively-determined problems in living' (p. 20). He further points out that although other studies in this area might be methodologically sound, '. . . they do not attempt to relate the experiences described as being meaningful within the individual's cosmology, but they are evaluated within a medical or descriptive psychiatric model' (p. 28). Thus, to conceptualize an auditory or visual experience as being hallucinatory or delu-sional is to delimit the phenomenon to abnormal or pathological mental conditions, and hence denigrate the meaningfulness of that experience in the individual's *Lebenswelt*.

Schweitzer draws upon phenomenology in explicating the meaning structures of various categories of experience '. . . by viewing man and world as being in continual meaningful relationship' (p. 15). The methodological procedure used is similar to that already outlined. In brief, this entails engaging in the processes of intuition, reflection and description (Giorgi 1970), concentrating on that which is given prior to putting more specific questions to the data. Such a procedure enables one to study the phenomenon more fully since it is allowed to emerge as it is, rather than being primarily questioned according to specific preselected aspects of the phenomenon which have been defined in terms of a pre-given framework, which is possibly alien to the phenomenon as it actually is in its own 'horizonal field' (Gurwitz 1966). This is essential if one wishes to be rigorous since, as has already been emphasized, the researcher's conceptual framework (approach) and method prefigure the manner in which the data 'speak to the investigator'. To quote Schweitzer once again, 'A fundamental principle in the analysis of the data is to allow the data to speak for itself, and thus allow the relationships and organizational schemes to emerge from the data. The function of the analysis is to move from a description obtained in the field, to the conceptual structure of each category of experience' (p. 48).

Schweitzer goes on to give a detailed comparison of the Xhosa divination categories of experience and the Western medical nosology, suggesting the role of the diviner in contemporary mental health services. Since this does not directly concern us, however, we shall move on to a final example of human scientifically-inspired research conducted in the Psychology Department at Rhodes University.

Eppel (1976) conducted research into the experience of closeness – more specifically, the experience of feeling close to a particular person or persons in a particular situation. Accepting that the most direct way to obtain data about a person's experience is to ask him, being constantly aware that language – reflective as it is – can never fully express the dynamic of the lived-experience itself, Eppel conducted a non-structured interview aimed at pre-scientifically explicating the feeling of closeness.

Perusal of phenomenological literature resulted in Eppel developing '. . . a single methodology in which there was an interdependence between the phenomenon of closeness, the interview question, the structure of the interview and the method for data explication' (p. 43). As such, his research is highly rigorous since at all times Eppel was acutely aware that the facts that were emerging were doing so owing to the specific perspective which he had adopted. This awareness that the investigator is very much a participant in the research forced him to choose carefully the type of question he put to the subject concerning the experience of closeness.

Apart from the selection-criteria already mentioned, Eppel asked the subject prior to the interview proper whether she had ever felt close to someone. Had her answer been in the negative, she would not have qualified as a subject, since clearly, 'Someone who has never felt close[ness] will not have the experience to explicate or will not be able to identify with a scientific description of that experience' (p. 46). Remaining true to the subject's experience, Eppel allowed her to freely explicate whatever experience she felt was *her* feeling of closeness. During this pre-scientific phase of the research, he attempted to be as 'non-directive' and non-manipulative as possible.

The scientific phase of the explicitation which followed was closely similar to that already outlined except that phase two (emergence of NMUs) occurred only after non-significant and repetitive data had been eliminated (phase three). Having thereafter listed all the NMUs, he proceeded to derive an essential description of the experience of closeness.

The description of closeness *per se* is not – for our purposes – of immediate concern. What is important, however, is to realize that closeness as an experience – not the physiological concomitants of feeling close to another person – cannot be studied adequately by any other method. Questionnaire-administration would be of no avail since, as has already been pointed out, the questionnaire itself would have, in the first instance, to be based upon our intuitions concerning the experience of closeness. In other words, the most important criterion for assessing the efficacy of a test is its validity; that is, the extent to which it measures or describes what it purports to measure or describe. Yet, how does the scientist know that what the questionnaire is measuring or describing is, in fact, the experience of closeness, unless he always already knew that experience by virtue of his own feeling-close-to-someone? That is to say, the scientist bases the questionnaire on his own experience and then verifies this by using the traditional techniques for obtaining the degree of reliability and validity of a questionnaire. This, however, indicates to the scientist only the extent to which the questionnaire measures or describes consistently and accurately the original experience. It does not signify that this experience is really – in this case – the experience of closeness. Hence if this very first phase of explicitating the experience of closenss is . faulty, then the following elaborate procedure is in vain. For this reason, phenomenology must be and always is (although in many instances only implicitly) propaedeutic to any form of scientific psychological research (cf. Giorgi 1975).

Pursuing his interests in phenomenological inquiry, Eppel (1978) further determined to investigate the experience of psychotherapy as it is lived by the client. Eppel considered that an exploration of the client's retrospective experience of psychotherapy would allow for a holistic encounter with the client's lived-experience of therapy which would be more comprehensive than would a study conducted with a client while undergoing psychotherapy.

In scrutinizing the literature it was found that questions concerned with psychotherapy have been divided into two broad categories – process and outcome. While the former is concerned with the rationale, technique and dynamics of psychotherapy, the latter category is concerned with evaluations of the efficacy of psychotherapy and the differential effects of various factors upon the outcome of psychotherapy. Although previous research has explored characteristics of the client, the therapist and the technique, as well as the quality of the relationship between the client and the therapist, the major emphasis appears to have been a quantification of and correlation between the above areas and such variables as client age, socio-economic status and educational level. That is, to date, the research on psychotherapy has had as its major aim the quantification of certain factors associated with psychotherapy, including research on the client-experience in psychotherapy (Howard & Orlansky 1968, 1970).

Eppel pertinently points out that to remain true to as well as open to all possibilities concerning the client's experience of psychotherapy, one cannot use a traditional psychological paradigm in which there is the inherent striving to quantify the investigated phenomenon – in this case, the client's retrospective experience of psychotherapy – so as to make it readily accessible through means of a measuring instrument of some description, for example, a questionnaire or a rating scale. Such an attempt at quantification is not a viable procedure (as we have already seen) for two major reasons. Firstly, it would presuppose that the categories made explicit in the questionnaire and/or rating scale are the only components of the client's experience and secondly, following from the above, there would be no formal possibility for the client being allowed to expand on the pre-given categories, that is, the client would merely indicate, in a questionnaire or on a rating scale, those aspects of his experience that were enquired after. Experiential aspects not asked about would tend to remain covered, so resulting in a failure on the researcher's part to remain faithful to the data before him.

Eppel's methodology comprises an interview and an explicitation of the protocol conducted along the lines previously recommended.

The forte of Eppel's research is that he was able to conduct a post-research interview which served as an additional form of validation for his research as well as being the source of further data. Several researchers (Giorgi 1970; Romanyshyn 1971; Von Eckartsberg 1971) have repeatedly stressed the incorporation of the subject's experience of the interview to be crucial in the overall research. The post-research interview allowed Eppel to ascertain whether his *Essential Description* of the client's experience – retrospectively reported – was accurate and, if not, the subject could serve as an assistant to the researcher in his striving to achieve a more precise description of the subject's experience – in this case – the retrospective experience of a client's experience of psychotherapy.

Since phenomenologically-orientated research methodologies will always remain in the neophyte state – each method developing in a dialogue with the phenomenon to be explored – it is imperative that the method presented in this chapter not be accepted as absolute but rather as one way of delineating general phenomenological principles of research. For too long the subject-matter has held a lowly position in deference to the privileged position of method and quite clearly this is anathema to any researcher wishing to conduct rigorous investigations in a psychology conceived as a human science.

CHAPTER V

Phenomenology, Psychopathology and Psychotherapy

PSYCHOPATHOLOGY AND PHENOMENOLOGICAL PSYCHOLOGY

The first question that raises itself, especially in view of the growth of the so-called anti-psychiatry trend, is the question as to whether there should be a science called psychopathology at all. One may well ask, if it is possible to understand the person, whether a special science called psychopathology should be erected for a special class of persons labelled abnormal whereas psychology should be for all the rest of us? The main thrust of the anti-psychiatry school has been towards the danger of labelling, thus putting a question mark behind the whole process of diagnosis.

THE MEDICAL MODEL

The medical model bases itself largely but not exclusively on the pioneering work of Emil Kraepelin. Kraepelin systematized the knowledge of his time and delineated nosological entities in the field of mental disorders in the same way as entities were delineated in the field of general medicine. Thus, dementia praecox, so-called by Kraepelin, but later renamed schizophrenia by E. Bleuler, was seen as a sickness in the same way as a disorder such as cancer or diabetes. It was supposed to have a definite etiology, course and outcome. In order to cure such a disorder it would be necessary to find out its causes and to struggle against these causes by using some form of physical or other therapy. It was Kraepelin's conviction that dementia praecox was caused by a metabolic irregularity, that it was of early onset, that it had a definable course and that it was incurable.

The modern medical model of schizophrenia would be that this is a form of psychotic behaviour or behavioural disturbance characterized especially by thought disturbance. The pattern includes withdrawal, being self-centred, and irrational. Although there may be large variations within individual cases, the common pattern is further characterized by affect which is inappropriately linked with verbal communications, delusions and hallucinations, whilst speech is often disordered and confused.

Kraepelin (1973) conceded that 'it is true that, in the strictest terms, we cannot speak of the mind as becoming diseased, whether we regard it as a separate entity or as the sum total of our

140

subjective experience. And, indeed, from the medical point of view, it is disturbances in the *physical foundations* of mental life which should occupy most of our attention. But the incidents of such diseases are generally seen in the sphere of psychical events, a department with which the art of medicine has dealt very little as yet. Here we are not so much concerned with physical changes in size, shape, firmness, and chemical composition, as with disturbances of comprehension, memory and judgement, illusions, hallucinations, depression and morbid changes in the activity of the will.' (Emphasis in the original.) It seems then that although Kraepelin looked upon schizophrenia and manic depressive psychosis, in particular, as basically physical disorders he did not consider the symptoms of a condition such as schizophrenia to be a *bodily* complaint. Even taking into consideration the amount of progress made since the time of Kraepelin, the symptoms of schizophrenia cannot be identified through the use of medical technologies such as blood-pressure gauges, thermometers, electroencephalographs, X-rays and so forth. The symptoms, however, are framed in terms of the application of a disease model to people's talk and conduct, their beliefs and communicated experiences.

A diversity of activities, beliefs and communicative experiences may lead to the diagnosis of schizophrenia in a specific person (Coulter 1973, p. 4). Since what is called schizophrenia has no fixed attributes, attempts to give a general description of this disorder are bound to represent only partially what is routinely included in this category in psychiatric practice. We cannot say that we are dealing here with conditions whose parameters are more or less fixed and determinate. However, the disease model of schizophrenia is essentially predicated upon the assumption that such reifications are permissible for *theoretical purposes* (Coulter, p. 5). However, since we lack precise and reliable operational descriptions enabling us to have a clear-cut and integrated picture of a disease called schizophrenia, it seems unlikely that research can establish the *causes* of such a heterogenous descriptive category.

Eugen Bleuler, who, under the influence of psychoanalysis, moderated Kraepelin's one-sided somatic emphasis, divided the symptoms of schizophrenia into primary and secondary signs. As main primary signs certain disorders of affectivity and associations were noted. 'The disorder in the affectivity', says Bleuler, 'is the tendency of the feelings to work independently of each other, instead of working together, which becomes evident for instance in the ambivalence, in inadequate affective reactions, simultaneous crying and laughing, and many other observations which occur very frequently in schizophrenics' (Bleuler 1973, p. 19).

The psychic mechanisms, Bleuler thought, were most clearly

seen in paranoia. He sees paranoia as typically arising where a person is frustrated and finds it impossible to blame himself for his failure and so looks for causes elsewhere. Such suspicions of being unfairly treated can arise in the mind of a healthy person; however, he felt paranoia arose when there were *primary* lesions causing the affect to exercise greater influence on the process of thought than usual and causing the counter-concepts to be suppressed and thus for suspicions to become convictions and hence delusions and feelings of persecution would follow. According to Bleuler, even a healthy person believes in what he wishes; 'but the sick person knows it and actually *is* the founder of a religion' (Bleuler, p. 20). As an instance of the primary physical disturbance Bleuler mentions schizophrenic thinking (p. 21). According to him, the disturbance of thinking has shown itself to be in no way dependent on psychic influences, but solely on the seriousness of a fundamental process. This he saw in some of the accompanying symptoms arising in an acute state such as catatonia and dyskinesis which are accompanied by bodily symptoms such as raised or lowered temperature, albumin in urine, metabolic disturbances, gnashing of teeth, etc. Here we can see an attempt on Bleuler's part to treat the symptom constructs as if they discriminated among *biologically* relevant dimensions.

However, the great hopes held out for this point of view have failed to materialize in the field of biochemical research in schizophrenia. Kety (1973, pp. 92–104) has summarized the extensive research done in this area. He reviews a large number of theories all of which have been rejected or have failed to prove valid on replication. The so-called genetic factors in schizophrenia, which started out by the finding of a very high concordance rate for monozygotic twins, have proved disappointing as the concordance rates were successively reduced in subsequent research. It should be pointed out that with adopted schizophrenics where environmental forces can be more successfully controlled, research has shown some importance of genetic factors but it seems that what we can look for here, at most, is a susceptibility to schizophrenia or to a variety of personality or character disorders. Kety suggests that personality or intelligence may be more appropriate models for schizophrenia than phenylketonuria (p. 99). He is further of the opinion that a polygenetic inadequacy of some sort may be interacting with particular life situations.

In this connection, the major review of research by Manfred Bleuler (1966) should be taken into consideration. He stated *inter alia* that clinical experience can easily be summarized in the statement that the large majority of endocrine patients are not schizophrenics and the large majority of schizophrenics have no endocrine disorders as far as we are able to ascertain at present (p. 8). He furthermore took the view that the genetic transmission theory of schizophrenia has become quite improbable. Family histories, he continues, as well as the incidence of schizophrenia amongst relatives of schizophrenics, do not support such an assumption. A further important argument against the Mendelian theory of schizophrenia, according to Manfred Bleuler (1970), is to be found in the fact that schizophrenics are much less fertile in comparison to the general population. If we had been dealing with a simple biological disorder based on genetic transmission, the number of schizophrenics should have been decreasing but so far no tendency in this direction has been observed, but rather the opposite.

In his 1966 review of the research Manfred Bleuler has suggested that the research into the causes of schizophrenia has been unsuccessful and he ascribes this to the possibility that there is no cause. He further states that in the existence of the healthy persons there is hidden a chaotic life which goes on without consideration of reality and that a healthy psychic life is hidden behind the morbid mask of the schizophrenic. It seems to me that Bleuler's position is not incompatible with the idea that schizophrenia is a highly diverse and confusing set of problems in living and that the cause–effect model is not a suitable approach to understanding this disorder. This may be comprehended in terms of the built-in legacy of misunderstanding in that the human being, for purposes of schizophrenic research, is considered as somehow being enclosed within his own skin. In other words, both diagnosis and research procedures are based upon the supposition that we are dealing with man as an encapsulated entity, closed off within himself, and that as a closed entity in this sense, he may then be seen as having been invaded by a disease process which has as its symptoms communicational problems such as those occurring in schizophrenia, manic-depressive psychosis, obsessive neurosis, etc. However, the gap between what goes on in the organism seen as a physico-chemical mechanism or corporeality and the level of communicational and inter-relational exchanges involved in the observance of the 'psychic' symptoms remains, in principle, unclosable.

PSYCHOANALYTIC APPROACHES TO SCHIZOPHRENIA

Freud's interests in schizophrenia were nowhere near as extensive as his commitments to understanding the neuroses. In 1911 he gave a most interesting study of the case of Schreber, who developed paranoia in later life. He ascribed Schreber's condition to repressed or latent homosexuality. (Parenthetically it should be pointed out that in a later work Morton Schatzmann has criticized

Freud for leaving out a lot of information which could have thrown interesting light on Schreber's condition. Schreber's father was a well-known doctor who wrote extensively on the education of children and devoted a great deal of time to his ideas on phsyical education. Schatzmann has tried to show how Schreber's 'delusions' reflect the injunctions, disjunctive relationships, prohibitions and directives of his father.) However, in 1928 Freud postulated that an ego-regression takes place in schizophrenia which means that libido is withdrawn from external objects. In the neurotic the regression is temporary and partial; the ego utilizes defence mechanisms in order to sustain a relationship with the external world. However, Freud postulated that in schizophrenia there was a regression to so-called 'primary narcissism' which is characteristic of infancy in which the ego has not yet been formed so that the total mental functioning is undifferentiated and a distinction between internal and external has not been arrived at yet. The nucleus of the schizophrenic experience is the break with reality during which the ego returns to its original, undifferentiated state in which it is dissolved wholly or partially into the Id. Freud's theory may be somewhat picturesquely represented as the schizophrenic ego throwing itself into the arms of the unconcsious or the Id.

Not only does the schizophrenic process seem to be marked by regression to narcissism but also, due to the impotence of the ego, a lot of primary process thinking takes place. In this early stage of infantile ego development, the infant's discovery of the body, hypochondriacal sensations as well as alterations of body sensations are said to cause a change in the body image which seems to be characteristic of schizophrenic regression. The disintegrating ego reacts to narcissistic regression by depersonalization and estrangement from direct experience. The delusions of grandeur and feelings of omnipotence are said to be similar to the magical thinking of small children because of the partial disintegration of the ego and their regression to early developing stages.

In addition to these symptoms of regression, Freud postulated that there were symptoms of restitution which are seen as evidence of the person's attempts to re-establish contact with reality and hence ego control. Hallucinations, considered to be perceptions of objects which do not really exist, are hypothesized to be projections of inner complexes, experienced as external perception. A simple wish fulfilment theory will not do in this case because many hallucinations are frightening rather than pleasurable and Freud therefore takes it to be the reappearance of part of the reality that was repudiated through regression. Thus, the hallucinations are both an attempt to escape from reality but at the same time indicate the failure of such an attempt. It is seen as a return of the repressed. Delusions seem to be at a higher level of integration where the patient attempts to reconstruct reality in ways that are less threatening to the ego.

Jung's theory of schizophrenia is predicated on his distinction between personal and collective dreams. Personal dreams, according to Jung, agree with the rules of a personalistic psychology; however, collective dreams have a character that exhibits a peculiar combination of mythological or archaic material and one has to turn to historical or primitive symbols in order to understand these.

In trying to work out a psychogenetic origin for schizophrenia, Jung feels that we may safely assume that personal matters and worries are sufficient to account for personal dreams but when we come to collective dreams which have weird and archaic images it is impossible to trace these back to personal sources. He finds that a study of historical and primitive symbols yields surprising and most enlightening parallels without which it is impossible to interpret such dreams. Comparative psychology is needed for the study of delusions because the symbols produced cannot be fully explained in terms of the personal history of such a person. Jung found that the qualitative analysis of schizophrenic conditions fully substantiates the need for such additional formation. Starting from Freud's personalistic medical psychology, Jung soon found that the basic structure of the human psyche is not personalistic at all but rather an inherited and universal affair. Jung hypothesized that the basic images and forms of imagination have more resemblance to *a priori* categories than to starting out as a *tabula rasa* and he furthermore found that schizophrenia yielded 'an immense harvest of collective symbology, neuroses yield far less, for, with a few exceptions they show a predominantly personal psychology. The fact that schizophrenia upsets the foundation accounts for the abundance of collective symbolism, because it is the latter material that constitutes the basic structure of personality' (Jung 1973, p. 134). Jung concludes that the schizophrenic state of mind yields archaic material and thus may be said to have the characteristics of a 'big dream' which he conceives of as an event with a numinous quality which primitive civilizations attribute to the corresponding magic ritual. We can see here some parallel with Freud's conception of the deterioration of the ego and the taking over of the daily life of the person by the Id against which a totally inadequate ego is struggling. However, Jung comes to an entirely different conclusion, pointing out that in primitive cultures and in medieval times the insane person had always been regarded as someone possessed by a spirit or haunted by a demon. This means that the unconscious had taken possession of the ego. However, this does not mean that the ego is enfeebled. On the contrary, the unconscious is thereby strengthened by the presence of a demon. This means that it is not so much the ego that is circumscribed but rather the unconscious which has been expanded and thus transgresses its boundaries. (As we shall see later, this aspect of Jung's theory has some affinity to the phenomenological approach.)

Jung comes to the conclusion that it is very difficult to answer the question whether the sole and absolute reason for a schizophrenia is a psychological one or not, but he says (p. 136) that the biology, anatomy and physiology of schizophrenia have had all the attention they want and that no definite results have come up. So, in view of the fact that we do not have an exact knowledge of heredity or of the nature of the primary symptom, he suggests that we should look to psychogenesis in the first place.

It seems therefore that Jung does not come up with a conclusive statement that schizophrenia is exclusively psychically caused, but he feels a fruitful line of investigation is open to us by concentrating on the psychic dimensions of schizophrenia.

We can see that Jung breaks with Freud in a certain sense. However, he does not break with Freud or with the medical model in that he does not reject the encapsulated view of man. Secondly, although Jung states (p. 135) that he is in agreement with the suggestion that the word causality or cause should be struck off the medical vocabulary and replaced by the term conditionalism he says so only because it is impossible to prove that schizophrenia is either an organic disease or that it has an exclusively psychological origin. However, in his own theorizing he does not make it clear that he has abandoned the cause–effect sequence because he seems to conclude that schizophrenia is caused by the increasing strength of the collective unconscious.

Harry Stack Sullivan formulated an interpersonal theory of schizophrenia. His standpoint was that personality manifests itself in personal relations and not otherwise. A study of schizophrenia would then be, for Sullivan, a mere variant on the study of interpersonal relations because personality, for him, evolves entirely from the individual's relations with the significant others in his environment. Interpersonal relations that corresponded with the development of schizophrenia come about through the conception of anxiety as a dynamic process. Anxiety passes over into terror or literal panic, usually during adolescence, under circumstances that cannot always be exactly specified. Anxiety was held by Sullivan to be the great disjunctive force in personal relations. In the insecure child, a very large part of experience is screened out of the self-system so that the child grows into an adolescent with a self that is narrow and fragile. However, because the demands arising in the adolescent period such as the demand for intimacy with the opposite sex and the need for self-assertion, ideas, stimulations, relations, etc., which had been ruled out of the system in early childhood, obtrudes into the self-system, giving rise to terror or panic. Anxiety then is a felt threat to or actual loss of self-esteem; owing to the actual, anticipated or imaginary disapproval of significant others or of disapproval of oneself owing to the values and ideals that one has been socialized into. The main defence mechanism hypothesized by Sullivan is dissociation of all material which contradicts the self-dynamism and which is unsuitable for the sort of life for which the self has been organized. There is a balance between the self-system and the associated elements or processes of a personality. In people who become schizophrenic there is an unusual balance between the two conditions that may have been obscurely evident for a while. Some specific event may trigger off a disturbance of the equilibrium and later panic may ensue in the form of unpleasant visceral sensations with a boundless and objectless terror.

As has been previously been pointed out, Sullivan moved away from a solopsistic view of human personality and, as we can see, from the encapsulated view of schizophrenia as well. Sullivan, however, was not able to devise an entirely consistent frame of reference within which these phenomena could be understood. However, he did approach the phenomenological view quite decisively.

From an interpersonal theory of schizophrenia to an understanding of this disorder as resulting from and embodying communicative disorders in the family seems a logical step. This led to a focus on the way communication and patterns of thinking of the parents (e.g. Bateson's double bind hypothesis) leads to a transmission of irrationality (Lidz) or mystification (Laing & Esterson). However, most researchers found that the ways in which schizophrenic families function presented a wide variety of shortcomings and distortions such as unstable, ineffectual, withdrawn or rivalrous, egocentric parents; failures of parental nurturance, a skewed or schismatic family structure due to the distorted relations between the parents; transgressions of generational or gender linked role boundaries and impaired socialization resulting in the child's failure to learn how to function adequately outside the home situation (Lidz 1975, pp. 14–16).

However, Lidz, from whose book the above summary has been condensed, still holds to an intrapsychic view of man in spite of his looking for causes in the family system (or perhaps *because* of it). Thought disorder, withdrawal of the child from society and so forth, are seen as being *caused* by the distorted family patterns *resulting* in gross failures of ego functions, lack of autonomy and fluid self-boundaries amongst other things. However, I must agree with J. Coulter, writing from an entirely different perspective, that it is inappropriate to try to translate cultural-interactional data into causal accounts. To do so 'is to espouse a programme which illicitly construes the human social world in non-moral terms, on the model of a field of interacting particles . . . and . . . to the apportionment of blame in the guise of scientific explanation' (Coulter 1973, p. 38). Another difficulty with these theories is that the authors tend to construe the experiences of the victims rather than to obtain first person accounts of what it is like to be a victim of, for example, a double bind.

However, from the point of view of a phenomenological psychology, these studies certainly constitute an incipient geography of the personal relations landscape in which persons who later have schizophrenic episodes or careers grow up. We note further that all the psychoanalytically-oriented theories including family models remain essentially biographical-historical ones emphasizing the past development of the person. However, a study of Dasein-as-history should be fully open for the future as future (rather than as a mere derivation of the past), i.e. for the life project, and hence the family findings are not directly translatable into a phenomenological existential theory.

THE BEHAVIOURIST APPROACH TO PSYCHOPATHOLOGY

I shall restrict myself in this presentation to the work of B. F. Skinner and his followers and in particular to an article entitled 'What is Psychotic Behaviour?' (by Skinner in Millon 1973, pp. 282–93). It seems that Skinner's radical behaviourism provides no special conception of psychopathology and restricts its formulation entirely to the observation of objective behavioural processes. Skinner makes it quite clear that he is not interested in understanding as such. He is not interested in finding out to what extent our fellow human beings are accessible to us but only to arrive at what he calls 'a true scientific understanding of man' implying that 'we should be able to prove this in the actual prediction and control of his behaviour' (p. 283). His well-known emphasis on the empty organism is reflected in his statement that the most important aspect of a behavioural description of an organism is the probability of the emission of behaviour. Skinner rejects the intrapsychic view of behaviour. However, whilst the intrapsychic view is undermined, the world is reduced to a mere system of facts such as are described by the natural scientific disciplines. (For Skinner the Newtonian universe is alive and well and flourishing in the psychology department at Harvard.) Skinner seems to accept that concepts such as 'conscious or unconscious mind' could be acceptable provided their physical extent could be described. In other words, the emphasis is not merely on the observable: we can after all, 'observe' a dying man gasping for breath but this is not quite what Skinner is after. There is a built-in *physicalism* as well – because he says (p. 287) that 'in abandoning the dimensional systems of physics and biology' we abandoned the techniques of measurement 'which would otherwise be a natural heritage from early achievements in other sciences. This is possibly an irreparable loss.' A description of the dying gasp is not scientifically admissible unless it is amenable to measurement, e.g. a measure of air displacement and muscle movement or emitted responses. He further says: 'the loss of the opportunity to measure and manipulate in the manner characteristic of the physical sciences, would be offset only by some extraordinary advantage gained by turning to inner states or conditions'. From this it is clear that Skinner is not interested in discussing the question as to whether the methods of physical science are applicable to the study of the human being as such. Instead, he is solely interested in using the measurement devices and strategies developed by the physical sciences to measure whatever is measurable about human behaviour. The question as to whether these methods will be able to encompass the total field of human behaviour certainly is not raised by Skinner in any of the books that I have consulted. The possibility that some psychological phenomena may not be readily accessible to the measurement methods of the physical sciences is not seriously considered by Skinner because, e.g. in reference to anxiety, he states: 'the number of references to anxiety in treatises on behaviour must greatly exceed the number of references to punishing episodes, yet we must turn to the latter for full details. If the details are not available, nothing can take their place.' In other words, Skinner is telling us that it is going to be respectable only to understand anxiety to the extent that the contingencies needed for this condition to arise can be specified in physicalistic terms. The possibility of anxiety being triggered off by an event which is still to come, such as one's own death, cannot readily be accommodated in this frame of reference. Whilst he has nothing but scorn for Freud's intrapsychic concepts, he shows himself as a Freudian in the sense that he looks for the reasons for present behaviour in terms of the reinforcement *history* of the organism. This is exemplified in the statement that 'eventually, of course, the affect must be explained – for example, by pointing to some earlier connection with more important events' (p. 288).

Furthermore, Skinner seems to feel that we should bracket any prereflective understanding or prescientific knowledge that we may have of the human being except in so far as such knowledge can be specified in terms of a physicalistic science of behaviour.

Thus, he makes the extraordinary statement: 'no behaviour is *itself* aggressive by nature, although some forms of behaviour are so often a function of variables which make them aggressive that we are inclined to overlook the inferences involved.' In other words, to be a true behaviourist, one has to act as if one is a being from another planet.

Another feature of Skinner's position is the devaluation of experience which he describes as incorrectly representing our information about a stimulating field (p. 288), which means that the world to him is simply a system of bare physical facts giving off stimuli and it is from this meagre basis that we have to describe and understand human behaviour. As could be expected, he does not accept the representational theory of consciousness and suggests that what goes on inside the organism is something to be relegated to physiology. On this question we need not differ with Skinner if he feels that what we see is what is there to be seen rather than a picture in the mind or the brain and that what is called physiological psychology may as well be assigned to physiology. We note again that where he assigns the outside world to the physical sciences, he does the same to the body in which he hardly differs from psychoanalysis and remains a true child of Descartes. A second instance about the evaluation of primary experience is that he agrees with some psychiatrists that the testimony of the individual regarding his mental processes, feeling, needs and so on, is, 'as the psychiatrist above all other has insisted', unreliable. This means that Skinner will have no difficulty at all in accommodating his behaviour science to the needs of organicist psychiatrists and would not feel embarrassed by the lack of communication that often characterizes the interchanges between organically oriented psychiatrists and patients.

As a contribution of behaviourism to the understanding of psychotic behaviour Skinner cites an experiment being carried out at the Boston Psychopathic Hospital where a patient is observed for one or more hours per day in a small pleasant room. This room is furnished with a chair and contains a device similar to a vending machine where the patient can then 'emit responses' by pressing buttons or pulling a plunger. This machine then spews forth reinforcements, such as candy or cigarettes, and a continuous record of the behaviour is kept, so permitting a ready inspection and measurement of the rate of responding. Here again, one can see Skinner's conception of the human being as an encapsulated organism or object; in spite of his insistence on his lack of interest of what is going on *inside* the skin, he is interested in what such an organism can emit.

The objection that such a procedure reduces the human subject to the status of an animal is easily (and to this reader, callously) shrugged off by pointing to medical research where experimental work on *animals* has ameliorated the human condition. Another objection, namely, the oversimplification introduced by the *absence* of a fellow human being, is met by the argument that this was a deliberate preliminary measure due to the need to control the variables in an experiment. By the same token, however, Skinner finds it quite appropriate to study psychotic behaviour outside its interpersonal context without considering whether psychosis can even be said to exist *outside* such a context.

From the foregoing it is clear that, however radical Skinner may be in his approach to the study of normal and/or abnormal human phenomena, he is philosophically still a child of Descartes. Although he would refute and reject Descartes' *cogito*, he certainly accepts Descartes' *res extensa*, arguing that there is only a physical reality and that experience is simply an incorrect representation of environmental information. It seems then, that in order to achieve the project of a scientific description of human behaviour, we must sacrifice our primary experience and also sacrifice our elementary understanding of what it means to be a human being. Furthermore, although Skinner rejects the Cartesian *cogito*, he fully accepts the definition of man as being an encapsulated organism. So, although he denies an interest in what is going on inside the skin, he still sees the organism simply as a mechanism that emits behaviour. He sees the organism as interacting with the environment but not as existing in relation to the environment. Furthermore, his emphasis on reinforcement history puts him on a par with Freud in that he similarly is unable to accommodate future as future. It is hardly possible, using the methodological approach given priority in operant conditioning, to observe the future as being reinforcing.

A PHENOMENOLOGICAL APPROACH TO SCHIZOPHRENIA

Let us again raise the question whether a psychopathology is needed at all in a phenomenological approach. The radical phenomenologist may argue that human life is indivisible and that there is no difference in principle between the life of a so-called normal person and a so-called abnormal or mentally ill person, i.e. people who have had experiences or who have lived certain contingencies that brought about their being labelled mentally ill. If we think of the dimensions in terms of which we stand out towards the world and if we assume, as a radical phenomenologist does, that man lives in and as relationship to the world, then it follows that the basic principles which would suffice for the experience of everyday life should also be sufficient for the experience of conditions known by various names within the science of psychopathology. If we move away from the encapsulated view of man, we necessarily have to move away from the encapsulated view of mental illness. 'Mental illness', then, is not something that happens to a person, but a set of relations which this person holds and carries out which, however, is of such a nature that it is regarded by some people as being so out of the ordinary and so incomprehensible that it requires to be labelled deviant and to be assigned to one of the categories by which people are considered to be not fully in control of their lives or not fully able to live their lives in a socially acceptable manner. If we look at the matter this way, then there is no science called psychopathology and our interests should therefore only be in the way in which people can relate to the world that brings about such categorizing and furthermore we should be interested in the process of insanity ascription. This means that what we would call schizophrenia or anxiety neurosis, cannot be divorced from the societal reactions thereto, in fact, cannot be divorced from the reaction of significant others to what happens in the world and what the identified patient experiences. In other words, a radical phenomenology would see what is called psychopathology, e.g. schizophrenia, not as a sickness that somehow attacks a person, but rather as a state of being in which the person starts relating to the world and fellow man in ways which are not readily comprehensible, i.e. socially validated, and that the study of neurosis or psychosis would then include not only the person's experience, but also his experience of how other people react to his communications and behaviour.

However, it seems that some phenomenologists at least are prepared to live with the medical model and to put a Daseins-analysis of a state of being such as schizophrenia side-by-side with the medical conceptualization of mental illness. An example of this is Ludwig Binswanger. Ludwig Binswanger shows that the diagnosis of a person as mentally ill is a cultural process and that people are judged in terms of a norm of social behaviour (Binswanger 1957, p. 45).

That the psychiatric diagnosis of mental disorder is a cultural process has been made clear by Rosenhan in his definitive study of being sane in insane places (Rosenhan 1974). Binswanger points to the well-known fact that an assessment as to what is mentally disordered differs from culture to culture and also from one cultural epoch to the other within the same culture. For instance, in the time of the flowering of Pietism what we see nowadays as a morbid introspection or sickly consciousness of sin would then have been seen as an expression of great piety. He further points out that this judgement stands on pre- and irrational grounds and stems from the area of communication. Binswanger further points out that this being based on the understanding of interactional phenomena, the diagnosis is also inevitably grounded in social-ethical norms (p. 46). However, psychiatrists are attempting to find a system for the judgement of mental illness outside the culture, that is, in nature. Their scientific ideal is to be able to translate culturally related human behaviour into naturally determined events (p. 46). Binswanger further argues that the terms illness and abnormality are not completely synonymous. In other words, what natural scientifically oriented psychiatry would be striving after would be a system of co-ordinates which is neither a cultural one nor a pure natural scientific biological one but a medical one, that is, a system of co-ordinates of medical pathology. Binswanger suggests that in psychiatric mental illness diagnostics we are not acting in the same way as when we are talking about a purely physical bodily behaviour and therefore are no longer in the area of pure biological assessment, but are looking at biology in terms of a consideration of *aims*. Health and illness are value conceptions forming the material of a *biological* aim judgement. Therefore, when the psychiatrist considers a life historical phenomena as a schizophrenic disease, he is in fact trying to say that he conceives it to be abnormal behaviour in that he sees in it danger, limitation or suffering. However, he cannot stay here. He has at least to try to show that this danger or limitation is to be reduced to processes in a natural object to which he has thus to reduce the human being. This natural object in psychiatry will then be the organism in the sense of the totality of life and achievement coherences of a *human individual* (p. 47). This means that in the last instance all medical diagnoses must rest upon an encapsulated view of the organism and therefore it also requires a philosophical argument to indicate why it is that, whenever one speaks of sickness, one should in the last instance think in terms of the individual organism. In view of this, it is not surprising that Binswanger is convinced that schizophrenia cannot be understood purely from an idealistic (functional) or psychogenic point of view because this disorder, he says, falls into a biological rather than a psychological category in the last instance (Binswanger, p. 282).

This may be taken to show then that Binswanger himself did not overcome the subject/object split entirely, although he made immense efforts in this direction and is the father of the well-known saying that the dualistic split stemming from Descartes is the cancer of all psychology. Nevertheless, he does contribute valuable insights in his extensive study of unfolding schizophrenic careers (Daseinsverläufe). He used all forms of case history material that were available and his epoch-making study included the famous case of Ellen West. On the basis of these extensive studies, he was able to come to the following general conclusions regarding the schizophrenic Daseinsform.

As foundational conception for the understanding of a Dasein described as schizophrenic, he noted the falling *apart or disintegration of the consistency of natural experience*. Natural experiences are the unreflected, unproblematic and hardly noticed sequence of events which are characteristic of the everyday contact of Dasein with the things (Preller 1977, p. 120). The inconsistency comprises the impossibility to 'let the things be' in an unmediated encounter, in other words, the impossibility of having an undisturbed 'dwelling with' the things. A very clear example of this is to be found in the case of Ellen West. We see her, says Binswanger (1957, p. 13), trying to arrange the things independently, trying to *dictate* to them how they should be. In her case, the main preoccupation of her life was that her body must not be stout but had to be slim. Moreover, she herself should not have been the way she was, but different. She repeatedly prayed to God to create her once again but to create her better. Moreover, in her existence she could not accept human society as it was; it had to be different. This last example shows that a letting-be-ness is not a sort of quietism, which lets things be by not participating but, on the contrary, even the revolutionary who wants to overthrow the social order is able to sojourn unmediately and without disturbance with the things as they are in order to be able to involve himself with them, because otherwise he will not be able to master them in order to overthrow them. In the case of Ellen West and the other schizophrenics, studied by Binswanger, they suffered from the way things were, or, more accurately put, they suffered from the fact that the things were not the way in which they would have wished them to be and thus their relationship to the things was characterized by a wishing that they were different and a striving after an ideal. The Dasein of all the cases considered by Binswanger was found to have been turned into a life full of suffering because the patients could not reconcile themselves to the way things were but were always looking for ways to reinstate the ideal order which they saw as having been disturbed. They had an unquenchable thirst for restoring the lost order to fill in the gaps in their experience with new ideas, undertakings, ideals and so forth.

If no way out can be found, then in some cases like that of Ellen West, death is seen as the only way out and therefore the only real happiness. For instance, a poignant example was found in her writings where she gives an analogy in which she sees herself as being surrounded by enemies. Whichever way she turned, it seemed to her that a man with a drawn sword was opposing her. She uses the simile of the stage: 'the victim rushes towards the exit, but halt, a heavily armed man meets him. He tries the second or third exit. All in vain. He is surrounded, he cannot get out anymore.'

What we lack in adaptation or adjustment to the life situation should not be looked at merely in the 'practical' inefficiency of the approaches used, but to the deepest extent in the fact that the method itself shows all signs of the inconsistency of natural experience. Thus, another of Binswanger's probands, Ilse, put her hand into the fire and sustained serious injuries because she wanted to do something which would show her father how greatly she loved him and through that would be able to persuade him to ameliorate his harsh, inconsiderate behaviour towards her mother. However, burning her hand and arm cannot be seen as a goal-directed act in the technical sense nor as a consequence of her feeling. This action in reality contradicted authentic 'feeling logic' in that this does not show itself as a deed or gift of love which is to be received as a gift, but merely as an exhibition of a martyred suffering 'out of love'. The fact that this does not constitute properly motivated suffering makes it inconsistent with the predicate 'I love you, father'. As a result her suffering was not able to bring about a bond of love and thus did not show her a way out of the intolerable life situation.

The second main feature of schizophrenic Daseins-courses is the splitting apart of the consequences of experience into alternatives, that is, into a rigid either/or. Schizophrenia is, amongst other things, an attempt to bring a halt to the disorder of inconsistency. In order to achieve this, there is an overstrained forming of ideals. Dasein now puts everything into the ideal of holding this upright, in other words, to follow the overstrained ideal through thick and thin. This ideal is also overstrained in the sense that it is completely unsuitable for the total life situation and therefore does not offer an outlet but leads the person up against a wall. Dasein is then unable to find its way out of this overstrained taking hold of an ideal and, in fact, this overstraining in the either/or situation then, by and large, *becomes* the Dasein. The overstrained ideal formation represents one side of the alternative while the other side takes in everything which opposes such an ideal. The schizophrenic Dasein 'pulverizes' itself in these alternatives. In the case of Ellen West we see the two alternatives, namely, to be thin and yet not being able to do without eating on the one hand and her complete and utter rejection of getting plump on the other. Her conflict can be traced back to a more original splitting of experience into the alternatives of life and death, of ideal and reality, of nature or fate versus the ideal.

A further constitutive conception for Binswanger's research was the conception of covering-up or concealment. What is referred to here are the persistent attempts to cover up the fended-off, intolerable side of the alternative with a view to underpinning the supremacy of the overstrained ideal. Thus, Ellen West had per-

156 PHENOMENOLOGY, PSYCHOPATHOLOGY, PSYCHOTHERAPY

petually to take exercise and purgatives to prevent putting on weight. In another of Binswanger's case studies, namely, J.Z., this same rigid either/or came to light in J.Z.'s relations with others. His life was dominated by the possibility that he would be exposed as a worthless individual and so he had a permanent compulsion to identify himself as a person belonging to a class which could not be embarrassed. This he contrasted with the possibility of being a failure, sinking down to the proletarian level and thus being blameworthy and exposed in the eyes of the others.

J.Z. always had to stress whatever possibility in himself identified him as belonging to a better class of person and could in no way surrender himself to just being human. Thus, J.Z. had the feeling that people would be able to see when he had an erection. He therefore preferred winter when he could wear an overcoat to summer when he was more scantily dressed. Around this particular problem he built a whole life style which prevented him from falling back into the situation where he was open and exposed to others. Similarly, in the case of Ellen West, the elaborate series of strategies that she used in order to prevent her gaining weight was the covering or protection she used against letting the alternative to her overstrained ideal emerge.

A last constitutive conception is that of the ripping apart of Dasein which means the culmination of the antonomic tensions in a resignation or a refusal to carry on with life involving such insoluble antonomic problematics. Ellen West took the most desperate way out of her problem by committing suicide. In the case of J.Z., the ripping apart of his Dasein culminated in his withdrawal from life, his attempt to live in a nirvana and thus forgo the tensions of trying to live his life outside the institution. (He was a well-qualified person.) These delusions are a completely involuntary way of withdrawing from Dasein. In this step, Dasein does not voluntarily withdraw from life or from society but what happens is that life as a independent self surrenders itself to that which is foreign to itself (*Selbst-fremde Daseinsmächte*). We shall see later that this conception is closely allied to M. Boss's conception of fallenness to a particular segment of the world.

Medard Boss (1975) questions the priority of the natural scientific method and denies the validity of the world and the body as a system of mere facts. It is, he says, a peculiarity of human bodiliness that it is accessible to natural scientific methods of investigation, but he denies that this is the only or privileged approach and that it could be expected to lead us to the full truth of what it is that medicine, in the wide sense, has to deal with. He denies that the human reality of sickness whether 'physical' or 'psychical' can ever be encompassed in a description, in natural scientific terms, of an isolated body subject. By conceptualizing human existence in terms of a calculable, causal sequence of chemical and physical processes and organ structures, one can make great progress and biology can then be reduced to physics and molecular biology, physiology to biochemistry and so on. Therefore, these disciplines, at the moment, are basic sciences for medicine besides anatomy. According to this framework, then, the whole of human existence can be interpreted on the basis of conceptualizing the human body as a physical-chemical system. As a consequence of the great success of the natural scientific approach in general, and the success of this approach in medical science in particular, we have become quite reconciled to think that all therapeutic manipulations based on this model stand most chance of success (Boss, p. 21).

However, to deduce the existence of a depression or disturbed thought processes from a brain structure is not only undemonstrable but, in principle, impossible. If we search the brain, we shall find synapses, nervous tissues, hormonal effects, physical, chemical and electrical reactions: however, we shall not find thought. The more we look in the brain or other parts of the body, the more we shall be puzzled by what we nowadays call psychosomatic disorders and other forms of 'mental illness'.

The health of man in the broader sense can be delineated only as being the ability to carry out the realization of the basic categories or dimensions of being human as explicated in a previous chapter. A really human medicine and general pathology should explicate all the possibilities in which the carrying out or actualization of the basic dimensions of being human are being limited or partially destroyed in its carrying out and in its behavioural possibilities. In other words, sickness can be seen as a lack of freedom, as a limitation on the extent to which the sick person can be involved in being-in-the-world and the extent to which he can carry out in free activity his intention in view of what is given to him in his world. This means that we must be able to move from an image or conceptualization of a human corporeality, i.e. the human body seen as a biochemical factory or machine, to an insight into the bodiliness of Dasein. Similarly, we have to move away from the conception of a psyche to an understanding in Daseinsanalytic terms of the being-in-the-world of a human being. Moreover, we have to move from a classical, representational theory of consciousness to an understanding of the essential openness of human existence. We have to move from the conceptualization of a psychic unconscious to a thinking about human ability to hide oneself from oneself and from fellow man. We have to overcome Freudian and other instinct or drive conceptualizations in order to arrive at a conceptualization of the relational possibility of the human being in his *Mitwelt*.

We further have to move from a conceptualization of psychic faculties to an existential understanding of the great variety of behavioural possibilities open to a human being. Furthermore, we do not need a theory of empathy or *Einfühlung* but rather an insight into the unmediated understanding of the other as fellow human being, and, last but not least, we have to move from the conceptualization of psychic causes and psychodynamics to an understanding of how motives cohere within the openness of a life project.

These conceptualizations mean, then, that we can retain the metaphor of illness but we shall see that what this amounts to then is a change in understanding, and instead of looking at a mental or any other illness as being somehow characteristic of an encapsulated psyche or organism, it will be viewed as an expression of the entire existence of an individual involving a limitation on his freedom of expression and action. This conceptualization is revolutionary. It amounts to a rejection of the entire view of reality initiated by Bacon, Copernicus, Galileo, Descartes, Newton and Harvey. According to this Renaissance view, reality is disclosed to us as a dimension independent of man, by looking at the thing and a body as an ob-ject which we pro-ject out there, the truth of which we should disclose by an attitude of non-involved neutrality (objectivity) using an agreed-upon method which consists of measurement operations. According to the point of view defended in the present book, measurement operations can only disclose one profile of reality. A phenomenological psychology therefore does not, as we have seen, concede man's body and his world to natural science but concedes that valuable aspects of man's bodiliness and spatiality or worldliness may be disclosed by the methods of these disciplines.

Let us return to the person mentioned in the first chapter who felt himself controlled by the chair and by other things in his world. It was stated that the structure of this person's life had undergone a catastrophic change, that he had lost distance, and that the invitational character of the world had turned into a command. Another way of putting this is that, instead of his being able freely to choose how he responds to the invitation of the world, he has become a captive of certain features of his world openness. This means that in a sense, he had lost his world openness or, put more accurately, his world openness had become at the same time boundless, thus enabling him to see things in a radically different profile, not open to people in general and at the same time he had fallen for a particular aspect of this world openness. This is the same as saying that there is a catastrophic limitation of his freedom. This same client, after he had seen me once or twice, was taken to a psychiatrist who diagnosed thought disorder which is a euphemism for schizophrenia. Although the intention of his parents and the psychiatrist that he should be admitted to a mental hospital for treatment was not realized and he preferred to go into psychotherapy instead, he then 'fell' for this diagnosis and for months afterwards he could not stop thinking about the words of the psychiatrist 'thought disorder'. In other words, in his transaction with the psychiatrist he was not able to shake off this one particular happening which he experienced as another command against which he had to defend himself all the time. Examples of such extreme narrowing down of existence to a relatedness to one very limited aspect of one's total world openness are not hard to find. Thus, I have seen an intelligent young clerical worker shock his fellow workers when he came in one morning and on seeing a couple of specks on the floor he sat down and started studying these, refusing to get up. He was eventually removed to a mental institution. Similarly, as we have seen in the case of Ellen West, her existence narrowed itself down to a dialectic between her unbridled appetite on the one hand and her need to be thin and ethereal on the other.

What we have said so far can be summarized in that schizophrenia is a manner of being or a Dasein in which the actualization of the foundational characteristic of being human, namely, openstandingness and freedom is severely limited. This means, however, that the entire existence is a fallen one and therefore that all other categories must be disturbed as well. If we study the existence of the schizophrenic, then, we shall see that it is not only in relation to his freedom of choice but also his temporality, his spatiality and his being with others which are all disturbed. The so-called triad of symptoms which is definitive for schizophrenia, namely, the thought disturbance, the disturbance of activity and the disturbance of ego-feelings in the sense of a subjective depersonalization, can therefore be understood only from the point of view of the total disturbance of the existence of the person. This means that the existence is not disturbed because of the so-called primary and secondary symptoms but rather that these changed functions can only be ascertained because the existence as a whole is fundamentally disturbed.

Boss (p. 489) cites the case history of a young man observed over seven years in which the main features of beingschizophrenic were strikingly exhibited. This was possible because the young man was very intelligent and had a great capacity for explicating his experience. He complained that as long as he lived he would be compelled to 'surrender' to everything that he encountered. Every chair that he saw could force him to sit upon it and he had to obey – as would a slave – the things and the people he met. Phenomena such as these can be ascribed by psychiatry to thought compulsion or thought crowding, but the person himself did not experience this as a problem with his thinking but rather for him it exclusively had to do with the unfree appeal going out from the encountered things themselves. The compulsion could not be experienced by him as being within himself but as emanating from the things encountered in his world. He realized too, that tomorrow or the day after or after a year he would still be 'falling' for the things and for fellow man in much the same way. This means that, in a sense, this young man had lost time. He no longer had his own time but simply lived the time of others. An ecstatic living into his own time became closed for him. Thus he was living in an inauthentic present and past.

The particular way of his schizophrenic existence could be summarized in his own words that things cannot let him be in peace and neither can he leave anything in peace. When he was a child and he went for a walk in the forest with his mother, his mother would all the time point to things of interest and draw his attention to the things he should know about the plants, insects, trees and so on in the forest. This means that in his present existence he was still living the dictates of his parent according to which he always has to do something with something, always has to be busy because one does not progress in life otherwise. If it should happen that this young man could go into a forest and simply let the forest be forest, that would already show great progress in overcoming his schizophrenic existence (Boss 1975, p. 491).

The schizophrenic existence becomes even clearer in Boss's example of the 'Sun Man', a young, intelligent and physically small person who was admitted to a clinic and who quickly made progress so that it was possible for his doctor to discuss the nature of his situation with him within a couple of weeks after admission. It transpired that shortly before he was admitted to the clinic, he had seen the sun throughout a whole night. He was lying in his bed, the window was closed and it was quite dark in the room. However, he suddenly saw the sun on the wall opposite his bed. Underneath the sun there was a sleeping man.

We would say that this client was hallucinating. He was hallucinating both the sun and the sleeping man. The aim of a phenomenological understanding is to see what it meant to the person concerned, or, more exactly, to see in what shape his world was during this particular experience. It transpired that the sun was as real to him as the electric light on the ceiling and, furthermore, that he was filled with anxiety and that he had the feeling that he could not take his eyes away from the sun because if he did something catastrophic would happen. The sun was something stronger than the human being and he had to ensure that the sun did not turn itself upon him. He did not dare risk closing his eyes for a single moment because then he would have stopped seeing the sun altogether. The sun was so clear that he was quite sure that if anyone else had been with him, he too would have seen the sun. The person knew quite well that this was not the 'real' sun. Even before that evening, he had been compelled to think of the sun for days; he then had the feeling that his penis was somehow connected with the sun and that the sun could bring about an erection. Should he stop looking at the sun now appearing on the wall of his bedroom, the sun would have come too near the earth so that the earth would have gone up in flames and his anxiety concerning this possibility became very great.

A year after this episode, the case was followed up. The 'Sun Man' had again taken up his previous occupation, namely, a fairly routine job in a factory, he was living with his parents again and, apart from them, he mixed with no one else except close blood relations. It then transpired that a time before his schizophrenic break, he had had an unfortunate experience in which a friend, the only one he had ever had, left him in the lurch by not keeping a certain appointment and by failing to contact him afterwards. Apparently this young man had been able to lead a meaningful although narrow existence in that he was open only to a very restricted portion of the world. However, when the friend showed himself to be unreliable, it broke up the boundaries of his narrow everyday existence lived within the confines of his house, his friendship and the factory where he was able to encounter the same trusted things over and over again. What followed was that a catastrophic widening of the boundaries of this existence structured an openness which had no limits to it. In other words, pulled out of the trusted context of everyday life, being no longer able to run smoothly in the grooves that he had cut for himself, his existence suddenly became a boundlessly open one. The possibility of living in the fashion of an ordinary fully grown wakeful person was wiped out of his Dasein and this loss he could see from the 'hallucinated' appearance of the man who was sleeping under the 'sun'.

This suggests (p. 501) that his being-a-self has been severely undermined. As a corollary of his unfree helplessness, his encounter with the world became such that the significant thing in his life shows itself to him as a cosmic structure and dominates his existence. In his life, the sun was the origin of all vitality and growth but at the same time the sun was that which can consume and destroy everything. The sun thus overcame him as the knowledge of something that embodies both being and at the same time non-being.

Put another way, it seems that what happens in the case where an acute schizophrenic episode takes place is that, due to the disintegration of the usual boundaries of existence, the person becomes confronted with the boundlessness which is the true and ultimate form of our existence which in this, then, reality presents itself to him in a different profile. Put differently, it means that the person who is trying to categorize his experience and make sense of his life happens, in some cases, to be the product of trying to live an impossible existence, as the work of Laing has made clear. In this 'impossible' existence the person can no longer share socially validated reality. However, he does not thereby cease relating to the world or perceiving the world in a meaningful fashion. The world presents itself to him in a hitherto unexperienced fashion. His usual attunement to the world falls away and he now becomes attuned in anxiety. Anxiety then, in this context, means a loss of one's hold on the usual attunedness that one has with the world.

As a further example, the same client whom I have previously mentioned in connection with the chair commanding him, told me that he was one day sitting by himself on a lonely hill and he was thinking. He was looking at the clouds and then he saw God in the clouds. He immediately told himself that God could not possibly be in the clouds but, none the less, he could see God in the clouds. In an age such as ours which is said to be characterized by the radical absence of God, such a statement seems extremely improbable and cannot be said to be scientifically verifiable or socially validated in any going sense of those terms. But since God remains a part of our total possible cosmic reality, it is, in principle, possible for a human being to see God in the clouds. Although I could not experience this with him, and although I myself have not seen God in the clouds, it nevertheless remains possible for one to relate to the world in such a way that God will show Himself to us in some way. When we speak of the absence of God, it could also be interpreted to mean that God shows Himself by His absence. Something showing itself by its absence, is, in principle, possible for us and not foreign to our experience. We may remember the example of Van den Berg's friend showing himself by his absence when Van den Berg looked at the bottle. One waits for a friend at a certain place but the friend does not show up. However, the friend is very much present in the shape the world takes, the forlornness or desolation of the place where we are waiting for him. Godot is very much present in the play 'Waiting for Godot'.

To say then, as conventional psychology does, that a hallucination is a perception without an object which, it is implied, should be traced to some form of brain dysfunction or some irregularity within a container called psyche would be to overlook the nature of the experience of being able to hallucinate. Describing it as a subjective perception is simply another way of discrediting the experience. The alternative view is to see the 'hallucination' as a perceptual act by which an alternate profile of reality appears. What Westerners term hallucinations may be acceptable perceptions of reality in another culture.

Thus the Xhosa diviner is, amongst other functions, a seer. It is his function to *see* evil influences in his patients and initiates and to rid them of these influences. A diviner said: 'I had a case of ukupambana [madness]: in the course of treatment I saw a bat coming out of his mouth. Sometimes I myself dream that the affected initiate has the impundulu' (Kruger 1978, p. 475). Both the impundulu (lightning bird) and the bat (ilulwane) are highly negative and powerful forces of evil in Xhosa cosmology. Both are as real as magnetic functions and molecules are in Western scientific cosmology.

In the case of the 'Sun Man' as well as the young man who saw God in the clouds, it is simply undescriptive to state that these were 'objectively' speaking, perceptions without object. The 'Sun Man' clearly said that he knew that he was not looking at the sun in the ordinary sense of the term, but he was nevertheless also not saying that the sun as it appeared on his wall constituted an 'objective' perception. If we say that only 'objective' perceptions are real, we pretend that we have a hold on reality in all its manifestations and by what right can we do this except possibly by absolutizing the empiricistic, positivistic, materialistic approach of natural science and demanding tangibles. If we do that, how then do we explain the phenomenon of the after image? This also, after all, reflects a perceptual experience for which there is no tangible object in terms of contemporary natural scientific thinking. To the 'Sun Man', his perception of the sun on the wall was so clear that he was convinced that anyone standing next to him would have been able to see it as well. However, he realized the dependence of this sun on its relationship to him because he said that he was afraid to close his eyes in case it would vanish. It was therefore to him, at that moment, a valuable experience. However, in both this case and that of God in the clouds we note one feature which is important for any 'hallucination'. That feature is that the perceiver is alone. He is not able to share his reality with someone else. Psychopathology may be described, in the words of J. H. van den Berg, as the science of loneliness.

The schizophrenic who hallucinates has a profile of the world, but for himself alone. He thus has a world of his own that is grounded in loneliness. Even the 'normal' person who is subject to complete isolation, will 'hallucinate' after a while, as has clearly been shown by experiments on sensory deprivation.

When we try to understand the hallucination of the schizophrenic by asking ourselves about the object of this perception which would be 'there' for us as well, it means that we are equalizing hallucination to ordinary perception 'which in turn means to wish that the mentally ill would stop being ill. The mentally sick person, once he is better, can tell us nothing sensible about his hallucinations. His hallucinations, his inapproachability and the fact that he cannot be understood, are all one and the same thing: his illness' (Van den Berg 1972, p. 103). It should be clearly understood that from the perspective of the ordinary person a schizophrenic's existence is different and also incomprehensible. This leads to the somewhat nihilistic conclusion by Jeff Coulter that the logical status of the concept of madness is such that if we could understood it, it would cease being madness. However, it is clear from previous examples that although we cannot necessarily share the world of the schizophrenic in the sense that we can 'see' his 'hallucinations' the structure of his world can be understood and his experiences remain communicable and credible. As long as we view the schizophrenic from an external scientistic frame of reference his 'symptoms' will be incomprehensible and bizarre; if we are able to consult his experience of his world, this experience becomes meaningful and coherent.

Similarly, the person who has delusions is alone in his world. The paranoid schizophrenic has a structure of the world in which he is persecuted by others. However, as we have seen it depends much on what is accepted as relevant and what is screened out as being irrelevant. We are all dimly conscious of the fact that even our friends are not entirely positively tuned towards us which means that our friends do have some reservations about our likeableness, our intelligence and so on. However, in the ordinary course of events, we do not allow this to become a theme in our being-with-others. However, persons with delusions of grandeur and persecution are people who are attuned to the world in such a way that this aspect of people's interactions is very prominent in their being-with-others in a shared world.

The question now arises whether the approach sketched here can come to grips with what has been called (in psychiatry) the primary symptoms of schizophrenia, namely, disturbed thought processes, affective disturbances, and disturbance of the ego-feeling in the sense of a subjective depersonalization. If we start from the premise that being-in-a-schizophrenic-state, as it is sketched above, means trying to live a life of shattered boundaries and overwhelmed by a salient, restricted aspect of being we should attempt to understand these symptoms in terms of what happens in the life of a person to whom a profile of reality that is not socially validated has been revealed. Let us suppose that one is in a schizophrenic episode and one is walking through a park at night. One hears the wind through the trees. However, in one's new relation to the cosmic totality, it could well be that the wind in the trees can no longer be conceptualized simply as the movement of air through the leaves which creates a certain level and quality of sound due to the friction of these leaves. If this is no longer one's reality, how does one then describe one's present reality? *Where does one find the words?* However, if one is none the less under pressure – as one will be because one continues to live interpersonally – to give some sense to what one has been experiencing and to give some explication of the way one has been living, then one must nevertheless try to say what is happening in one's life. Since ordinary words and sentences are inadequate to describe this, it follows then that one cannot give an adequate account of one's experience and, lacking this, one would hardly be able to think in terms ordinarily regarded as logical.

From the point of view of socialization in our society one's affectivity too would appear to be inappropriate. Let us go back to the case of Mandy who, it appears, did not become schizophrenic but whose experience is sufficiently idiosyncratic to serve as an example of one of the possibilities of a schizophrenic existence. Let us suppose that she, as an adult, had become extremely upset at a tree being chopped down, it is most likely that people around her would have regarded this as an abnormal reaction, as a sign that there was 'something wrong with her'. Such an expression of distress, a verbalization of 'you are killing the tree', crying over the tree, being shocked at the signs of the tree bleeding, all this would have been taken as inappropriate emotion or an affective disturbance.

As regards the feelings of depersonalization, we may speculate that in the examples sketched above there is a change in the person's relationship to the world. There is a change therefore in the person's being a self, i.e. having a secure relationship to the world which is his. He is now suddenly confronted with a profile of the world which he cannot accept as being his, cannot carry out in socially acceptable forms of behaviour, cannot actualize in the usual ways. He therefore cannot relate to others in the ways he has done up to now. With the change of his world, fellow man changes as well. Fellow man becomes peripheral to his world, fellow men become strange, alienated creatures with whom he cannot communicate and share. Fellow man can no longer be related to within the trusted context of being-in-the-world in the same way as I am. Fellow man, by going about his ordinary business, contradicts the reality of the schizophrenic and therefore he becomes an incomprehensible being. Thus, the prereflective being-with-others is shattered and this, together with the loss of being-a-self in freedom, leads to depersonalization.

THE CLINICAL PSYCHOLOGIST IN THE HOSPITAL

The clinical psychologist often has to work in a mental hospital, which means that he has to work within the classic paradigm of mental illness. In some cases the position of the clinical psychologist is further confounded and complicated by legislation which seems to aim at protecting the psychiatrist from undue competition with the clinical psychologist. Thus, in South Africa, the clinical psychologist is not *legally* allowed to make a diagnosis. However, in actual mental hospital work, it is the clinical psychologist who studies diagnostic features of any one case extensively and supplies a diagnostic work-up to the psychiatrist. It is only when it goes out of the hospital that the clinical psychologist has no right to put his name to it. Although clinical psychologists in South Africa can give expert testimony on mental states to courts of law, this inconsistency is to be ironed out in new legislation which will ensure that only psychiatrists can present such expert testimony. However unfair this may seem to the clinical psychologist, it is the identified patient for whom we should be concerned, and the first task of the clinical psychologist should be to serve his interests, protect his humanness and help him return to a dignified existence in the community. If we look at the issue from this point of view, then the important facet of the present mental health system is not so much the question of the reduction in stature of the clinical psychologist, but rather the question of the reduction of stature and humanity of the identified patient (Kruger 1976).

In order to make the best of the situation in the mental hospital, the clinical psychologist can participate in reforms that may be possible within the system. He will thus not allow his energies to be restricted to purely diagnostic routine work, but will also be involved with the enterprise of the quality of life of the mental patient, the nursing staff, the relations, employers, family and friends of the identified mental patient and, last of all, of himself. He should keep in mind the following:

Firstly, man characterized as being-in-the-world has as an essential feature, an originary understanding of being, i.e. of himself, fellow man and world. The schizophrenic or any other person labelled mentally ill by no means loses the basis for understanding, nor do other people lose their ability to understand him. However, there is a communication barrier and the clinical psychologist should not do anything to elaborate this barrier but rather understand the reasons for its being there at all. The clinical psychologist should be fully cognizant of the fact that scientific diagnosis, in the sense of placing a person into a specific category, serves the needs of society. The temptation to do this is great, because we are usually in the position where we have to face our fear of the unknown when we come across a person who has stepped off the narrow bridge spanning the void. There is something uncanny about the schizophrenic. The praecox feeling of which Rümke spoke is real and authentic, but it should not be misconstrued as revealing something that is either *in* the patient or *in* the psychiatrist. Rather it should reveal to us the uncanny nature of the *encounter* with someone who has broken with aspects of a shared reality in which we usually live and feel at home. Because this encounter is frightening, making a classification into nosological categories may be a defensive strategy. The clinical psychologist should be aware to what extent his satisfaction in doing this work serves his own need rather than that of the identified patient. By rather holding on to the fact that this fellow man, called schizophrenic, has not lost his basic understanding of being, he is keeping open the possibilities for meaningful communication.

A second important point is to realize that clinical psychology is not an applied science, i.e. is not the application of psychology as constituted now. The good clinical psychologist is not the person who knows experimental and physiological psychology (although this may be handy), who knows how to measure, who knows about correlation coefficients, factor analyses, etc. The clinical psychologist is a person who fearlessly and calmly strives to open himself up to the reality of the other person. He can face the anxiety generated by an encounter with a person whose life is entangled. He is not afraid to reach out into the void sometimes and not scared to listen to someone whom he cannot, for the moment, understand. He has a certain faith in his fellow man which leads him to believe that no matter how uncommunicative and incomprehensible the fellow man (called patient) may be at a certain moment, the nature of man's existence will enable him to reach out and thus to succeed in serving as a bridge on which the struggling person can again tread the path which he can share with others in a common world.

Thirdly, the clinical psychologist is no technologist. We are fond of using the medical profession as a model and one of the main things that strikes us about the contemporary medical profession is that it has a large armoury of technical procedures at its disposal. Being a doctor means that one is powerful, but this power is derived from technology and not from something inherent in the medical enterprise. Clinical psychologists would sometimes like to develop technology. A formidable example, the Rorschach, became a symbol of their power because it created in fantasy (seldom in practice) the impression that a clinical psychologist could 'read your mind', that he did not need your own powers of understanding to come to an understanding.

We cannot, however, develop a Rorschach technology because the Rorschach is not really a technique in the sense that its results are self-revealing to the experienced operator who knows the rules. The rules of Rorschach interpretation are only a start; in the real sense one always remains a beginner. The main challenge of interpretation is always the attempt to enter the world of a testee. Thus, the test will always remain a challenge to the psychologist as a person to articulate his understanding and experience of fellow man. The many attempts to psychometricize the test (e.g. that of Holtzmann) combine a fine regard for statistical manipulability with a profound indifference to the human experiential reality.

Although man is, in the last analysis, inherently unpredictable, technocracy, in view of its long-range production, marketing and social planning, demands predictable human 'responses'. This is certainly not what clinical psychology is all about. Its endeavour should not be to make man predictable but to enlarge his existence by helping him to increase the sphere of his freedom. Should the role of the clinical psychologist require him to participate in predictive processes, he should point out to the client that these are requirements imposed by society and what is 'measured' cannot evaluate his humanness. It only helps to constitute the outer contours and restraints of his situation.

PHENOMENOLOGICAL PSYCHOTHERAPY: AN EXAMPLE

The phenomenological approach to psychotherapy has been called Daseinsanalysis by Medard Boss, Ludwig Binswanger and others. Whether we use this term or not, this approach may be defined as a situation in which one human being (therapist) is available to other human beings (clients) as fellow human being in the attitude of *Gelassenheit* or let-be-ness which is a special and active rather than passive participation in the unfolding being-ness of the other person aimed at grasping those relational meaning coherences of the world that are specifically the client's, so as to facilitate his taking upon himself that existence which is his own. Psychotherapy, in this sense, is essentially an enterprise by which client and therapist strive towards a common aim, namely, to disclose what the meanings of their respective lives are. This is the same as saying that authentic existence aims at a fearless disclosure of life's meanings. The therapist–client relationship implies that the therapist already has a better hold on what his life is uniquely about than does the client on his own life, but that every experience of the client represents to the therapist also a growth towards meaning, whereas for the client the idea is that the whole relationship should essentially revolve around his efforts to arrive at the meaning structure which constitutes his life.

How do we do this sort of therapy? The approach of Daseinsanalysis may be characterized as a set of attitudes rather than a set of techniques. In fact, Daseinsanalytic or phenomenological therapy is quite indifferent to techniques to the extent that one may be practising the method of psychoanalysis, Frankl's paradoxical intention, client-centred psychotherapy or even a form of behaviour therapy and still be a Daseinsanalytic therapist. In what follows I am going to illustrate the Daseinsanalytic approach to 'psychopathology' and psychotherapy from the point of view of a client who underwent a major therapy. Most, if not all, of the case histories and therapeutic interactions described in the literature, are delineated from the point of view of the therapist. However, in this present case study, the whole therapeutic experience is described in terms of its meaning structures for the client. This is possible because, after completion of the therapy, M. Eppel (1978) researched the client's experience of psychotherapy and this I am using as a basis for what is to follow. Obviously the important thing about psychotherapy is the client's experience thereof.

The therapist's report is briefly that the woman, who is identified in the protocol by the pseudonym of Sara, was a married woman in her early twenties when she was first seen in a major psychotherapy which lasted more than two years with certain interruptions. She was unhappy in her work and changed jobs soon after starting in psychotherapy. Although she was a qualified teacher, she did not want to return to her profession but changed to a different post in which she was also unhappy. She suffered from various 'psychosomatic disorders', namely, frigidity, eczema and asthma and, in addition, developed a stomach ulcer whilst in the early stages of therapy. She stated that her husband was a good, intelligent and understanding person and the fact that she was sexually frigid was very distressing to her. She also stated that she was almost child-like in her dependence on him and that he did a lot for her which most married women do for themselves, e.g. shopping etc. Much of her childhood had been unhappy, especially her relationship with her mother who drank rather heavily. Her parents' marriage, as she described it, could be characterized both as unhappy as well as schismatic. She had one sister who was unhappy in the home situation and unlike Sara actively rebelled against the parents.

Sara was unhappy at school and often was sick, unable to cope, but she did manage to do quite well in certain subjects. Some of her teachers she found quite difficult to get on with, whilst one or two inspired her to a great interest in literature which she has retained. At times she wrote both poetry and prose but she had never published anything.

At the first interview, Sara impressed the therapist as being a submissive, non-assertive, unhappy person. Throughout the therapy she was easily moved to tears. She had great difficulty in relating to her parents although she loved her father very much but she could not entirely trust him either.

The therapist was impressed by the fact that, although Sara seemed to be quite an attractive woman, she was dressed in a rather dowdy manner, wore spectacles that made her look even more turned into herself and he also received the impression that she was quite anxious.

During the second year of therapy, according to Eppel (1978), it so happened that both the therapist and Sara's husband, Bobby, were away at the same time. At this stage, Sara went to her physician and said that she had decided to leave her husband. His advice to her was not to do any such thing but to try again. However, she remained adamant, and when her therapist came back she told him that she had decided to leave her husband. He accepted this and simply asked whether she would like to tell him why. In her own words, 'I then broke down and this was our first real contact'. What she meant here was that, before that time, she had found it impossible to open herself up in therapy, to really and genuinely face up to her problems, and this time when she had taken the decision which was accepted by the therapist, she started being really herself. She then had the brief affair with a young man whom she found very attractive, but soon left him on a mutually agreed basis because she felt that, although she could have an exciting time with him, she was not genuinely in love with him.

Later on, she took up a relationship with a man called David. Sara, herself, had returned to full-time study in the meantime. When therapy ended Sara had changed into a beautiful, attractive, sexually warm and creative person.

It is possible, in view of Eppel's research, to describe therapeutic change in terms of the basic characteristics of being human as outlined in chapter II. However, we shall restrict ourselves to one aspect only, namely, the change in Sara's being-a-body and then consider how Sara experienced the psychotherapy process.

According to her therapist, when Sara was at school, her teachers, who were nuns, told the children, pointing to the figure of the crucified Christ, that if they were naughty they would be hammering more nails into the suffering body of Christ. When this was said, she somehow felt herself being pierced. Her frigidity tied up with the fear of being penetrated and she was anxious about using tampons. Shortly after her divorce and on the insistence of her ex-husband, the therapist arranged a joint interview. At one stage in this interview, when her husband was quite bitter about the broken relationship, certain questions were put to her and certain statements made to her by her husband. The therapist observed her having the beginnings of an asthma attack and he asked her what was happening and how she was feeling. She then stated: 'I am being invaded.' Here we can clearly see how 'psychosomatic symptoms' were part and parcel of the bodiliness of this client. More specifically, her bodiliness is characterized by what she herself calls her need for a large personal space. It is certainly not only in relation to her psychosomatic disorders that her bodiliness is manifested in her report of her experience of psychotherapy. For example, she also says (Eppel, 1978): 'people around tend to hassle me quite a lot because I like being on my own and people intrude on my personal space all the time. And I go to X and I say, what can I do? He says, you know, "you got the right to be on your own" and then suddenly I think, Ja, why not, I have a right as an individual to be myself and I don't have to justify myself to other people or try and make them like me.'

She also states: 'So my therapy was incredibly traumatic for me. In fact, I got much worse and I had sort of physical symptoms, like I started an ulcer during therapy and I got quite bad asthma attacks, because I just didn't want him (the therapist) to find out what was going on.'

That her bodily being-in-the-world was involved in her problematic life and her therapy is illustrated by the statement 'you know, we had this thing, afterwards (X and me), we developed a sort of image of me as a rag-doll, because I had a dream once that I was a rag-doll, and everyone was throwing me around. We sort of decided that this was in fact what I am or was, you know, a rag-doll: I was allowing everyone else to live my life for me and I just didn't have the courage to say "this is what I want".'

How her bodiliness was changing during the course of the therapy also became clear in the assertion: 'Every session I went to, I realized what was happening to me, how much I was getting out of it. Everytime I walked out of his room, I felt lighter, whereas before, I felt heavier. Before that time, I wanted to cry and go to sleep to get away from it, to get away from what was emerging in therapy.'

How the psychosomatic problem was and is being resolved by Sara is illustrated by the statement: 'I realized that I had to admit to myself that I'd been using all these psychosomatics, that I'd been a big fraud and that I'd been play-acting all the time and that I'd been wanting people to feel sorry for me.' Further on the

same page she says: 'whenever I get a cold or I get asthma or
something now, I say to myself, you're not fooling me.'

The existential meaning of the upright stature is expressed by
her in a later statement: 'You'd think that it would have left me
sort of faltering and not sure, but it left me discovering a fantastic
pair of healthy legs (this was after her seeing that her
psychosomatics served as an excuse) and thinking "but all this
time I have been going round on crutches when I got the best legs
in the world to stand on".' Her identity is related to her bodiliness: 'The fact is that X had the insight to see it beneath all that
stuff that I used to cover it up, and the insight to see that I could
throw off all my sickbed crutches and all that, and *be* myself
without those aids. You know, when I went to X I had no
identity.' The pact between body and world is well illustrated by
her remark: 'I hated my body, I hated this thing that has
represented me and the fact that I didn't want to be inside my
body because it represented my marriage, my whole sickness sort
of somatic thing. It represented me, the dominated child by my
parents. But there, somewhere inside me, *was* a spirit which was
me.'

J. H. van den Berg says that the body shapes itself in accordance with its task in the world. We can clearly see here that
Sara's body shaped itself in accordance with her world in which
she cowered away from contact and confrontation with others. It
was a body which had the task of covering up her true feelings but
thereby also made her-as-body an object in the eyes of the other.

In the research interview she put this clearly, stating that
'because my body symbolized my interaction with the world, and
I wasn't interacting with the world, so by withdrawing from my
body, I was trying to cut off my interaction with the world. And
once I got *back* into my body and I accepted my situation in the
world, I could have a balanced sort of life again.' When therapy
started changing Sara, she became very aware of her need for
personal space and she became very aggressive to people who
intruded into it. However, this problem was solved because she
said: 'slowly I learnt to make my personal space more logical, that
in fact it isn't my body that is so important. I've learnt not to hate
my body, you know. I am allowed my personal space.'

The 'process' of psychotherapy

Apart from the changed bodiliness, the other categories of
Sara's experience of psychotherapy can, no doubt, also be read in
the following account, e.g. timeness, life history and spatiality of
which we have already seen something in 'personal space'. However, in what now follows we shall try to get to grips with the

movement that takes place in therapy. Eppel (p. 174 et seq.) was able to divide the client's experience into five categories:

(a) The actual sessions and movement from the initial stages to the more meaningful later stages.
(b) Her experience of insight.
(c) Her experience of the therapist and her relationship to him.
(d) The value of her therapy in terms of how she presently experiences her existence.
(e) The client's general experience of her therapy and her evaluation of this.

(a) Eppel finds that, in the first year in therapy, the client avoided confronting her life situation, because she found it too painful. She found it traumatic and anxiety provoking to face herself and although she was not fully aware of avoiding her problems, she feels that 'somewhere she must have known that being open with the therapist would mean a rather painful confrontation with her life'. Initially she experienced her therapy as just another demand which she could not fulfil; this being quite typical of her response to various other demands in her daily life. She felt threatened by the therapist, in that she saw him as challenging her to be open with herself and to change, and she felt inauthentic in that she wasn't really changing.

However, after the first year, she made her first really honest contact with her therapist. This breakthrough resulted from an insight between the sessions. This was at a time when the therapist was away and, during his absence, she felt that she had to leave her husband. When she told this to X, he calmly asked her to tell him why she wanted to do this. In her own words, 'and I broke down and that's when we made our first contact'. She realized that when she told him this 'secret of hers' that she was being totally honest with him and with herself for the first time. She then became increasingly aware of herself as a self-sufficient person and she could, for the first time, allow herself some genuine aggression. This signified for her the beginnings of true self-expression and acceptance of herself as a whole person who could live and express herself through her body. She then came to accept body and self as one.

(b) *The client's experience of insight.* Sara felt that insight was the integration of her greater ability to see into herself with the experiencing of this increased understanding which meant for her greater freedom in living her life.

Insight did not necessarily occur in the sessions. Sara came to insights on her own but she feels that it was particularly meaningful to her when she came to this insight *outside* the therapy session. Although the insights could develop suddenly in the actual session, either through a comment from the therapist or a dream explication, insight for her was mainly a process of gradually coming to some realization. However, the insights did not bring about a change in her life. This was because an insight in itself required time to work through and greater courage in order to live or experience that insight in her daily life, and, secondly, when she had the courage to tell her therapist that she had been a fraud, this was the beginning of a greater freedom in her life. By that also, she took an irrevocable step, namely, to take full responsibility for her life. As we have seen in the section on the unconscious, progress in therapy means enlarging the scope of one's responsibility, taking responsibility for what one would otherwise blame on circumstances or the 'unconscious'. Although the insight did not necessarily free her from these specific problems of psychosomatics, she became aware of the fact that these were under her control and so when she 'gets' psychosomatics, she can decide to do something about it and not give in to it as she always did in the past.

(c) *The client's experience of the therapist and her relationship to him.* Undoubtedly, Sara experienced her therapist as a crucial factor in facilitating growth and development. She attributes the rediscovery of herself and the unfolding of her existence to her relationship with the therapist. In retrospect she realizes that during the first year of therapy the therapist was conscious of the fact that she was avoiding confronting her life. However, although she was sure the therapist had the insight to see the basic person that she was, and although she experiences her therapist as having 'uncovered her with the shovel of therapy' he did not tell her this; he never pushed her but waited for her to grow at her own pace, to discover her own answers.

The relationship was experienced by her as a non-specific one and so she cannot point to any specific techniques used by the therapist. There was nothing specific that the therapist said. If he gave her courage to confront her life it was not by what he said, but rather by his whole attitude towards her which she saw as being always flexible – he could be indirective or directive, giving her clarification as he saw it, and even in his more directive attitudes some valuable insight could result for her. She was deeply aware of the therapist's caring attitude 'that he was determined to help her and that he had faith in her own capacity for growth'. She was also emphatic that the therapist helped in that he was always available. She experienced these therapist attitudes as giving her stature and the most important thing was that she believed that his attitude was totally genuine. She experienced the therapist as non-judgemental, as living her feelings with her; as gauging them as important and making them important to her by 'exploding' them. 'Exploding' refers to the fact that the therapist enabled Sara to confront a particular issue in her life by highlighting it. This enabled her to feel free to express and explore her own life and in this way she could develop an identity which she herself could accept and like.

(d) The client's experience of the value of her therapy. Sara had a very low self-esteem when she came into therapy, and hardly had an identity. In retrospect she sees the 'symptoms' such as 'psychosomatics' as an inauthentic way of life that allowed her to maintain some sort of relatedness to the world because she could at least get some sympathy from people around her. By this very same token, however, she could not open herself up to the world and therefore could not really encounter the world as herself. We can see, if we refer back to the section on Bodiliness how strongly this feeling was, in terms of helplessness, alienation from the body, feeling of intrusion and lack of personal space and her inability to satisfy her own need for personal privacy because she felt she had no rights of her own.

As therapy developed, Sara came to realize that her basic personhood was there all the time, but through therapy she could develop the courage to become the person that she always was – she has become more of what she already was. In other words, psychotherapy was a rediscovery of herself and will continue to be a discovery of herself in the sense that she will continually discover herself as the drama of her life unfolds over time.

She assimilated certain values from therapy, the most important of which was that she can now live a life and that she can be what she is without justifying it to other people. She is prepared to take life on with all the uncertainties and insecurities that it involves. She accepts both the negative, suffering parts of life as well as its fullness and its joy. With her newly found freedom she has become more self-assured and self-sufficient and feels herself to be a strong and vital person. She still has a great need for personal privacy and she can defend her personal space assertively if it is violated.

(e) The client's evaluation of her therapy. The client experienced her therapy as having been truly successful when both she and her therapist agreed that a definite positive transformation had taken place. The experience of success is, however, not in the sense that therapy changed her into 'someone else'. Rather she experienced therapy as successful in that it stimulated self-openness and helped her to accept responsibility for and to help her to become herself. She evaluated her therapy in terms of feeling that the therapist was always *available*, that he was someone with whom there existed a mutual faith, someone she knew understood her and had confidence in her ability to become what she now is. She

said: 'I think that was a sort of a fight against myself because I wanted to very much change because of his attitude of hope for me and obviously his faith won because it was stronger than my will not to grow.'

Sara does not see the value of therapy as having given her specific answers to specific questions. Therapy did not teach her to overcome problems or take her depressions away. She was never told how to live her life and, in fact, she never discussed some of her specific problems or symptoms. Therefore the vital part of therapy was not specific by-products such as being able to sleep at night, overcome her psychosomatics, or stand in bus-queues. The vital part was that therapy gave her a richer and deeper experience of life so that she was more aware of herself as a whole person living more genuinely as the person she is and not refusing to meet certain aspects of life because they might involve pain or suffering. She thought there was a magical quality to her therapist because she could not really isolate what actually happened in the sessions or what the therapist specifically did. Another important aspect of therapy that came out was that therapy did not happen in the session so much as it happened in between sessions and how she lived her life after the sessions. For her, therapy was really the place which opened up her life so that she could live it. When therapy was terminated after approximately two years, this was certainly not the end of her therapy. The outcome of her therapy was not as a static entity but as a continual growing and developing through life. She felt that much of what happened in therapy would only unfold in her life at a later stage. Eppel puts it this way: 'so she did not merely live her life in therapy at the time because her therapy dialogues with her life and her life dialogues with her therapy.' Her therapy stimulated self-openness and much of what she did not verbalize to the therapist became apparent to her only after the sessions. Her growing therefore took place outside the sessions and therapy was a place which opened up her life so that she could live it. This means that what happened in therapy has been integrated into her everyday life and so therapy, in a sense, never ends because it has meaning in terms of the unfolding of her life.

Eppel (pp. 190–3) gives the following essential description of the client's holistic and retrospective experience of psychotherapy:

'The client does not experience psychotherapy as an isolated event or series of events in her life. Therapy for the client does not end and has no specific result. The meaning of her therapy experience, which for the client is the most crucial part of her total experience of therapy, is not experienced as specific behaviours which she can now perform, but as a new qualitative enrichment of her whole life. This is because psychotherapy for the client is experienced as the medium through which she unfolds the meaning structures of her existence and gets to know herself, and from which she rediscovers herself learning to take on the life that is essentially hers, learning to confront all that which "speaks" to her in the world. This is a life-long process and psychotherapy is experienced by the client as an *initiation* into this process – a vital stimulating phase in her life's journey towards the discovery and experiencing of herself as a whole being, experiencing herself in and through her body, living and relating authentically to the world. Psychotherapy for the client does not end'.

'What is crucial for the client *retrospectively* is not what actually happens in the sessions, but the way she lives her life after the sessions, and therapy's residual nature which acts as a springboard for her whole life. She experiences the dialogic co-operative encounter of the therapeutic relationship as really the beginning of movement towards the process of change the nature of which is so subtle that the client is not fully aware of it at the time because it only gains momentum and is assimilated into her total life project as she goes on living her life. Therapy is therefore experienced by the client as having meaning for the rest of her life and increasing in meaning and value as she encounters new situations in her life. Therapy for the client is experienced as the trigger mechanism for a whole new life experience towards the process of growing and becoming what she already is. But the client only understands her experience of psychotherapy and its meaning for her as she gradually discovers herself, becomes what she is, and as her life unfolds through time and increasing world experience. Therapy for the client is not an event or place that changes a specific bundle of symptoms. Instead, the client experiences therapeutic change as a gradual process of becoming what she already was by learning to be open with herself.

'The client experiences actual therapy as a withdrawal to a place without outside pressure, a place where she is in battle with herself and her life situation, a struggle with herself in the attempt to discover or rediscover her core being so that she can take on the life that is hers. But this struggle does not come to a halt at the end of the sessions.

'Initially the client experiences the pain of self-confrontation and the confusion as to the direction of therapy. While there is a longing for growth, there is also a desperate fear of growth – the fear of unfamiliar freedom and openness of being and the desire to remain within the familiar but encapsulated security of her unhappiness or reduced world openness. Thus the confusion as to what to do in therapy and how to do it and the avoidance or denial of those areas of her life that she cannot face. But at the time, the client is not fully aware of her avoidance of her life situation.

'The client experiences her therapy as initially hoping to find something definite or permanent on which to depend. She refuses to take responsibility for her own life, not being fully aware of this at the time, and experiences a need for the therapist to provide answers. Instead the client begins to realize and experience that the answers lie within herself, that life is unpredictable and that she has to learn to live with the security of insecurity. Therapy is not experienced as providing answers or focusing on specific symptoms but as enabling the client to take responsibility for her own life, to face the inevitable joys and sufferings that go with life and to live with and through them.

'In the struggle towards the development of courage to confront all possibilities of her existence, the relationship with the therapist is experienced by the client as crucial. Within the safe encounter of this relationship, the client experiences the therapist as providing the framework within which she can explore her life. But that framework represents her own standards of authenticity and self-honesty. The client experiences her therapist as leading her along her own life path without giving explicit direction so she is not aware of his lead, only his reassuring presence. Thus the client discovers that the meaning of her life can only be revealed not explained. The therapist's listening to the client is not experienced as merely hearing the client but rather an active listening that reflects also the kind of person he is. The client experiences her therapist by what he is not what he does.

'Through the relationship the client begins to experience a commitment to her own struggle. But that commitment includes for the client, the commitment of the therapist towards that struggle. The client experiences this commitment in the form of attitudes conveyed from the therapist and not techniques. She experiences and feels the therapist's genuine but flexible attitudes of faith, total acceptance, respect and availability and feels that these attitudes enable her to develop courage to open herself to herself and to confront her life situation, to articulate those aspects of her life which she has been denying, to explore the landscape of her life, to develop, integrate and experience insight and to begin to come to terms with her life situation accepting the person that she is and experiencing the freedom that is hers. Psychotherapy is experienced by the client as an initiation into the process of unfolding and living her true potential and the actual sessions are the medium through which she learns to be open with herself – in order to live and experience an authentic existence. What happened *in* the actual sessions and its ever increasing meaning and value for her whole life cannot be meaningfully separated. For the client they are part of the same process.'

The above makes clear that what is essential in psychotherapy is not an exploration of the derivation of symptoms as such. The therapist in the therapy sketched above did not focus on the symptoms. What he did was to allow the client to unfold her life meanings progressively as she experienced them, to create the necessary atmosphere in which she could express these, to be available as fellow man to the client during the entire process of psychotherapy. As the client progressed in therapy, it became clear that the key to understanding was not through the symptoms themselves, but rather through the way in which the client lived her life, the strategies which she used in order to avoid challenges, suffering and encounters with others and the world. As she got a grip on these, as she was able to take those aspects of the world that had special meaning for her upon herself, her psychosomatic symptoms started retreating and eventually, as we have seen, she was able to realize that she was using her 'symptoms' as a crutch, thus establishing her mastery over them and being able to live without them in that she could now take upon herself the joy and suffering that constituted her life.

CHAPTER VI

Concluding Remarks

In chapter I we had a look at the dilemmas posed to psychology by Cartesian dualism and noted that the different schools of psychology were attempts to overcome these. Having looked at the possibilities of building psychology on an alternative paradigm, namely, on a prescientific encounter with man as articulated by an anthropological philosophy based primarily upon the ontology of Martin Heidegger, we can see how we could redefine the subject.

It should be clear by now that a phenomenological psychology rejects the intrapsychic view of man. Psychology therefore cannot define itself as the study of individual behaviour. There is no 'individual' in the sense of an isolated subjectivity. The task of psychology is to study human *existence* in the sense of how we live our lives. For the same reason, psychology cannot define itself as the 'scientific study of the behaviour of organisms' because the view of the human being as organism would simply give us the encapsulated organism instead of the encapsulated psyche and would mean that we substitute a scientific conception for the human being as we encounter him in everyday life. We have further seen that it is impossible to do experimentation in such a way that all 'variables' can be 'controlled'. The person only lives in and as relationship to the world and the project of experimental psychology cannot overcome the contextual embeddedness of the person and therefore it is, in principle, impossible to predict human behaviour.

The elucidation of cause-effect sequences is inherently part and parcel of the project of natural scientific psychology, whether this be seen in the context of discrete schools or eclectic psychology. One may be tempted to believe that meanings may emerge from an explanation based on a causal account, but this view is in error. In natural science, mechanical determinism can only mean that once a certain set of necessary and sufficient contingencies (A) has been specified, a further event or effect (B) will *follow*. It can never be said that B *arises out of A*. It is therefore, impossible, in principle, for meanings to be explicated through a causal account. It is sometimes argued that causality in the social sciences is different from or independent of the physical science paradigm. In such a case, however, it would be incumbent on the advocates of social or psychological 'causality' to formulate a logically consistent and generally acceptable alternative paradigm.

180

Whilst cause-effect thinking is implicit and evident in all natural scientific psychologies, radical behaviourism distinguishes itself by its insistence, in blatant disregard for the human nature of its subject-matter, that the science of psychology can be projected only on the basis of the prediction and control of behaviour. Whilst the other schools of psychology, including the eclecticists, are at least trying to remain true, to some extent, to humanness as it is encountered in everyday life, and to try to live with the confusion engendered by Cartesian dualism and the setting up of the priorities of the natural scientific method, the behaviourists – in order to make man amenable to the method of their choice – are distorting and devaluating the human being into an object that emits responses (like a charged battery). It is an assumption of the phenomenological attitude that the scientific method used in research shall dialogue with the subject-matter. However, the only way in which behaviouristic approaches can be seen to be dialoguing with their subject-matter is in the nature of the human being as he is distorted by the bureaucratization of a technological order. In view of the fact that the human being is inherently unpredictable, the behaviouristic approaches seem to be in dialogue with technology: large-scale enterprises and long-term planning of production of marketing schedules require predictable human 'responses' and behaviourism is a suitable way of speaking of modern man openly in the sense and to the extent that he can be distorted to fit into an engineered society.

The basic assumption with which psychoanalysis *started* can be accepted by a phenomenological psychology. This basic assumption was that symptoms, and therefore by extension all acts of human beings, can be seen as meaningful. Furthermore, the biographical approach in which man is seen as history and in which his identity can be seen to be co-constituted by time is acceptable. However, a phenomenological psychology must reject the reductionistic emphasis of psychoanalysis as well as the inner view of man. It can go along with the psychoanalytic rejection of the concept of rational man. However, in so far as rational man is self-determining man, psychoanalysis went too far in its rejection of rationalism and its positing man as essentially determined by passion which in turn reduces to energy. However, psychoanalysts remain much less blatant in their rejection of the moment of truth contained in rationalistic conceptions than the behaviourist. Truly great men such as Freud and Jung lived far too near the realities of being human to be guilty of such gross over-simplifications.

Psychology cannot be indifferent to the image of man that it projects to the public. So fascinated are behavioural and related approaches to the problem of man by mechanomorphic models that the experienceable and well-known human phenomenon of being able to reflect and evaluate one's behaviour is conceptualized and thinned down to a concept of feedback and a mechanical concept like governor is taken over from mechanics rather than to question the 'words governor or governance to uncover its originary meaning in our lives. It is degrading that psychology should look for its models in mechanics while mechanics itself looks for its models in the lived world of everyday experience.

From this it follows also that psychology cannot be an ethically neutral enterprise. As has been pointed out several times in preceding chapters, man's existence cannot be understood except in the sense of being related to various aspects of the totality of meanings called world. Dasein therefore means a taking upon one's self, a caring for of those aspects which specially appeal to one. Care may thus be said to be the being of being-in-the-world (Heidegger 1972, pp. 191–9). In this pervading care structure of life, then, the contradiction between 'is' in the sense of 'exist' or existence of man and 'should' is overcome. In our encounter with fellow man, in the mood of letting-be-ness and in our explication of this encounter, a science of psychology unfolds as an endeavour to describe the meaningfulness of lives which are themselves processes of unfolding.

Psychologists cannot but take the initiative in describing human potential and therefore must necessarily identify societal structures which inhibit, thwart or confound such unfolding. The psychologist must name and describe these; must not be afraid of being a social critic. A science and profession of psychology cannot be true to itself if it supports distorted postures of humanness, required by at least some aspects of the present system. A psychology which designs itself in such a way that it 'fits' people into systems, designed by and for a self-validating and self-perpetuating technology and its concomitant technocracy, which 'adjusts' people to conditions which should not have existed in the first place, can only be scorned. The ultimate horror is the behavioural technologies which are now being peddled for use in mental hospitals, prisons and other institutions of which it may well be asked whether they 'treat', rehabilitate or 'demolish' the inmates (Rothman *et al.* 1972; see Illich 1977, p. 261). Furthermore, even their use in non-hospitalized populations must be seen as part of the overall strategy of 'human engineering to fit populations into engineering systems' (ibid.).

The psychological profession can assure itself of both influence and affluence by setting up a psychocracy (the powers-that-be will gladly co-operate provided psychologists can promise 'to deliver the goods' – and psycho-technology cum behaviour modification seems to be the most promising for this dismal project) but can only do so by failing to be *true* (there is no difference in the ethical and cognitive dimensions of this term in the present context) to its subject-matter. A psychocracy seems to be purchasable at the price of technologizing man's existence. In this way then, the governance of man's life becomes not only an organizational control of his physical and industrial environment, but the bureaucratization and computerization of his personal life as well. But when life and its joys are thus computerized and efficiency is the only value left, such an enterprise stands unveiled in its hostility to life itself.

The following definition can be proposed:

Psychology is an intersubjective, communicative science, systematically studying the structures of human existence by explicating lived (historical) experience.

The word *intersubjective* indicates that psychology must be a shared, validated enterprise. It is not necessary that we arrive at this intersubjectivity in the same way as in natural science where experiments can, in principle, be replicated in order to test the results of previous ones. It should suffice if the same or similar themes can be explicated in the same field by different researchers. The word *communicative* indicates that psychology is a science which must be built up by what people can communicate about their experience and action. Undoubtedly, language will be the most important medium and certainly it will prescribe the boundaries of the science. Language, says Heidegger, is the house of being and in that house man dwells. This implies that the meanings conveyed to us in the world of everyday experience are structured in language. What cannot be put into language cannot be material for science. The question then remains whether body or other 'languages' will be left out. There are many situations in which spoken and written language is not equal to the task of structuring our experience. Things that cannot be said in spoken-written language, can be said in music, in the dance, in drawing, etc. The lived body will give expression to what has not been said, or is unsayable, by the subject. It is obvious that body language is an inherent part of the phenomenological understanding of man but, at the same time, it means that body language, in order to be intersubjectively communicable between a community of scholars, will have to be turned into a communicable language. Illustrations may help, so may video-tape recordings. To be material for science, however, it is imperative that a verbal description should also be rendered. There are many problems and difficulties, but these can be overcome in a co-operative endeavour between the subject and the researcher. As we have seen in the case of Sara, the radical body language of her 'psychosomatics' was eventually understood and mastered. She articulated these in terms of her despair in her inability to face the challenges in her interpersonal, spatial and time world. The problem is therefore not insoluble, but the extent to which it will be solved in the practice of a science of psychology based on the phenomenological approach can be proved only by extensive research.

In the definition we talk about the *structures of human existence*. This is the same as saying that psychology should explicate the unwritten constitution of everyday life. Let us try to clarify this by means of an example. Two men are walking towards a river. When asked why they are doing this, one man replies that he is going in order to test for impurities in the water which he defines as a combination of hydrogen and oxygen atoms. The second man states that he is going to the river because he wants to make a sacrifice to his ancestors. Their encounter with the river is going to be an entirely different one. The structure of their existence, too, will be different. This gives us a clue to how psychology should set about the explication of the constitution of everyday life. If both these people are followed, they will also encounter, apart from the river, fellow man, future, past and present, natural and cultural artefacts, sickness and death, etc. The structures that we have to study are, for a defined population, e.g. contemporary Western man in South Africa, or Black persons belonging to a situated traditional group, or Western man in general, or urbanized (partly) Westernized Blacks in South Africa, etc., and to delineate for each population things of the world or meanings typically encountered by people in everyday life. However, what we study will also be determined by what is specially questionable so that the interests of psychology, in the abstract, cannot map unknown territory completely, but must let itself be guided by those questions which seem pertinent from a number of points of view.

Within the South African situation the contemporary encounter between Black and White constitutes a potentially explosive situation of which the experiential dimensions just cry out for explication and clarification. On the one hand what is the meaning of White fears and White identities etc. in terms of bodiliness, spatiality, being-with-others and historicity? On the other hand how are Whites perceived by Blacks?

The many attitude surveys that have been undertaken do not really answer the question and have not even been quoted by the one Black psychologist who has been trying to articulate the experience of being Black in South Africa (Manganyi 1973, 1977). What does it mean to be a Black person and how does the Black constitute himself as a person in relation to a society dominated by an affluent, powerful, White minority? Manganyi (1977*b*) raises the possibility of the negativity of the Black man's bodiliness in so far as he constitutes his being-a-body in terms of the dominant White sociological schemata. What is the nature of the dialectic between the body alienation of Western White industrial man and the negative body schemata of the semi-Westernized Black industrial worker? A somewhat bizarre light on these questions is thrown by the statements of Black 'schizophrenics' in a recent publication (Erasmus & Minnaar 1978, p. 4). Thus, a hospitalized Black aged 29 stated 'that he was born of an English father and an Afrikaans mother at Scotland Yard in England. . . . He maintains that he belongs to the English nation through his father but that his home language is Afrikaans through his mother.'

Erasmus & Minnaar also report a paranoid patient as looking carefully around him and saying: 'Sir, they are persecuting me for this: I am a White man in black skin. Please respect me accordingly.'

Erasmus & Minnaar comment that '. . . resentful identification with the privileged position of Whites in western society still forms part of the delusions of the mentally ill Black.' This comment can be accepted within the framework of classical concepts of mental illness. However, from the contextual point of view defended in this book, it should be seen as an extreme and blatant statement of the alienation of the lived body which may become evident as possibly part of everyday life in more wide-ranging research of being-black-in-the-world. The extreme loss of world openness and being free (see chapter V) is also clear.

By explicating man's various encounters with the world, psychology can contribute to man's articulated dialogue with the problems of being human in the historical epoch of the third quarter of the twentieth century.

Furthermore, psychology should explicate *lived (historical) experience*. It is impossible for a person to be involved in, for example, making love and to explicate this at the same time. However, it can be explicated afterwards. Here again we can see another limitation that cannot be overcome although it can be ameliorated. One can ask a person to explicate his experience of psychotherapy, but memory being what it is, one would not expect the subject to be able to explicate this fully. Therefore, various aids to memory, e.g. tape-recordings, video-tapes, etc., can be used. However, a complete exposition, in the sense of leaving absolutely nothing out, is impossible because explicating all experience will then encompass the whole of life. What are to be explicated are the essential themes of any such experience.

The emphasis in the definition on lived (historical) experience raises the interesting question whether a phenomenological approach to psychology can grapple with the question of historical psychology. J. H. van den Berg has undertaken an impressive and intriguing series of metabletic studies into human bodiliness (1959, 1960), spatiality with special reference to church architecture, the changing mathematics since the Renaissance and man's spirituality (1965, 1969, 1977), the changing personal landscape of man with special reference to childhood, puberty, adulthood, the unconscious and plural existence (1956, 1963, 1971, 1971) and has thereby greatly contributed to an understanding of contemporary Western man in terms of how he came to be where he is at *now*. He himself describes this method as a phenomenological one to a certain point only. Husserlian phenomenology in its later phases restricted itself to a study of consciousness or a cogitating ego whilst bracketing the world out there. With phenomenology Van den Berg shares the principle of non-interference. As a phenomenologist, he is inspired by respect for what he can see and hear and he describes what he sees in the way he perceives the phenomena. With phenomenology, then, he shares the definition of this as a science of phenomena in the way these phenomena appear. However, he says (1971*d*, p. 283) that when it comes to the principle of reality he parts from the ways of phenomenology because the phenomenologists in the Husserlian sense will answer that they are not concerned with the question of whether what they see belongs to a concrete 'objective' material world of reality. Van den Berg considers the fact that Husserl, who paved the way for phenomenology, started by pulling down the wall between subject and object, but in his reversion to a neo-Cartesianism, Husserl more or less restored this wall to its original state. Possibly this was not possible in Husserl's time, but it is possible now. Life as such, in the second half of the twentieth century, can end this reserve of philosophical idealism. 'Today, the human race, falling with great gusto on matter as never before, eating, drinking, bathing, travelling, in brief, enjoying the fruits of the earth, makes this reserve seem ridiculous' (p. 283).

Clearly then, Van den Berg's interest is not in a human being, a body or a spirituality that delimits itself from the world. His interest is very much in man as a mundane, incarnated being, embedded in a cosmic totality. We must agree with Van den Berg that such a bracketing, delimiting approach as is conceptualized in the later Husserl is no longer tenable and therefore it does not seem that Van den Berg's metabletics need distantiate itself from the phenomenological psychology expounded in the present book, in which the approach defended is a hermeneutic phenomenology rather than a phenomenology of consciousness in the Husserlian sense. Metabletics being founded on the postulate of change, can be well reconciled with the attitude defended in this book. A phenomenological psychology must delimit itself quite clearly from psychology in the usual sense which is founded on the postulate of immutability and which would view life in past ages as a variation on a well-known theme. However, if we think of man as mutable, it becomes easier to understand that in earlier generations life was truly different from ours. History, to Van den Berg, is not that which continually flows out of something, but that which discontinuously happens. Historical psychology is not a mere looking back which is devoid of life, but rather the metabletic method requires one to go *into* the moment of history to experience it, 'to be there when it happens, to be with Descartes, Breuer and Freud at the moment of their discoveries and to share their feelings filled with concern for the consequences' (Claes 1971, p. 82). This approach is then not a historiography but rather a living-as-history, a merging with the past in the moment of happening.

Although Van den Berg has pioneered this method he is not entirely alone. Thus, Bertha Mook (1977) has made a study of Dutch family life in the seventeenth and eighteenth centuries using studies of cultural historians as well as the work of writers and painters of the time. She was able to demonstrate decisive changes in the relationship between adults and children, between family and neighbourhood, in the position of women and in the first signs of neurosis at the end of the eighteenth century, thus confirming and amplifying certain of the findings of Van den Berg and the historian Phillipe Aries.

It is only because historical psychology is very much embedded in the specific view of life that man is open and discontinuous and ever new that the terms 'history' and 'psychology' as they are commonly used are somewhat deceptive in describing this approach. Therefore, the approach needed a new name, Metabletics. However, should phenomenological psychology establish itself in this area, there is no reason in the present climate why the term historical psychology should not be used as well and why this approach should not be applied outside the context of European history.

The question now arises whether research on a natural scientific basis should be used at all. What has been said in this book essentially means that human existence cannot be understood by the empirical, deterministic, and objectivistic procedures of natural science. This may be interpreted to mean that the natural science approach has no place in psychology whatsoever. We believe that it is important that psychologists should consider this matter most carefully. As has been made clear in the chapter IV, phenomenological research may be seen as propaedeutic to all research. However, this restricts itself to the factual position of contemporary research and does not debate the position of the natural science approach, so we still have to consider on what principles this issue is to be resolved. One possibility which seems important is that human behaviour can be seen as both intentional and functional. It is true that the intentional pole is sometimes the most important; on another occasion, the functional may be predominant. Probably the behaviour that is important most of the time is intentional. One lights a cigarette in order to smoke; smoke has a certain meaning for one. We go to a friend to talk to him. We pick up a child because we love this child.

We could also divide behaviour into 'action' behaviour *v.* process behaviour. The examples mentioned so far may be described as action behaviour, i.e. acts with a certain goal. However, to use one of the same examples: behaviour may also be process behaviour because one sometimes acts automatically. The act of lighting a cigarette may be entirely automatic when one is engrossed in something else.

It cannot be denied that a fairly large segment of behaviour can be understood in terms of habits, conditioned reactions, and reflexes. This could be seen in terms of mans' historically changing nature. That the human penchant for acting in a reflex manner can itself be understood in a phenomenological and metabletic way has been illustrated by J. H. van den Berg (1973). At the threshold of the industrial era, man was undergoing a great change, he was preparing himself for a great task, namely, that of a totally different existence from previous centuries. During the nineteenth century, the reflex became increasingly important and reached its climax in the work of Pavlov. Modern man would be unthinkable if it were not possible for him to mobilize his reflexes in order to drive a car, hammer a typewriter, and perform a variety of industrial tasks. All these, once fully mastered, may be classified as process behaviour and therefore one of the obvious fields in which research on a natural scientific basis should be continued is that of traffic. It is impossible for one to drive a motor car and take oneself safely through the city if one is unable to change one's acts into a series of learned reflexes, i.e. into process behaviour. In research such as this, one would have to ask questions like: will the motorist react better to sound rather than to colour, or will the motorist react better with a combination of colours A *v.* a combination of colours B? In a case like that, one requires yes or no answers and if one thinks in terms of the behaviour of a great number of people (as one has to in the present state of society), and if one wants to have a model of average behaviour of the motorist, the experience of those persons is not the decisive question. In such a case then, by arriving at some formulation of the question in terms of how long? how many? how frequent?, etc., as well as being able to count or measure calculate correlations and significant differences, this approach should be able to continue to be useful for many purposes. It is unlikely that the lived human reality of an individual existence can be disclosed by measurement operations. This is the task of phenomenological-experiential research. However, once this has been done it may be deemed necessary to compare an individual with a population or populations with each other. In such a case a measuring device based on the findings of experiential research may be used. Let us suppose that the management of an organization wants to know how satisfied Black workers are with their jobs, their pay, etc. A survey is done and the researcher then tries to relate his findings to other measurable parameters, e.g. rates of pay, opportunities for advancement, working hours, availability of facilities, etc. Various correlations, significant differences and so forth are found and the interpretation of these is the conclusion. But it is possible that such a survey will not disclose the reality of being-a-black-worker in that organization. Thus, A. S. Alverson (1975) found the secret of survival for the Black industrial worker is to keep the White man as ignorant of him as possible (p. 290). In the organization studied, it transpired that there were a number of informal Black leaders who advised their new workers how to 'handle the Whites' with whom they were likely to come into contact. Most Blacks had very little usable knowledge of the intricacies of the formal and informal hierarchies in the factory. The formal organization required that all orders be passed down through recognized channels. Informally the Blacks knew that their welfare was also dependent upon the extent to which they could comply with the informal dominance of Whites within the organization. This informal dominance still means, by and large, that any Black is supposed to do the bidding of a White and sometimes a single Black would be given instructions by various Whites who had no formally instituted authority over him. Some 'satisfactions' of Blacks, in this organization, were obtained entirely outside the structure provided by management. These included information and guidance provided by 'old hands', illegal distribution of liquor and dagga, consultations with the Inyanga (diviner or herbalist) who provided magical means for coping with the contingencies of the industrial environment in which the Black is much more powerless to cope than his White counterpart.

These experiences are unlikely to be incorporated into the typical psychometric research approach, which frowns on 'impressionistic reports and requires hard data' (Baran 1975, p. 267). A phenomenological approach may rather be described as a 'soft empiricism'. It was Freud's insistence on the 'hard data' of human eros that led him to seek its reality in libido and energetic conceptions whilst the phenomenologist will try to understand sexuality in terms of the encounter, the bodiliness of man and woman and the spatiality of closeness and distance. The glance, the touch, smell and taste are just as much involved in sexuality as the hardening of the penis. The 'reality' of death is not merely the failure of the breathing apparatus and the cessation of perceptible and measurable brain activity, but is experientially describable as distantiation from the trusted context of life, as parting, loneliness, anguish and the possible overcoming of these, above all as the final horizon of life as being in the world and thus as decisive co-constitution of that unique, always varied, sad/joyful life which is the possession of thee and me.

With the above argument, not all forms of psychometric research are being discounted. We are arguing that it is, in principle, impossible for human reality to be *disclosed* by means of measurement operations in the same manner as the profiles of physical reality are being disclosed by the methods of the natural sciences. However, most psychometricians will probably concede this but will argue that the contours of the human situation can be better understood through a measurement study provided the phenomenon being studied has been clearly formulated and is able to generate a theory. Thus, a large amount of research into psychotherapy has been done by using ratings to compare therapeutic outcomes with therapeutic process using variables such as warmth and empathy (Traux & Karkuff 1959). However, the fact that warmth and empathy facilitate some therapies was not discovered by measurement operations but rather through the insights and intuitions of Carl Rogers and worked out by him in detail before the measurement studies were undertaken. On the other hand, the research has shown up facets that were not clear in the original therapy itself, e.g. that it is the therapist as a person rather than his particular theory or set of techniques that seems to be crucial in the therapeutic situation. What is even more crucial, however, is to establish whether the client experiences therapy as being divisible into process and outcome variables such as is hypothesized in most research on psychotherapy. Perhaps once we have made extensive phenomenological studies of how therapist and client experience psychotherapy, i.e. once we have delineated the main themes of what it means to be in a therapeutic relationship with another person, more meaningful psychometric research into the subject can be made as well. As regards the thousands of psychometric studies already made, these should be used pragmatically in our dialogue with the phenomena being studied.

The phenomenological approach to psychology is by no means a closed system. No human experience is disqualified. The door to the spiritual and transpersonal is kept firmly open. Phenomenological psychology is already a transpersonal psychology in the sense that the world is not restricted to tangibilities and mere facts but can only be conceptualized as a system of infinite possibilities and meanings. Explicating our understanding of an individual existence may take us to the edges of the vast cosmic backdrop of human life as we have seen in the case of the 'Sun Man'. In the last instance being and life itself remain a mystery. L. Binswanger could argue that Heidegger's being-in-the-world does not exclude being-beyond-the-world. Phenomenological psychology develops, in the first place, as explication of man's immanent existence, but does not restrict the content of the 'in-dwelling' or 'inhering'. It is not the task of psychology to concern itself with theological arguments concerning the absence or presence or death of God, but has as its task to note these themes in theology, philosophy, literature and poetry as an aspect of the life of contemporary man. Individuals may experience the presence of God, the infinite or the numinous in meditation, in trance states, in worship or ritual, in ecstasies or in schizophrenic states: the phenomenological psychologist is not content to label these hallucination, illusion or delusion but accepts the reality of these and will help the subject in mutual trust to explicate them. Realizing that we are moving into a field in which exaggerated claims can be made, we should remember that phenomenological research, being a co-operative venture, cannot be done with subjects who do not trust the researchers: the latter, however, should also not do research with subjects whom they do not trust. The validity of research, in the final analysis, rests upon the integrity of both subjects and researcher. There is no way in which this limitation can be overcome. It has to be stressed at this juncture because phenomenological psychology is both pretentious and naïve: it questions the phenomenon and dialogues with it through human experience and hopes to delineate the encompassing contours of human existence. It does not want to leave out the grey areas in the vast field of being human where intersubjective validity is difficult to achieve yet it cannot deny the fact that the human being is able to lie and to hide himself from himself and fellow man.

The classical example of how a dialogue between a researcher and his subjects can go wrong is afforded by Freud's experience with his first psychoanalytic patients. Freud believed that hysterics suffered from reminiscences – the cause of the patient's present predicament was to be found in the past. In the past, Freud believed, there was a trauma of some sort but always of a sexual nature. Within this atmosphere the patient believed that her condition was caused by an event that she had forgotten and that she could be cured by *remembering*. If no trauma could be recalled the impasse remained. The patient would search the *possibilities* of her past and from these possibilities imagination could construe a 'screen memory' of something forgotten; could select this possibility as the answer, i.e. the event that was required, and offer this to the psychoanalyst who would then be satisfied that the root or *cause* of the trouble had been found. This was the hard datum required by early psychoanalysis. However, when Freud later checked this information he found, to his discomfiture, that none of these stories was true in the hard empiricistic sense at all – these events had not actually taken place.

The transpersonal also includes the so-called psi-phenomena. These phenomena are in principle understandable in terms of the openness of existence. Ecstatically and existentially man is open to fellow man and to the future, and lived human spatiality is not measurable extension. It frequently happens in psychotherapy that a therapist who is congruent with his own experience verbalizes the thoughts of the client and sometimes the reverse happens. Xhosa diviners, speaking in a language congruent with their own tradition, make statements like the following with great confidence, in speaking about those whom they are healing:

'I know what is wrong with the person; these have been revealed to me in dreams.'
'Some I just look at and I know what is wrong with them.'
'I use the vumisa procedure and during the process my ancestors come to me and tell me what is wrong with that person.'

African selfhood has been formulated in the following terms: 'I am because we are and we are because I am.'

The statements above are not at all incredible if we accept that the boundaries which Western man erects around himself in that he sees himself as encapsulated, do not reflect the reality of being-with-another in a common reality. The Xhosa diviner does not have to contend with this encapsulation and there is thus nothing mysterious for him in the accessibility that he may have into the meaningful life structures of those who come to consult him (Kruger 1978*b*, p. 476).

Phenomena such as clairvoyance and telepathy may be understood in terms of such world openness and, additionally, in terms of the primary non-linear nature of lived time, bodiliness and spatiality. We have seen in Mandy's report how she became one with the tree although the measured distance between her and the tree remained unchanged. We all know that we can be very close to someone who, in terms of measured distance, is miles away from us. We all know the phenomenon of 'synchronicity', e.g. one thinks of something important and resolves to phone someone about it at the same time as that same person has been thinking about the same thing and is actually engaged in phoning one. Most of us have had the experience of having a feeling that something, not clearly defined, is going to happen and then it happens as if the coming event has been throwing its shadow forward. A smaller number of us have had experience in which the contours and details of a coming event were clearly foreshadowed. M. Boss (1974, pp. 202–17) reports a number of telepathic or prophetic dreams including the famous and well-authenticated dream of Bishop Joseph Lanyi who had a vivid and detailed dream of the murder of the Grand Duke Franz Ferdinand (1914) before the actual murder took place far away from the bishop's residence. Freud, too, did not deny the validity of telepathic dreams but suggested that the real core remained the wish-fulfilment.

If one accepts that being human means existentially and ek-statically standing out towards the world, the future and *Mitwelt*, then these phenomena are, in principle, understandable but have to be systematically explicated by trustworthy subjects and researchers.

Phenomenological psychology is a *human* science and not a *humanistic* one. This does not mean that phenomenology needs to distantiate itself from the humanistic trend or third force, in American Psychology, but it can be clearly demarcated within this field in general. It is, however, necessary to note that phenomenological psychology does not make the human being the measure of all things. The philosophical movement of humanism includes a rationalistic set of ideas and ideologies according to which man is complete within himself. In what is called humanistic psychology the encapsulated view of the human being has, for the most part, not been overcome. This is the clearest difference between phenomenological psychology and the rest of humanistic psychology. Another, but related, difference is illustrated by the fact that the transpersonal psychologists in the U.S.A. refer to themselves as the Fourth Force in American Psychology (Bruno 1977). As we have seen, phenomenological psychology is already a transpersonal psychology and does not need a special area because man is already open to the spiritual and transpersonal in this conception. If we interpret the dream as Erich Fromm does on the basis that dream phenomena are the symbolic expression of nothing more than *our* wishes, *our* thinking, and *our* virtues, then we are, in fact, cutting off an access to transpersonal areas which are kept open in the psychologies of both Freud and Jung. This we can see in Freud's description of drives or instincts as 'mythological beings of unknown origin' as well as Jung's collective unconscious. Phenomenological psychology is therefore, in principle, open-ended as to the potentials of being human rather than restricting its definition of humanness to that which is consistent with the general rational conception of humanity.

THE FUTURE

Whether phenomenological psychology can become *the* psychology of the future remains to be seen. In the countries of Western Europe: Germany, France, Switzerland and Holland where it originated, it has not progressed as much as its initiators could have hoped; has even suffered setbacks. In the U.S.A. it has had an impact but has been largely assimilated into humanistic psychology so that the overcoming of Cartesian dualism has not been the central emphasis in the work of Rogers, Jourard, Maslow, and others that it could have had. In Pittsburgh, the Department of Psychology at Duquesne University has done outstanding pioneering work in endeavours to systematize research in phenomenological psychology. In addition to the journal of phenomenological psychology, they have published at least two volumes of research studies. The pioneering work of Rollo May has certainly helped to introduce phenomenology, but more in its existential nuances, to the American psychological and psychotherapeutic scene.

In South Africa, the visits of J. H. van den Berg during the 1970s have made a considerable impact and the South African Institute for Psychotherapy was largely started under his influence (although this institute is eclectic rather than Daseinsanalytic). However, while his ideas have penetrated clinical psychology and psychotherapy, and while at least one department of psychiatry (the University of the Orange Free State) has some pehomenological orientation, there is only one university department of psychology where courses in phenomenology are offered at both undergraduate and post-graduate levels. However, this Department at Rhodes University is certainly not exclusively phenomenological. Moreover, if we look at the two main research institutions in South Africa, namely, the Human Sciences Research council and the National Institute for Personnel Research of the Council for Scienctific and Industrial Research, we note that both these institutions do psychological research but almost exclusively of a psychometric nature. The Human Sciences Research Council shows very little, in psychology anyway, of its Afrikaans title: Raad vir Geestewetenskaplike Navorsing. The *Geisteswissenschaftliche* aspect of this institution has not been actualized and we note that of its twelve institutes there is no institute for psychological research, but only an institute for *psychometric* research. One hastens to add that the Council has not discriminated in any way against students wishing to do Masters or Doctoral degrees in phenomenological psychology but has treated these applications on exactly the same basis as all others. However, when it comes to awards for major projects, one wonders how the Council would regard an application to do a major phenomenological research project and how they would calculate the value of such an undertaking.

If one looks at the implications of phenomenological psychology for the future training of psychologists, one is struck by the fact that the differences between psychotherapy and phenomenological research tend to become blurred. In both cases a relationship of trust and sharing, i.e. being-with-one-another in a common world, is required. It also means that good phenomenological researchers will have to undergo some of the same sort of training as that of psychotherapists, which means that the future researcher should explore his own humanness in much the same way as the future therapist currently has to do. In all courses on psychology, there should be a considerable emphasis on personal growth. The future research psychologist should be open to the way he experiences other people and the way other people experience him. In a society in which contact across colour lines is still taboo in many ways, one may wonder about the amount of freedom that will be allowed in order to explore this area. Recently the Department of Health closed an important therapeutic division of a certain mental hospital, allegedly because, in this institution, there was said to be undue physical contact across the colour line. There is no way in which phenomenological research requires permissivity or promiscuity. There is, however, a need for freedom: the freedom to explore and to test out the dimensions of being human.

There is, however, a set of contingencies which do not arise from the *Umwelt*, i.e. from the social organization of present-day society (especially in South Africa), but rather from within the paradigm of phenomenological research itself. Phenomenological research still remains completely within the dyad model elaborated by Freud and Jung. No doubt this model is enormously important and will probably continue to be the main research model as well. However, the work of the family researchers in schizophrenia has opened up another set of possibilities which has to be met by some form of dialectic, namely, how experience is structured by the words and actions of others. In family therapy, for instance, the way the family reacts in the therapeutic session gives one a clear idea of the personal relational landscape of the identified client or patient. Should phenomenology fail to expand its paradigm in such a way that these phenomena may be accommodated therein, it may represent a formidable limitation on its future growth.

It is clear, therefore, that phenomenology will have to cope with its limitations in future research if it is to expand and reach its full expository depth and power. However, its merit is undoubtedly that it opposes tendencies to reduce us to thing-like qualities, that it has taken the human being out of the confines of the Cartesian cogito, the Freudian 'psychic personality', the Skinnerian response emitting structure and the Rogerian 'inner self'. It resituates man in his true habitat: the world in which we journey and dwell.

REFERENCES

ALLPORT, G. M. (1968) *The Person in Psychology*. Beacon Press, Boston.
ALVERSON, H. S. (1975) Africans in South African Industry. In: Morse, S. J. and Orpen, C. (Eds.) *Contemporary South Africa: Social Psychological Perspectives*. Juta & Co., Cape Town. pp. 280–94.
BAKKER, R. (1965) *Merleau-Ponty, het Wêreldvenster*. Baarn.
BARAN, S. (1975) Zulu acculturation in South African Industry. In: Morse S. J. and Orpen (Eds.) op. cit. pp. 267–79.
BARRELL, J. J. & BARRELL, J. E. (1975) A Self-Directed Approach for a Science of Human Experience. *Journal of Phenomenological Psychology* **6**(1): 63–73.
BERGER, J. (1975) *Ways of Seeing*. BBC and Penguin Books, Harmondsworth.
BESHAI, J. A. (1971) Psychology's Dilemma: To Explain or to Understand. *Journal of Phenomenological Psychology* **1**(2): 209–33.
BESHAI, J. A. (1975) Is Psychology a Hermeneutic Science? *Journal of Phenomenological Psychology* **5**(2): 425–39.
BETHGE, E. (1970) *Dietrich Bonhoeffer*. Chr. Kaiser Verlag, München.
BINSWANGER, L. (1957) *Schizophrenie*. Verlag Gunther Neske in Pfüllingen.
BINSWANGER, L. (1964) *Grundformen und Erkenntnis menschlichen Daseins*. Ernst Reinhardt Verlag, München.
BLASIUS, W. (1976) *Problems of Life Research: Physiological Analyses and Phenomenological Interpretations*. Heidelberg, Springer-Verlag.
BLEULER, E. (1973) The Physiogenic and Psychogenic in Schizophrenia. In: Millon, T. (Ed.) *Theories of Psychopathology and Personality*. W. B. Saunders Co., Philadelphia.
BLEULER, M. (1966) Conceptions of Schizophrenia within the last fifty years and today, reprinted from *International Journal of Psychiatry*
BOSS, M. (1957) *Psychoanalyse und Daseinsanalytik*. Hans Huber, Bern.
BOSS, M. (1974) *Der Traum und seine Auslegung*. Kindler Verlag, München.
BOSS, M. (1975) *Grundriss der Medizin und der Psychologie*. Hans Huber, Bern.
BOSS, M. (1976) *Das Verhältnis von Leib und Seele im Lichte der Daseinsanalytik, Separatdruck aus Psychosomatische Medizin*, Heft 3/4, Band 6.
BRANDT, L. W. (1970) Phenomenology, Psychoanalysis, and Behaviourism: (E = S) v (E ≠ S)? *Journal of Phenomenological Psychology* **1** (1): 7–18.
BRANDT, L. W., & BRANDT, E. P. (1974) The Alienated Psychologist. *Journal of Phenomenological Psychology*, **5**(1): 41–52.
BRUNO, F. J. (1977) *Human Adjustment and Personal Growth*. J. Wiley, New York.
BUGENTAL, J. F. (1973) Confronting the Existential Meaning of 'my death' through Group Exercises. *Interpersonal Development* **4**(3): 148–63.
CATTELL, R. B. (1970) *The Scientific Analysis of Personality*. Penguin Books, Harmondsworth.
CLAES, J. (1971) Metabletica or a Psychology of History. *Humanitas* VII/3; 279–90.
CLOONAN, T. F. (1971) Experiential and Behavioural Aspects of Decision Making. In: Amedeo Giorgi *et al.* (Eds.) *Duquesne Studies in Phenomenological Psychology*, Vol. I. Duquesne University Press, Pittsburgh. pp. 112–31.
CLOONAN, T. F. (1975) Body-Subject and Dialogue of Perspectives in the Perception of Letters traced on the Head. In: Amedeo Giorgi *et al.*, *Duquesne Studies in Phenomenological Psychology*, Vol. II. Duquesne University Press, Pittsburgh. pp. 104–29.
COLAIZZI, P. F. (1968) The Descriptive Method and the Types of Subject Matter of a Phenomenologically based Psychology: Exemplified by the Phenomenon of Learning. Unpub. Ph.D. Thesis, Duquesne University.
COLAIZZI, P. F. (1971) Analysis of the Learner's Perception of Learning Material at Various Phases of the Learning Process. In: Amedeo Giorgi *et al.*, op. cit. pp. 101–31.

COULTER, J. (1973) *Approaches to Insanity*. Martin Robertson, London.

CRUSE, L. (1974) *Räumliche Umwelt*. Walter de Gruyter, Berlin.

DE WAELHENS, A. (1967) The Phenomenology of the Body. In: N. Lawrence & D. O'Conner (Eds.) *Readings in Existential Psychology*. Prentice Hall, Inc., Engelwood Cliffs, New Jersey. pp. 149–67.

DUBLIN, J. E. (1972) Language as Expression of Upright Man: Toward a Phenomenology of Language and the Lived Body, *Journal of Phenomenological Psychology* 2(2): 141–60.

DUFRENNE, M. (1967) Language and Metaphysics. In: Lawrence N and O'Connor D. (Eds.) *Readings in Existential Phenomenology*. Prentice Hall, Inc., Engelwood Cliffs, New Jersey.

EPPEL, M. D. (1976) Towards an Essential Description of the Experience of Closeness – A Phenomenologically Based Study. Unpub. Honours Project, Rhodes University.

EPPEL, M. D. (1978) A Phenomenological Explication of a Client's Retrospective Experience of Psychotherapy. Unpub. Master's thesis, Rhodes University.

ERASMUS, P. F. & MINNAAR, G. G. (1978) The discriminative Ability of the TAT-Z with regard to hospitalized and non-hospitalized Groups of Black Men, Human Sciences Research Council, Pretoria.

ERIKSON, E. H. (1973) *Childhood and Society*. Penguin Books, Harmondsworth.

FISCHER, W. F. (1974) On the Phenomenological Mode of Researching 'Being Anxious'. *Journal of Phenomenological Psychology* 4(2): 405–23.

FREUD, S. (1955) *Das Unbehagen in der Kultur*. Fischer Bücherei, Frankfurt.

GILBERT, G. S., & RAPPOPORT, L. (1975) Categories of Thought and Variations in Meaning: A demonstration Experiment. *Journal of Phenomenological Psychology* 5(2): 419–24.

GIORGI, A. (1970) *Psychology as a Human Science: A Phenomenologically Based Approach*. Harper & Row, New York.

GIORGI, A. (1970) Toward Phenomenologically Based Research in Psychology. *Journal of Phenomenological Psychology* 1(1): 75–98.

GIORGI, A. (1971) A Phenomenological Approach to the Problem of Meaning and Serial Learning. In: Amedeo Giorgi *et al.* (Eds.), op. cit., pp. 88–100.

GIORGI, A. (1971) Phenomenology and Experimental Psychology. In: Amedeo Giorgi *et al.*, op. cit.

GIORGI, A. (1974) Meta-Psychology of Merleau-Ponty as a Possible Basis for Unity in Psychology. *Journal of Phenomenological Psychology*. 5(1): 53–74.

GIORGI, A. (1975) An Application of Phenomenological Method in Psychology. In: Amedeo Giorgi *et al.*, op. cit., pp. 82–103.

GIORGI, A., FISCHER, C., & MURRAY, E. (Eds.) (1975) *Duquesne Studies in Phenomenological Psychology* Vol. II. Duquesne University Press, Pittsburgh.

GIORGI, A., FISCHER, W. F., & VON ECKARTSBERG, R. (Eds.) (1971) *Duquesne Studies in Phenomenological Psychology* Vol. I. Duquesne University Press, Pittsburgh.

GRAUMANN, C. F. (1970) Conflicting and Convergent Trends in Psychological Theory. *Journal of Phenomenological Psychology* 1(1): 51–61.

GROF, S., & HALIFAX, J. (1978) *The Human encounter with death*. Souvenir Press, London.

GURWITSCH, A. (1966) The Phenomenological and the Psychological Approach to Consciousness. In: Maurice Natanson (Ed.) Essays in Phenomenology. Martinus Nijhoff, The Hague. pp. 40–57.

HANNUSH, M. J., (1973) ADORNO & SARTRE: A Convergence of Two Methodological Approaches. *Journal of Phenomenological Psychology* 4(1): 297–313.

HEIDEGGER, M. (1943) *Vom Wesen der Wahrheit*. Vittorio Klostermann, Frankfurt.
HEIDEGGER, M. (1972) *Sein und Zeit*. Max Niemeyer Verlag, Tübingen. Translated as *Being and Time* by J. Macquarrie & E. Robinson. SCM Press Ltd., London. Page references are to the German edition except where otherwise stated.
HOWARD, I. H. & ORLANSKY, D. E. (1968) The patient's experience of psychotherapy: some dimensions and determinants. *Multivariate Behavioural Research*. Special issue, pp. 55–72.
HOWARD, I. H. & ORLANSKY, D. E. (1970) Affective experience in psychotherapy. *Journal of Abnormal Psychology* 75(3): 267–275.
ILLICH, I. (1978) *Limits to Medicine*. Penguin Books, Harmondsworth.
JOHNSON, H. H., & SOLSO, R. L. (1971) *An Introduction to Experimental Design in Psychology: A Case Approach*. Harper & Row, New York.
JUNG, C. G. (1973) On the psychodiagnosis of schizophrenia. In: Millon, T. *Theories of Psychopathology and Personality*. W. B. Saunders Company, Philadelphia.
KANTHACK, K. (1959) *Das Denken Martin Heideggers*. Walter de Gruyter, Berlin.
KELEMAN, S. (1974) *Living your dying*. Random House, New York.
KELLY, G. A. (1973) Personal Construct Theory. In: Millon, T. (Ed.), op. cit.
KETY, S. S. (1973) Biochemical hypotheses of schizophrenia. In: Millon, T. (op. cit.)
KOCH, S. (1974) Psychology and emerging Conceptions of Knowledge as unitary. In: T. W. Wann (Ed.) *Behaviourism and Phenomenology*. The University of Chicago Press, Chicago.
KRACKLAUER, C. (1972) Exploring the Life-World. *Journal of Phenomenological Psychology* 2(2): 217–236.
KRAEPELIN, E. (1973) Clinical Psychiatry. In: Millon, T. op. cit., pp. 14–18.
KRUGER, D. (1976) To diagnose or not to diagnose. *Psychotherapeia* 2/3: 19–26.
KRUGER, D. (1978a) The Xhosa Diviner: Ways of Understanding. *Koers* 43/5: 456–83.
KRUGER, D. (1978b) Psigodiagnose en psigologie as menswetenskap. *Psychotherapeia* 4/3: 15–24.
KULLMAN, M., & TAYLOR, C. (1966) The Pre-Objective World. In: Maurice Natanson (Ed.) op. cit., pp. 116–36.
KVALE, S. (1973) The Technical Paradigm of Psychological Research. *Journal of Phenomenological Psychology* 3(2): 143–59.
LAING, R. (1956) *The divided Self*. Penguin Books, Harmondsworth.
LANDMANN, M. (1974) *Philosophical Anthropology*. Tr D. L. Parent. Westminister, Philadelphia.
LANGAN, T. (1959) *The meaning of Heidegger, a critical study of an existential phenomenology*. R. Paul, London.
LA POINTE, F. H. (1972) Merleau-Ponty's Phenomenological Critique of Psychology. *Journal of Phenomenological Psychology* 2(2): 237–55.
L'ECUYER, R. (1975) Self-Concept Investigation: Demystification Process. *Journal of Phenomenological Psychology* 6(1): 17–30.
LEVEY, C. E. (1973) Toward Primordial Reality as the Ground of Psychological Phenomena. *Journal of Phenomenological Psychology* 6(2): 173–86.
LIDZ, T. (1975) *The Origin and Treatment of Schizophrenic Disorders*. Hutchinson and Co., London.
LUIJPEN, W. (1969) *Nieuwe Inleiding tot de existentiële Fenomenologie*. Het Spectrum, N. V., Utrecht.
LYONS, J. (1970) The Hidden Dialogue in Experimental Research. *Journal of Phenomenological Psychology* 1(1): 19–29.
MANGANYI, N. C. (1973) *Being-Black-in-the-world*. Spro-cas/Ravan, Johannesburg.

MANGANYI, N. C. (1977a) *Mashangu's reverie*. Ravan Press, Johannesburg.

MANGANYI, N. C. (1977b) *Alienation and the Body in racist Society*. N.O.K. Publishers, New York.

MARCUSE, H. (1970) *Der eindimensionale Mensch*. H. Luchterhand, Neuwied and Berlin.

MARCUSE, H. (1972) *Eros and Civilization*. Sphere Books, London.

MARKESON, E. W. & GOGNALONS-CAILLARD, M. (1971) Talks with Father William. *Journal of Phenomenological Psychology* 1(2): 193–208.

MASLOW, A. (1961) Existential Psychology, What's in it for us. In: May, R. (Ed.) *Existential Psychology*. Random House, New York.

McCONVILLE, M. (1978) The Phenomenological Approach to Perception. In: Valle, R. S. & King, M. *Existential Phenomenological Alternatives for Psychology*. Oxford University Press Inc., New York. pp. 94–118.

McINTYRE, A. C. (1976) *The Unconscious*. Routledge and Kegan Paul, London.

McCLELLAN, D. (1977) *Marx*. Fontana.

MERLEAU-PONTY, M. (1962) *Phenomenology of Perception*. Humanities Press, New York.

MOOK, B. (1977) *The Dutch Family in the 17th and 18th Centuries*. University of Ottawa Press, Ottawa.

MOUSTGAARD, I. K. (1975) Phenomenological Description after the Manner of Edgar Rubin. *Journal of Phenomenological Psychology* 6(1): 31–61.

MOWRER, O. H. (1963) *The new Group Therapy*. D. van Nostrand Co. Inc., New Jersey.

MUNRO, M. M. (1975) The meaning of Ordination for a Sample of United Methodist Ministers: a Phenomenological Exploration. Unpubl. Ph.D. thesis, Boston University Graduate School.

MURRAY, E. L. (1974) Language and the Integration of Personality. *Journal of Phenomenological Psychology* 4(2), 469–489.

NATANSON, M. (Ed.) (1966) Essays in Phenomenology. Martinus Nijhoff, The Hague.

PARKER, P. (1977) An Ideographic Study of Bisexuality. Unpubl. Master's thesis, Rhodes University.

PARSONS, A. S. (1973) Constitutive Phenomenology: Schutz's Theory of the We-Relation. *Journal of Phenomenological Psychology* 4(1): 331–61.

PINES, M. (1973) *The Brain Changers*. A. Lane, London.

PIRSIG, ROBERT, M. (1977) *Zen and the Art of Motorcycle Maintenance*. Corgi Books London.

POSTMAN, L., & KEPPEL, G. (1969) *Verbal learning and Memory*. Penguin Books, Harmondsworth.

PRELLER, A. C. N. (1977) *Harry Stack Sullivan en die fenomenologiese Psigiatrie*. Boekenhout Uitgewers, Pretoria.

PSATHAS, G., & BECKER, P. (1972) The Experimental Reality: The Cognitive Style of a Finite Province of Meaning. *Journal of Phenomenological Psychology* 3(1): 35–52.

ROBINSON, DANIEL, N. (1976) *An intellectual History of Psychology*. Macmillan, New York.

ROMANYSHYN, R. D. (1971) Method and Meaning in Psychology. The Method has been the message. *Journal of Phenomenological Psychology* 2(1): 93–113.

ROMANYSHYN, R. D. (1973) Copernicus and the Beginnings of Modern Science. *Journal of Phenomenological Psychology* 3(2): 187–99.

ROMANYSHYN, R. D. (1975) Metaphors and Human Behaviour. *Journal of Phenomenological Psychology* 5(2): 441–6.

ROSENHAN, D. L. (1974) On being sane in Insane Places. In: Zax M., & Stricker, G. *The study of Abnormal Behaviour*, Macmillan, New York. pp. 66–86.

ROSZAK, T. (1972) *Where the Wasteland Ends*. Faber & Faber, London.

ROTHMAN, DAVID, J. *et al.* (1975) An Historical overview: Behaviour Modification in Total Institutions. In: Illich, I., op. cit., p. 261.

RYCROFT, C. (1966) *Psychoanalysis Observed*. Constable, London.

SARDELLO, R. (1978) A phenomenological Approach to Memory. In: Valle, R. S., & King, M., op cit., pp. 131–51.

SCHATZMAN, M. (1976) *Soul Murder: Persecution in the Family*. Penguin Books, Harmondsworth.

SCHWEITZER, R. D. (1977) Categories of Experience Amongst the Xhosa: A Psychological Study. Unpubl. Master's thesis, Rhodes University.

SHAPIRO, K. J. (1976) The Elusive in Experience. *Journal of Phenomenological Psychology* 6(2): 135–152.

SHOTTER, J. (1975) *Images of Man in Psychological Research*. Methuen, London.

SKINNER, B. F. (1974) Behaviourism at Fifty. In: Wann, T.W. (Ed.), op cit., pp. 79–96.

SKINNER, B. F. (1973a) What is Psychotic Behaviour. In: Millon, T. (Ed.), op. cit., pp. 282–93.

SKINNER, B. F. (1973b) *Beyond Freedom and Dignity*. Penguin Books, Harmondsworth.

STEINER, GEORGE (1978) *Heidegger*. Fontana.

STEVICK, E. L. (1971) An Empirical Investigation of the Experience of Anger. In: Amedeo Giorgi *et al.* op. cit. pp. 132–48.

STRASSER, S. (1963) *Phenomenology and the Human Sciences*. Duquesne University Press, Pittsburgh.

STRAUS, E. (1966) *Phenomenological Psychology*. Tavistock.

STRAUS, E., AUG, R. G., & ABLES, B. S. (1971) A Phenomenological Approach to Dyslexia. *Journal of Phenomenological Psychology* 1(2): 225–35.

THINES, G. (1970) The Phenomenological Approach in Comparative Psychology. *Journal of Phenomenological Psychology* 1(1): 63–73.

THORPE, F. (1975) Unabhängigkeitserklärung der klinischen Psychologie. *Zeitschr Klin. Psychol. Psychother.* 23, Heft 1, s. 3–5.

TODRES, L. A. (1975) A Phenomenological Approach to the Practice of Transcendental Meditation. Unpubl. Honours Project, Rhodes University.

TODRES, L. A. (1978) An Exploration into the Meaning of Death. Unpubl. Master's thesis, Rhodes University.

TRAUX, C. B., & CLARKHUFF, R. R. (1964) Significant Developments in Psychotherapy Research. In: Abt, L. E. & Riess, B. F. (Eds.) *Progress in Clinical Psychology*, Vol. VI. Grune and Stratton, London.

VAN DEN BERG, J. H. (1959) *Het menselijk Lichaam*, Deel I, Het geopende Lichaam. C. F. Callenbach, Nijkerk.

VAN DEN BERG, J. H. (1963) *Leven in Meervoud*. G. F. Callenbach, N.V. Nijkerk.

VAN DEN BERG, J. H. (1968) *Metabletica van de Materie*. C. F. Callenbach, B. V. Nijkerk.

VAN DEN BERG, J. H. (1969) *De Dingen*. C. F. Callenbach, B. V. Nijkerk.

VAN DEN BERG, J. H. (1971a) *Dieptepsychologie*. C. F. Callenbach, N. V. Nijkerk.

VAN DEN BERG, J. H. (1971b) What is Psychotherapy? *Humanitas* 1971, 7(3): 321–70.

VAN DEN BERG, J. H. (1972a) *ZIEN, Verstaan en verklaring van de visuele waarneming*. C. F. Callenbach, N. V. Nijkerk. J. H. v. Schaik Bpk., Pretoria.

VAN DEN BERG, J. H. (1972b) *A Different Existence*. Pittsburgh, Pa., Duquesne University Press.

VAN DEN BERG, J. H. (1973a) *Kroniek der Psychologie*. G. F. Callenbach, N. V. Nijkerk.

VAN DEN BERG, J. H. (1973b) *De Reflex*. G. F. Callenbach, N. V. Nijkerk.

VAN DEN BERG, J. H. (1976) Have you Seen the Pantheon? *Journal of Phenomenological Psychology* 6(2), 121–34.

VAN KAAM, A. L. (1958) The Experience of Really Feeling Understood by a Person. Unpubl. Ph.D. thesis, Western Reserve University.

VAN KAAM, A. L. (1969) *Existential Foundation of Psychology*. New York, Image Books.

VON ECKARTSBERG, R. (1971) On experiential methodology. In: Amedeo Giorgi *et al*. op. cit., pp. 66–79.

VON ECKARTSBERG, R. (1972) Experiential Psychology: A Descriptive Protocol and a Reflection. *Journal of Phenomenological Psychology* 2(2): 161–173.

WEIL, SIMONE (1974) *Waiting on God*. Fontana Books, London.

WONG, E. (1975) Visual and Tactile Perception Reconsidered: From an Empirical Phenomenological Perspective. *Journal of Phenomenological Psychology* 6(1): 75–87.

WOODWORTH, R. S. (1931) *Contemporary Schools of Psychology*. Methuen, London.

ZIEHEN, T. L. (1924) *Leitfaden der physiologischen Psychologie in 16 Vorlesungen*. Gustav Fischer, Jena.

Index

Affectivity. *See* emotion
Alienation, 2, 33, 34, 58, 175, 185
Allport, G. M., 6, 7
Anger, 21, 66
Anxiety (anguish), 23, 56, 68, 69, 70, 146,
 147, 149, 152, 158, 161, 162, 167, 190
Approach (human scientific), 113, 115,
 118, 131
Attunedness. *See* mood
Authenticity, 64, 66, 77, 168, 175, 178

Bakker, R., 87, 88, 90, 92, 93
Behaviour, 1, 5, 16, 21, 85, 89, 90, 92, 114,
 148-151, 152, 176, 180, 182
Behaviourism, 5, 6, 20, 21, 28, 148-151, 181
Being-free, 54, 77-79, 157, 158, 159, 161,
 174, 175, 177, 185, 195
Being-in-the-world, 3, 24, 25, 26, 27, 28,
 98, 108, 118, 157, 161, 165, 191
Being-with-others, 28, 29, 30, 39, 70-77,
 86, 134, 157, 158, 166, 168, 179, 184,
 192, 195
Binswanger, L., 50, 69, 116, 152-156, 168,
 191
Bleuler, E., 141, 142
Bleuler, M., 142, 143
Bodiliness, 28, 30-38, 39, 89-92, 107, 121,
 133, 156, 170, 171, 172, 183, 184, 185,
 186, 190, 192
Boss, M., 13, 40, 50, 56, 66, 67, 68, 69,
 73, 74, 76, 77, 78, 95, 156-162, 168, 193
Bracketing, 128, 149, 186
Brain, 19, 20, 27, 30, 31, 36, 80, 81, 82,
 85, 90, 94, 95, 96, 97, 115, 157, 190
Brentano, F., 23
Buber, M., 61

Care, 174, 182
Cartesian. *See* Descartes
Causality. *See also* determinism, 17, 79, 105,
 108, 141, 143, 146, 147, 148, 157, 180,
 192
Communication, 18, 20, 28, 29, 30, 71, 118,
 141, 144, 150, 152, 164, 166, 167, 183
Consciousness, 10, 20, 23, 24, 40, 46, 53,
 108, 109, 114, 148, 150, 157
Cosmic, 41, 161, 186, 191
Coulter, J., 141, 148

Dasein, 26, 27, 56, 60, 64, 66, 67, 68, 69,
 70, 74, 77, 101, 153-156, 161
Dasein's analysis, 152, 168
Death, 56, 61, 62-66, 67, 68, 70, 79, 112,
 134, 154, 184, 190
Delusion, 46, 135, 140, 145, 156, 164, 185,
 191
Descartes, R., 8, 9, 10, 15, 38, 47, 49, 53,
 80, 82, 90, 105, 110, 111, 151, 153, 196
Description, 21, 119, 123, 127, 129, 130,
 131, 151, 156, 183
Determinism. *See also* causality 11, 12, 79,
 83, 108, 153, 180, 187
Dilthey, W., 23

Dreams, 8, 40, 42, 43, 112, 145, 171, 192,
 193
Dualism (Cartesian), 8, 9, 21, 26, 40, 71,
 73, 153, 180, 181, 186, 194

Empathy, 71, 158
Einfühlung, 72, 158
Emotion, 66, 141, 164, 165
Empirics, empiricism, 13, 96, 149, 190
Encapsulation, 14, 24, 27, 72, 143, 146, 147,
 150, 151, 152, 153, 158, 177, 180, 192,
 193
Engram. *See* Trace
Encounter, 69, 70, 76, 77, 98, 167, 177,
 178, 184, 185, 190
Eppel, M.D., 136, 137, 138, 139, 161, 170,
 173, 176
Erikson, E., 65
Existence, 19, 20, 22, 26, 27, 49, 54, 55, 64,
 66, 77, 90, 97, 103, 110, 111, 112, 119,
 154, 156, 157, 158, 159, 160, 161, 162,
 168, 180, 182, 183, 184, 189, 191, 192
Experience, 4, 16, 22, 23, 27, 28, 29, 38, 39,
 44, 46, 48, 49, 51, 53, 54, 56, 72, 75, 78,
 86, 87, 94, 114-127, 130-139, 141, 148,
 151, 154, 155, 160, 162, 163, 165, 173-
 178, 183, 184, 185, 191
Experimentation, 5, 17, 18, 116, 117, 118,
 123, 124, 150, 151, 180
Explication, 3, 24, 29, 53, 127, 135, 159,
 165, 174, 183, 184, 185
Explicitation, 127-139

Fallenness *(Ver Fullentheit),* 64, 156, 158,
 159, 160
Finitude. *See* death
Freedom. *See* being free
Freud, S., 2, 9-14, 22, 33, 56, 57, 61, 103,
 104, 105, 106, 107, 109, 110, 143, 144,
 149, 151, 157, 181, 190, 191, 193, 194,
 195, 196

Gelassenheit. See let-be-ness
Genetics, 142, 143
Giorgi, A., 113, 116, 119, 121, 122, 123,
 124, 126, 127, 136, 139
gnostic sensing, 49, 86, 87, 118
God, 37, 38, 154, 162, 191

Hallucination, 46, 135, 140, 141, 144, 160,
 161, 162, 163, 164, 191
Heidegger, M., 3, 24, 25, 26, 29, 49, 64, 69,
 71, 72, 77, 133, 180, 182, 183, 191
Historicity, 11, 59-62, 101, 148, 149, 151,
 172, 181, 183, 185-187
Human Science, 4, 28, 114, 115, 116, 118,
 120, 139, 183, 193, 194
Husserl, E., v, 22, 23, 71, 72, 88, 114, 186

Idiographics *vs.* nomothetic, 16, 17, 135
Imagination, 73, 74, 101, 102, 192
Insight, 108, 173, 174, 178

203

7729